17.50

D0936916

A Place Called Home

Mullins' Alley

According to Riis, John Wood erected a blank-walled block between Gotham Court and his neighbor Mullins's building to get even with him for being knocked down during an argument over property lines.

Source: Photograph by Jacob A. Riis, The Jacob A. Riis Collection, Museum of the City of New York.

A Place Called Home

A History of Low-Cost Housing In Manhattan

Anthony Jackson

The MIT Press
Cambridge, Massachusetts, and London, England

The research for this book was given generous financial support by the Canada Council.

This book was set in IBM Composer Theme by Technical Composition, and printed on Finch Title 93 and bound in G.S.B. 82 by Murray Printing Company in the United States of America.

Library of Congress Cataloging in Publication Data

Jackson, Anthony, 1926-
   A place called home.

   Bibliography: p.
   Includes index
   1. Rental housing—New York (City)—Manhattan (Borough)—History.
2. Housing—New York (City)—Manhattan (Borough)—History. I. Title.
HD7304.N5J32   301.5'4'097471   76-17659
ISBN 0-262-10017-7

To my father, Jankel Zelechin,
and all those who left
persecution behind and settled
in other countries, where we,
their children, had the good
fortune to be born

Contents

Illustrations

Preface

Since the Industrial Revolution, every generation has had its housing problem. This history of the supply of low-rental housing in Manhattan is a case study of how succeeding administrations tried to cope with the ever-present demands of a population seeking shelter. From a total reliance on private enterprise including its philanthropic wing, through private-public partnership, to public housing and government-financed support of private enterprise and its market, New York has been in the forefront of this search for solutions. That success continues to elude it and other North American communities is not a reflection on their ingenuity but an indication of the essential incompatibility between their ends and their means.

A Place Called Home

Prologue

"As a city grows in commerce, and demands new localities for traffic and manufacture, the store and workshop encroach upon the dwelling house and dispossess its occupants. At first the habitations of citizens are removed to a limited distance, because, with an industrious population, time is money, and neighborhood of residence and business secures both economy and convenience. The merchant and master, then, find it for their interest to dwell in the vicinity of their active operations; and so, likewise, do the mechanic, laborer, and all dependent on business life. . . . [Later] as our wharves became crowded with warehouses, and encompassed with bustle and noise, the wealthier citizens, who peopled old "Knickerbocker" mansions, near the bay, transferred their residence to streets beyond the din; compensating for remoteness from their counting houses, by the advantages of increased quiet and luxury. Their habitations then passed into the hands, on the one side, of boarding house keepers, on the other, of real estate agents; and here, in its beginning, the tenant house became a real blessing to that class of industrious poor whose small earnings limited their expenses and whose employment in workshops, stores, or about the wharves and thoroughfares, rendered a near residence of much importance. At this period, rents were moderate, and a mechanic with family could hire two or more comfort-

able and even commodious apartments, in a house once occupied by wealthy people. . . . This state of tenantry comfort did not, however, continue long; for the rapid march of improvement speedily enhanced the value of property in the lower wards of the city, and as this took place, rents rose, and accommodations decreased in the same proportion. At first the better class of tenants submitted to retain their single floors, or two and three rooms, at the onerous rates, but this rendered them poorer, and those who were able to do so, followed the example of former proprietors, and emigrated to the upper wards. . . . It was soon perceived, by astute owners or agents of property, that a greater percentage of profit would be realized by the conversion of houses and blocks into barracks, and dividing their space into the smallest proportions capable of containing human life within four walls. . . . Blocks were rented of real-estate owners, or purchased on time, or taken in charge at a percentage, and held for underletting to applicants with no ready money and precarious means of livelihood. . . . To this class, then, entire blocks of buildings, worn out in other service, were let in hundreds of sub-divided apartments . . . and they soon became filled, from cellar to garret, with a class of tenantry living from hand to mouth, loose in morals, improvident in habits, degraded or squalid as beggary itself."[1]

I

It was just a question whether a man would take
seven percent and save his soul, or twenty-five
and lose it.

Jacob Riis

1

The Problem Stated

The first New York building designed specifically as a tenement house was, according to the recollection of the octogenarian marine engineer Charles Haswell, built in 1833 by James Allaire near his famous engine works at the eastern end of Water Street in what later became Corlears Hook Park. On each of its four floors it housed one family. By this time the city already had its slums, though its population had just reached a quarter of a million. Apportioning blame for the high death rate in his report of 1834, the city inspector as chief health officer cited intemperance and "the crowded and filthy state in which a great portion of our population live, apparently without being sensible of their situation . . . we have serious cause to regret that there are in our city so many mercenary landlords who only contrive in what manner they can [to] stow the greatest number of human beings in the smallest space."[1] These conditions were more fully described eight years later by the then incumbent city inspector, John Griscom, a physician at the New York Hospital who had served in the public dispensaries. In a special report to the Board of Aldermen based on his investigations of underground and court dwellings, he stressed the ill effects of overcrowding, filth, and especially those "damp, dark and chilly cellars" whose "vapors, with malignant breath /

Rise thick, and scatter midnight death."[2] To protect the life and health of the poor, he asked the city government for regulatory legislation and sanitary police to enforce it; all he got was his dismissal. Supported by interested citizens including the renowned Peter Cooper, he repeated his views at a public lecture and then published them in *The Sanitary Condition of the Laboring Population of New York* just three years after his contemporary Edwin Chadwick had produced his similarly titled pioneering report in Great Britain.

In New York, immigration was the catalyst, multiplying the city's population eightfold between the War of 1812 and the Civil War, largely with the destitute of Northwest Europe. "The tide of emigration," asserted Griscom, "which now sets so strongly towards our shores, cannot be turned back. We *must* receive the poor, the ignorant, and the oppressed from other lands, and it would be better to consider them as coming filled with the energy of hope for happier days, and more useful labors, than they found at home. No one, I presume, seriously believes that they come with bad intentions, and then whose fault is it that they live here in cellars more filthy than the cabins of whose wretchedness we hear so much, and for whose existence, half the blame is thrown upon the government they have left. Let us first cast the beam from our own eye. We are parties to their degradation, inasmuch as we permit the inhabitation of places, from which it is not possible improvement in condition or habits can come. We suffer the sub-landlord to stow them, like cattle, in pens, and to compel them to swallow poison with every breath. They are *allowed*, may it not be said *required*, to live in dirt."[3]

By the early 1840s, the tenement house had joined the cellar, alley, and rookery as the abode of these newcomers, and another city inspector was deploring the "prevailing practice, which is becoming every year more general, of building houses for the poorer classes of our population, so as to cover the whole or nearly the whole area of the ground, and thus crowding a large number of families together in a space which is not more than sufficient for one."[4] Notwithstanding further demands over the following decade for authority to regulate the design and construction of this new housing type so that the "errors and mischief of misguided haste, and the vile promptings of pecuniary profit, would thus be despoiled of their injury and fatality,"[5] there was no government supervision of the erection of tenement houses except for the general requirements of fire prevention. The standards were those of private enterprise.

The most notorious of all tenement houses was Gotham Court. Located on Cherry Street a short way up from where George Washington had briefly lived at the time of his inauguration two generations before (when the street had been lined with cherry trees), the building was erected in 1851 by Silas Wood, who, according to the later reformer Jacob Riis, was a benevolent Quaker who wished to build a model tenement.[6] Although the *Evening Post* considered Gotham Court "a praiseworthy enterprise and well worthy of immitation,"[7] it soon took over from the Five Points the reputation of being the worst spot in town. Its deterioration was marked by its changing nicknames: Swipe's Alley, Guzzle Row, Hell's Kitchen, Murderer's Row.

So called because of the confluence of Baxter, Worth, and Park streets, now a few blocks from City Hall, the Five Points had been described by Charles Dickens in his *American Notes:* "lanes and alleys, paved with mud knee-deep, underground chambers, where they dance and game . . . ruined houses, open to the street, whence, through wide gaps in the walls, other ruins loom upon the eye, as though the world of vice and misery had nothing else to show: hideous tenements which take this name from robbery and murder."[8] The newly built tenements such as Gotham Court quickly came to equal the old converted ones.

Five floors high and stretching 234 feet back from a frontage of 34 feet, the block contained 116 apartments entered from two side lanes, graphically known as Single and Double alleys. Seven and nine feet wide, they were lined by the yards of buildings from an adjacent street and another row of five-story tenements. Inside the dwellings, reached by narrow winding staircases, small windows in two cramped rooms opened over the sickening smells that rose through the pavement gratings from the doorless privies in the vaults below. Heated by a fireplace in the living room, lighted by the tenant's own kerosene lamps, with water drawn from the courts, the low monthly rent was probably around $3.25 in 1856 and $5 fourteen years later, thus maintaining its value with postwar inflation. Described by the Association for Improving the Condition of the Poor two years after its completion as being "of the better class"[9] of tenement (although considered overcrowded and deficient in ventilation), it was found a few years later to be a "horrible place"[10] occupied by 120 wretched Irish families who spent as much in the "rum holes" as they did on rent. When inspected in 1864 by the Citizens' Association Council of Hygiene and Public Health, it contained 4 cases of smallpox, 8 of typhus, 4 of measles, 7 of scarlatina, 5 of dynsentery, 12 of consumption, and 27 of infantile marasmus (though its salutary condition was considered to be normal for tenements in the lower part of the city).

Its open drains, only occasionally flushed, ran along both sides of the vaults of the building into the Cherry Street sewer and served as a breeding ground for rats and "as places of refuge and dens of iniquity for all the small thieves and vagabonds in the

Gotham Court, 1851
Source: Jacob A. Riis, *How the Other Half Lives* (1890).

vicinity,"[11] especially the local gang named the Swamp Angels, who hid themselves and their loot in the tenement's cellars, which were located immediately behind the district police station. "I found myself in an entry about four feet by six," wrote an eye-witness in 1871 just before Sweeney's Shambles, as it was then called, was temporarily closed by the Board of Health in an effort to clean it up, "with steep, rough, rickety stairs leading upward in the foreground, and their counterparts at the rear giving access to as successful a manufactory of disease and death as any city on earth can show. . . . Every step oozed with moisture and was covered sole deep with unmentionable filth. . . . The walls of rough stone dripped with slimy exudations, while the pavements yielded to the slightest pressure of the feet a suffocating odor compounded of bilge-water and sulphuretted hydrogen. Upon one side of this elongated cave of horrors were ranged a hundred closets, every one of which reeked with this filth."[12] Serviced by the food and liquor stores that occupied the Cherry Street front-age, its tenants were apparently contented until evicted by the city, when "denunciations loud and deep were uttered against the officials who had thus considerately driven them from the filthy slough in which they were wallowing."[13]

The tale of Gotham Court did have a comparatively happy ending. In 1880 the lease of the building was purchased by a group of philanthropists. Fulton Cutting told the 1894 Tenement House Committee that he had first had Gotham Court pointed out to him by Jacob Riis, and the *Real Estate Record* named him and his brother as the lessees (though Alfred White believed them to be Bayard Cutting, William Dodge, and Willis James). When they took over the building, the water pipes had been torn out and sold, the window shutters used as kindling, and the "appearance of the tenants justified the conditions of their homes."[14] Under the firm management of two ladies previously associated with the City Mission, all this changed. They demanded cleanliness, rectitude, sobriety, and the prompt payment of rent, and in return they offered efficient management and individual concern. The apartments, which even at reduced rents had been only half occupied because of their notoriety, were now filled according to the reformer Charles Wingate with "decent, respectable tenants."[15] This model state of affairs lasted until the owner found another lessee who offered more rent, but soon afterward the building was condemned under the tenement law amendments of 1895. The city paid nearly $20,000 in compensation for the property that 45 years before had been assessed at $23,000, and the following year Gotham Court was demolished.

In its early days, however, it seemed as if the findings of the Association for Improving the Condition of the Poor were correct: that the construction of tenements was often superior to the living habits of their inhabitants. After all, over a third of the population of Ireland lived in windowless one-room mud cabins shared by pigs and poultry, with a dunghill outside the hole that served for door, light, air, and chimney; while even in Irish cities the poor used slop buckets rather than privies and got their water from a public fountain. "While no invidious distinctions are designated," a report by the Association for Improving the Condition of the Poor observed, "it were folly to ignore the facts, that three-fourths of our tenant-house population are families of foreign-born immigrants, consisting chiefly of Irish, Germans, and a liberal admixture of other nationalities . . . the worst portions of the city are chiefly inhabited by immigrants of the lowest class, whose disregard of *personal* and *domiciliary cleanliness*, would, if left to themselves, convert a palace into a pig-sty."[16] The association's judgment was based on firsthand experience. Formed in 1843 and financed by wealthy merchants and businessmen, its aims were to prevent duplication and fraud in the giving of charity while elevating the moral and physical condition of the poor. Believing that defective character was the chief cause of poverty manifesting itself through indolence, improvidence, and intemperance, it considered economic relief less important than a reformed character. But convinced of the link between physical and moral degradation, it almost immediately concerned itself with the improvement of those conditions that appeared to breed disease, crime, drunkenness, and promiscuity.

Its *Fourth Report,* published in 1847, summarizing its investigations into the environment of the poor, noted that their tenements were "generally defective in size, arrangement, supplies of water, warmth, and ventilation; also the yards, sinks, and sewerage are in bad condition. The occupants consequently often suffer from sickness and premature mortality; their ability for self-maintenance is thereby impaired or destroyed; social habits and morals are debased, and a vast amount of wretchedness, pauperism, and crime is produced."[17] If the standard of accommodation being offered was extremely low, the rent was not, and the association appealed to enlightened capitalists to provide decent housing at a fair return. To aid them in their philanthropic investment, it circulated lithographed designs that had originally been evolved for its own use but had been shelved when the project was judged impracticable.

The proposal was to buy a plot of land 200 feet square, divide it in half in one direction by a passage 20 feet wide, and into 4 in the other direction by three passages, 20, 10, and 20 feet wide, respectively. These eight 4-story blocks would be further divided into three houses with separate entrances, each containing eight apartments consisting of a living room 15 by 11 feet and two bedrooms 7 by 12½ feet. With their own sink and water closet, they would rent at $1 a week and at the same time "yield a handsome income"[18] to potential owners. Considering that the apartments in these plans provided almost 30 percent more space per family than Gotham Court, plus sanitary conveniences, at slightly more rent, and were half as densely packed on the site, it was not surprising that no developer offered to use them.

A few years later the association returned to the problem of providing adequate new housing for the so-called laboring classes and set up a committee to make recommendations. Its report, published in 1853, found that large profits were being made on slum dwellings and that even the better newly built tenements were "overstocked with inmates, and in many instances, very badly arranged: the sleeping rooms, for example, are frequently without means of ventilation, being dark, or having windows 18 inches square, with fixed lattices . . . and are on so contracted and penurious a scale, that they are actually inferior, as it respects the essentials of a human dwelling, to many of the old buildings whose places they supply."[19] Determined to show that good low-rental housing was a worthy economic venture and a necessary counterpart to regulatory legislation (reformers of this period having great faith in benevolent capitalism), it organized its own subsidiary to erect the first authentic model tenement in 1855.

The only building designed as a tenement house in the city which was larger than Gotham Court, the Working Men's Home, as it was named, was located on six lots between Mott and Elizabeth streets and designed by John Ritch, founding member and first treasurer of the American Institute of Architects. Its 87 apartments on six floors faced onto an alley 22 feet wide, which, while not the imposing thoroughfare shown in the architect's perspective, was two and a half times greater than that of Gotham Court. Wide-access galleries ran along an open well at its back, leading to iron stairs and separate toilets and into the apartments, which, theoretically, received light and air from them. But

Working Men's Home, 1855, hallway
Source: Jacob A. Riis, *The Battle with the Slum* (1902).

behind the front outside windows of each living room (with pantry alcove supplied with water), the apartments stretched 36 feet deep back to the gallery so that any practical ventilation of their two miniature bedrooms could come only from the flues set into the structural crosswalls. The inner bedroom was also completely dark. Looking back on it nearly half a century later, housing specialist Lawrence Veiller found it "hard to imagine how a worse plan could have been chosen. When we consider what has since been built on six city lots, or what easily could have been built then, it is amazing to think that any body of men could have been so blind."[20] The architect, a native New Yorker, had no precedents other than current sensibilities and Gotham Court. "If they had only copied it," commented Veiller, "the results would not have been so bad." Nevertheless, the 1856 Assembly Select Committee considered the Working Men's Home the best of the tenements it visited, and the executive secretary of the Association for Improving the Condition of the Poor, Robert Hartley, extolled the "commodious, well-ventilated" dwellings that enabled 348 "colored" persons to live comfortably.[21] It was a question of relative standards. The rents were comparatively high: $5.50 to $8.50 monthly at a time that white unskilled workers *when employed* earned about $6 weekly; and they returned 6 percent on the association's investment. Twelve years later the building was sold; the condition of the poor had not remained improved.

Although William Tolman of the association later cited the post-Civil War dispersal of blacks as the cause of its decline, according to Riis it was its long unsupervised corridors from street to street which not only gave doubtful through ventilation to the apartments but also indisputable through access to neighborhood toughs, whose presence drove respectable tenants out of the building. "The moral is plain," the later model tenement owner Alfred White observed: "A well-built house with fireproof halls and iron stairways, will become a residence of the lowest and dirtiest classes unless the manager or agent compels them to habits of neatness and order."[22] However, even the rigidly disciplined Five Points House of Industry failed in its turn to make the building financially self-supporting as a dormitory for working women, and in 1873 it once again changed ownership, to take its final form as the Big Flat until it was demolished in 1890. By this time the building was tenanted by a mixture of Polish Jews, Irish, Italians, and Chinese, with nearly a quarter of the apartments vacant. The upper rows of toilets had been removed, the alley built over at its ends, and its side light and air diminished by the backs of a solid mass of five-story workshops erected along Canal Street. Just before it ended its 35-year life, the building was again visited and described. "In a large proportion of the rooms," wrote Dr. Lucy Hall, "there is no means of ventilation, and a ray of sunshine has never touched the blackened walls, which a dimly burning match revealed covered with dampness and vegetable organisms. The air was thick with decaying filth and its products. The portions of the building where waste and excreta were, or should have been disposed of, were literally reeking, above and below, with what seemed the accumulation of years and yet we were gravely told that the place was cleaned (?) daily by the janitor. . . . As our guide proceeded we found ourselves in an everdescending scale of poverty, squalor, and wretchedness. The noisome air of the small, dimly lighted, and unkempt rooms was rivalled by that of the court-yards, where the masses of garbage, tossed recklessly in every direction, were made sodden by slops, water from the hydrants, and streams of excreta pouring unhindered from the dilapidated structure which occupied one extremity of the yard, destined for the common use of both front and rear tenements. Here were homes without bed, chair, table, or other furniture than a battered stove and a few benches. Men and women, many of them stupid with drink, and swarms of pale, sickly, prematurely old, and neglected children filled every available space."[23] This was a far cry from the architect's sketch with a well-dressed couple perambulating on a nonexistent sidewalk.

Gotham Court and the Working Men's Home were unique in their largeness and notoriety. They were also unusual in being among the very few specially designed apartment buildings in the city initially considered to be model tenements, though that such existed was denied by the 1856 Assembly Select Committee. "In a few of them," it reported, "the necessities of ventilation seem to have been somewhat considered, and in others the passages and stairways do not present the same trap for human life in emergencies of fire as in the less pretending houses built to 'hold' tenants; but in the important combined requisites of adequate drainage, abundant supply of water, separation of families, light, heat, dryness, ventilation, and appliances for health and cleanliness at all seasons, which *every* tenant-house, fit for human beings to dwell in, should be supplied with; there has been no building yet constructed which the Committee would endorse as a 'model.' "[24]

If the Association for Improving the Condition of the Poor, with all its research and professional guidance, failed to produce a satisfactory solution to the problem of providing low-rental dwellings, it was unlikely that the private builder without its resources would do any better. Individually owned by small investors, most tenements were constructed on the very restrictive standard 25-by-100-foot city lots originally established for home-building settlers and perpetuated by the Commissioners' Map of 1811 drawn up by the engineer John Randel. Bearing in mind "that a city is to be composed principally of the habitations of men," though not of tenement houses, which lay twenty years in the future, "and that straight-sided, and right-angled houses are the most cheap to build and the most convenient to live in,"[25] the commissioners imposed a gridiron over the hills of Manhattan. East-west streets from First Street, off of Houston Street above the disarray of old New York, to 115th Street were cut up into blocks by twelve south-north avenues with First Avenue by the East River and Twelfth Avenue along the Hudson. Only the old Bloomingdale Road (later renamed Broadway) idiosyncratically broke diagonally through this pattern.

The typical tenements of the 1850s, set into one of these minimal rectangles, consisted of a 25-by-50-foot front house, four or five stories high with dark interior stairs, having two lines of rooms on each floor with dark bedrooms in the center, and a similar 25-by-25-foot rear house at the end of the lot leaving a 25-foot-square internal court. Here stood the hydrant and the privies (when these were not in the cellar), normally unusable, dark at night, with their cesspool overflowing on the floor and seats so that slops were commonly thrown out of the windows to join the garbage on the sidewalk. Even the newest buildings soon became indistinguishable from existing slums. Reporting on a modern tenement in Hester Street which rented at the standard rate of $5 to $6.50 monthly for two rooms, the 1856 Assembly Select Committee described how the "place literally swarmed with life, but life of so abject and squalid a character as to scarcely merit the name. Dirty, half-naked children filled the cramped rooms and entries to suffocating populousness. There was no provision for ventilation; the drainage was insufficient; the sinks in wretched condition, and the entire structure thick with nauseating smells."[26]

The 1853 committee report of the Association for Improving the Condition of the Poor had recommended the erection of model tenements by philanthropists, as well as legislation to regulate tenement design. The first was inaugurated by the Working Men's Home; the second began with the appointment of the 1856 Assembly Select Committee charged with examining tenement houses in the cities of New York and Brooklyn and advising on what laws were necessary to protect their inhabitants. After a week of inspection, the committee reported that it had found "drunken and diseased adults of both sexes lying in the midst of their filth; idiotic and crippled children suffering from neglect and ill treatment; girls just springing into womanhood, living indiscriminately in the same apartment with men of all ages and of all colors; babes left so destitute of care and nourishment as to be fitted only for a jail or hospital in after years, if they escape the blessing of an early grave."[27] It asked for extra time to study questions of ventilation, cleanliness, cellar rooms, fire exits, and the prevention of prostitution and incest by the reduction of overcrowding. The realization that chastity could not be expected from girls forced to undress and sleep in rooms filled with family and lodgers was a stimulus to the nineteenth-century conscience and a significant factor in reforming zeal. The secretary of the committee, Augustine Duganne, a poet and writer of patriotic songs who became a one-term assemblyman during the Know-Nothing electoral successes of the mid-1850s, summed it up in verse: "Vice is a monster of so frightful mien, / As, to be *hated*, needs but to be seen; / But seen too oft—familiar to the face— / We first endure, then *pity*, then *embrace!*"[28]

The committee's request to be prolonged was turned down, but, having become personally involved, the five assemblymen persisted on their own and submitted their report the following year. Like the Association for Improving the Condition of the Poor, it found that tenements as built lacked air, light, space, water, cleanliness, and a proper arrangement of rooms. To remedy these defects, it proposed an unpaid board of three commissioners with the authority to have any tenement used for three or more families inspected between the hours of sunrise and sunset and to require it to be raised to an acceptable standard of fitness, occupancy, and upkeep or be vacated until it was. Applying only to existent tenements and not to those being continuously planned and erected, such retrospective action would have been of little use at a time when their construction was peaking toward sixteen new buildings a week. Nevertheless, the central issue had been clearly stated: the need for example and control to superimpose on a motley immigrant mass the modes and ideals of American standards. This leavening process was to pace the progress of housing reform.

"Blame not poverty that in desperation it yields to vicious example and seeks alleviation in the excitement of 'policy playing' or 'rum drinking.' Blame, rather, law and authority that they interpose not protection, nor establish incentives to industry, cleanliness, and the care of health. Blame, rather, philanthropy and justice! that they do not utter trumpet-tongued protests against the abuses allowed to exist, nor shake the very pillars of legislation with a demand for 'reform! reform! root and branch reform!.' "[29]

2

First Step

The 1856 Assembly Select Committee's recommendations for legislation were ignored. The only laws applicable to the erection of tenements before the Civil War remained those on fire-retarding construction and a later provision for fire escape stairs. At that time, in 1862, the first separate Building Department was set up and James McGregor appointed as superintendent. To curb the excesses of the tenement system, "that plan by which the greatest amount of profit is sought to be realized from the least possible amount of space, with little or no regard for the health, comfort, or protection of the lives of the tenants,"[1] McGregor proposed the most stringent laws and their vigorous enforcement. Unfortunately, even the 1862 law left its practical application to the discretion of the superintendent (as long as his decisions were upheld by the city's supreme court), while no standards at all were established for site coverage, heights, light, ventilation, or sanitary amenities.

Confronted by recurring epidemics before the nature of bacteria was understood, enlightened mid-nineteenth-century health officials believed diptheria, scarlet fever, and other contagious diseases to be filth diseases emanating from deleterious environmental conditions. The fact was that infection often coexisted with poverty. When Stephen Smith was physician in charge of hospital tents on Blackwell's (later Welfare) Island during the 1850s, he tracked the source of a typhus outbreak to a tenement but found that all he could do to improve its condition was to threaten to publicize his discovery. While the specific sources of infection, carried by lice in the case of typhus or contaminated food and water in the periodic attacks of cholera, were unknown, it was apparent that cleanly habits were an aid to health. In 1856, therefore, concerned doctors in the New York Academy of Medicine organized a petition to the state legislature, following it later with a draft bill, requesting the establishment of a Board of Health to deal with the sanitary problems engendered by mass immigration. This move, while frustrated by procedural subterfuges, resulted in the appointment of a Senate committee to investigate the existing health responsibilities vested with the city inspector.

The office of the city inspector had multifarious functions including keeping the streets clean, regulating the public markets, and protecting the public health. Originally headed by physicians, the department had become a political sinecure. The 1858 hearings took on the appearance of a tussle between the medical profession and the city administration, with the latter winning the battle of words and the former carrying the committee with it. Of 138 persons employed in the city inspector's department, only one clerk had any medical knowledge. The 22 health wardens included seven from the building trades, four liquor dealers, a butcher, a barber, an emigrant runner, and a policy dealer, each receiving $20 a week, or substantially more than a first-class craftsman. Despite an allocation of up to $400,000 a year for street cleaning, the streets were still unclean, but each incumbent was able to dip into this sum to fight for the retention of his office.

Giving evidence before the committee, Augustine Duganne once again enumerated some of the evils of tenement house living:

overcrowding through subletting and taking in lodgers encouraged promiscuity; darkness led to evil; halls and stairs were so cramped that often two people could not pass at the same time, and escape in case of fire was virtually impossible; lack of ventilation was the major cause of disease; the interior construction of these buildings was largely of light wooden lathing "so inflammable that the entire structure is like a mammoth tinder-box";[2] water was generally only in the yard and often in the barroom of the ground-floor grocery; and even when pipes were carried to the upper landings, they were never insulated and often froze and burst.

The Senate committee found that the city's excessive mortality was due to overcrowding, faulty construction, lack of light and ventilation, unwholesome food and beverages, poor housekeeping, insufficient sewerage, and unclean streets and wharves—in short, "a general disregard of sanitary precautions, the imperfect execution of existing ordinances, and the total absence of a regularly organized, efficient sanitary police."[3] But its recommendations for a Board of Health with a medical superintendent separated from an emasculated city inspector's office were rejected by the legislature after its New York City advocate in the Assembly withdrew his support on being told that three of his friends would otherwise lose their jobs.

During the committee hearings, a group of interested citizens had formed the New York Sanitary Association, with John Griscom as first vice-president and Peter Cooper among its council. When the New York Academy of Medicine gave up the fight, this new association tried in successive years to push a health bill through the legislature. In 1860 the Assembly again defeated the bill when two of its committee sponsors voted against it. In 1861, when the Assembly voted overwhelmingly for it, the Senate withdrew its earlier approval. The reason for its recurrent failure to pass was well known. "We understand," noted the *Tribune*, "that

$10,000 in cold cash went up from our city to Albany on Friday night to defeat the Metropolitan Health Bill. This was an *extra* sum, and is understood to be on account of street cleaning."[4] The extent of the corruption of the city inspector's department was brought into the open in 1864, by which time the notorious William Marcy Tweed dominated New York politics. A dissident superintendent, taking advantage of the emnity between his superior, Francis Boole, and the new mayor, Godfrey Gunther, against whom Boole had run for office, divulged not only that an offer to clean the streets without charge had been turned down because the city inspector expected to receive a quarter to a half of all expenditures but also that numerous salaries were paid to nonexistent employees and certified by the department's auditor, who happened to be the city inspector's brother. In the ensuing altercation the dissident superintendent was fired; Boole, suspended by the mayor, merely ignored him. "It is not true," he wrote to the Board of Aldermen, "that I possess a power which no honest man should desire to exercise. Power *may*, safely, be trusted in the hands of an 'honest' man."[5]

Amalgamating with Cooper's newly formed Citizens' Association, which had been organized to effect reforms in the city government, the Sanitary Association, or Council of Hygiene and Public Health as it was now called, made another abortive attempt to have a health bill passed in 1864. When this failed, the Citizens' Association, angrily determined to rouse public opinion against the machinations of the city inspector, donated $22,000 to enable a corps of young physicians to personally inspect every locality and building throughout the city. In the absence of the committee's secretary Elisha Harris, who was engaged with the United States Sanitary Commission in the Civil War then in progress, the investigation was organized by his contemporary Stephen Smith, who was on the surgical staff of Bellevue Hospital.

The city was divided into 29 sanitary districts, and each was examined as to topography, drainage, buildings, population, disease, and mortality. The individual reports, edited by Harris, made up a dirge of filthy streets polluted by the soiling and butchery of animals, overflowing sewage, overcrowded rooms shut off from light and air, degraded men and women finding their pleasures in groggeries, brothels, and lottery shops—a ululation virtually unrelieved except for a paragraph commending a group of cleanly, healthy, and industrious Germans living by the beneficent beer halls of the Bowery. The first sanitary district downtown on the West Side, where the old family residences had been taken over by Irish and German immigrants, held three churches—and 423 saloons. In the adjacent fifth ward there were 108 stables. Further north, in the sixty or so blocks that made up the eighth ward west of Broadway, there were 101 brothels. Where the wealthier people lived, private dwellings faced onto clean pavements and elegant shade trees, but just around the corner the streets were filthy, and alleys overflowed with "slops, water, garbage, human excrements, and urine."[6] Even the newer brick tenements between Broadway and the Bowery were despoiled by slaughterhouses and fat-boiling establishments, while those east of Third Avenue were found to have defective drainage, insufficient water, little ventilation, and tenants who thew their garbage into the streets rather than use the boxes provided outside.

Statistically, the survey counted 486,000 persons living in 15,511 tenement houses and a further 15,224 in cellars. There were over 9,000 tenements below Fourteenth Street containing nearly 300,000 persons, and the overall density of the eleventh and thirteenth wards along the East River was over 300 persons to the acre. Observing that the poor were becoming a segregated majority, overcrowded, sick, and morally, socially, and politically corrupt, the report demanded: "is it not reasonable and true that inasmuch as the causes of all these evils have been and are mainly physical—or at least always allied with material agencies which are under human control—in the same degree, and conversely and by redeeming conditions mainly of a physical nature, the evils we now deprecate, and the impending perils we now fear, may be and should speedily be averted and effectually prevented?"[7]

The Civil War draft riots in New York had occurred just the year before. Then an eyewitness had reported: "The high brick blocks and closely packed houses where the mobs originated, seemed to be literally hives of sickness and vice. It was wonderful to see, and difficult to believe, that so much misery, disease and wretchedness can be huddled together and hidden by high walls, unvisited and unthought of, so near our own abodes. Lewd, but pale and sickly young women, scarce decent in their ragged attire, were impudent and scattered everywhere in the crowd. But what numbers of these poorer classes are deformed—what numbers are made hideous by self-neglect and infirmity! Alas! human faces look so hideous with hope and self-respect all gone! And female forms and features are made so frightful by sin, squalor, and de-basement! To walk the streets as we walked them, in those hours of conflagration and riot, was like witnessing the day of judgment, with every wicked thing revealed, every sin and sorrow blazingly glared upon, every hidden abomination laid bare before hell's ex-pectant fire. The elements of popular discord are gathered in these wretchedly constructed tenement houses where poverty, disease and crime find an abode."[8]

The solutions that the report proposed were: the construction of improved dwellings by private investors, the improvement of existing tenements, the enactment and enforcement of sanitary laws, and the establishment of a research department to acquire and disseminate information on matters pertaining to the physical and social welfare of the working class. The first of these proposals continued to have little appeal or effect. The fourth found application in only a few charitable organizations. It remained for legislation to reflect the standards that were publicly acceptable.

Supported by the evidence of its investigations, the Council of Hygiene and Public Health submitted yet another bill to the legislature, but this was again defeated (the day before President Lincoln was assassinated) by the opposition preparing an alternate bill that gave the Assembly an excuse for holding back on the original, which had already received Senate approval. The outcome was another Senate investigation instigated by the Republican member from New York City, which took place during 1865 and was reported by the future first president of Cornell University, Andrew White, who was the only one of the three-man committee to be reelected the following year.

The committee's questioning of City Inspector Boole's assistants provided comic relief, if little else. After one of the health inspectors explained that he did not visit a person with smallpox because the family were "highjinnicks," that is, "persons who doctor themselves," the meaning of hygienics became a standard query by the committee. White later recalled, "some answered that they had them somewhat; some thought that they had them 'pretty bad,' others thought that there was 'not much of it,' others claimed that they were 'quite serious.' " Finally one of the health inspectors was asked on oath whether he knew what the word meant. "Yes sir," he replied. "It means the bad smells that arise from standing water."[9]

By this time, however, any further revelations of incompetence were unnecessary. On November 2, 1865, the steamship *Atalanta* arrived in New York harbor with fifteen dead from Asiatic cholera among the German immigrants crowded in the steerage. Fear of an epidemic and a postwar Republican electoral landslide combined to bring about reforms that had evaded a decade of agitation. In February 1866 an act was passed "for the preservation of life and health, and to prevent the spread of disease."[10] Abolishing the office of city inspector, (Boole, who under Tammany protection had survived investigation by the Board of Aldermen, Senate, courts, and governor, ended in a madhouse, according to Andrew White), the new law set up a Metropolitan Board of Health for the greater New York area consisting of nine New York area appointees: four new commissioners (including three physicians) nominated by the governor and approved by the Senate, the existing four metropolitan police commissioners, and the health officer of the Port of New York. With a staff of a sanitary superintendent and fifteen sanitary inspectors (ten of whom had to be physicians), the new board became responsible for keeping the streets clean, preventing disease, and removing any nuisances that were dangerous to life or health. These were myriad, including animals and their manure, slaughterhouses, bone boiling, markets, sewage, privies, garbage, rag picking, adulterated food and drink, and the environmental condition of cellars and tenement houses of which there were discovered to be 18,582, half of them in need of substantial improvement. The new board was an instant success. Lauding its anniversary, the *New York Times* recalled the bad old days of the year before when the "streets reeked with putridity: tenement-houses belched forth the pestilential odors of the charnel-house; slime and animal refuse clogged the gutters in the vicinity of slaughter-pens and fat and bone boiling establishments; and a hundred evils now comparatively unknown, if not forgotten, made the metropolis a stench in the nostrils of civilization."[11] That year the board's powers were further extended by the first tenement-house act of 1867.

From the beginning of its own formation five years earlier, the Building Department under James McGregor had tried to appropriate this responsibility for itself. In his second report, the superintendent had ventured the argument that "while it is not in the province of this Department to look after the sanitary laws governing the health and comfort of our citizens, yet the humanitarian considerations presented to our immediate notice, by coming so closely in contact with the abodes of squalid poverty in crowded tenement localities, have led to serious reflection as to whether an amendment should not be engrafted into the present code, providing for the size as well as the means of ventilating tenement and sleeping apartments, with a view of affording propers means of ventilation."[12] The following year he tried another tack, acknowledging that although the sanitary condition of existing tenements might be supervised by another department, no other department could enforce standards of potential sanitary fitness such as "the heights of ceilings, the dimensions of apartments, size of halls and stairways, methods of ventilation by means of the admission of light and air, and proper flues for the escape of impure air, all of which appertain to methods of construction."[13] By his fourth report of 1865, when it had become apparent that any new tenement law would be vested with the prospective Board of Health, because of the overwhelming concern for the health hazards of tenement life, McGregor had reluctantly yielded to "cheerfully accept any duty, however onerous, in aiding, to the fullest extent of my abilities, those who may be intrusted with establishing and executing salutary laws, designed to benefit that large class of our citizens occupying tenement houses."[14] Unfortunately, the graciousness of his words was not matched by his acts. His resentment and consequent lack of cooperation set a pattern that permitted the next 6000 tenement houses to be built without any significant improvements.

This conflict between control of the physical standards of housing and responsibility for what went on inside it remained unresolved until the end of the century. It also continued to be inherently ambiguous in the supply of housing, which was a major activity that spanned traditional occupations. The building industry and its related professions had little concern for the overall human consequences of their actions; social reformers largely ignored the technical problems of property development. There were very few housing specialists who combined both interests.

3

False Start

The unprecedented building activity of the 1850s, the outcome of the expanding commerce and massive immigration, had collapsed with the panic of 1857, and overextended speculators had difficulty in renting their buildings during the years leading up to the Civil War. By the end of the war, however, the interruption to private construction had created a new building shortage at a time of accumulated wealth, and the low cost of land and availability of labor and materials made tenements again a popular investment. From a low of 129 in 1864, the number of tenement houses completed each year rose to a high of 824 in 1871.[1] The 1867 act did little to improve this mass of new building.

The immediate source of the new act was the Assembly Committee on Public Health, Medical Colleges and Societies, which had been asked to assess the various resolutions that had been put forward in the legislature. Its report, based on collected testimony (and not on personal inspection), confirmed the need for regulatory action. While almost none of the Brooklyn tenement houses were found to be public nuisances, over one-half of New York's were considered to be in bad sanitary condition. However, of these 9846, the Board of Health noted that 5814, or nearly 60 percent, had reached the state they were in through neglect. On the one hand, the faulty design of tenements resulted in defici-

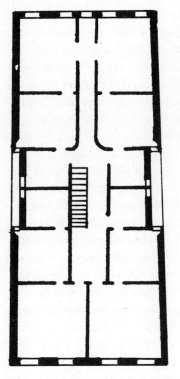

"Superior" tenement house, ca.1860, plan
Its superiority was attributed to its ventilation of the inner rooms and the staircase hall, its supply of water to every kitchen, and its high standard of maintenance.

Source: Citizens' Association of New York, Council of Hygiene and Public Health, *Report Upon the Sanitary Condition of the City* (1865).

encies in ventilation, light, drainage, toilets, and sometimes water supply and fire escapes; on the other, even suitable buildings would be useless "unless accompanied by constant watchfulness" over the tenants.[2] The report contained case histories of good and bad tenements, one of the former being at 89 Perry Street on the West Side. Though its plan was not considered anything unusual, it was included to show that under excellent management "a large number [20] of families *can* live together in one house without any gross violation of sanitary laws."[3] The Citizens' Association 1865 report also included the plan of this building, it being "so much superior . . . to other tenant-houses . . . [with] better ventilation than usual. . . . This house, as might be expected, *has been very free from sickness.*"[4] Its design was of interest in the history of rising standards, being a primitive dumbbell plan with air shafts 2 feet deep, a type that came into prominence twenty years later and then became obsolete after another twenty years. The committee submitted its draft bill, and two months later the new act was passed. For the first time the term *tenement house* was legally defined "to mean and include every house, building or portion thereof, which is rented, leased, let or hired out to be occupied or is occupied as the home or residence of more than three families living independently of another, and doing their cooking upon the premises, or by more than two families upon a floor, so living and cooking, but having a common right in the halls, stairways, yards, water closets or privies, or some of them."[5]

Improvements for existing tenements included an acceptable fire escape, the ventilation of inner bedrooms through outer living rooms and ventilated halls, the maintenance in good repair of roofs and stairs; the vacating of unsuitable cellar dwellings, and sufficient (one toilet for twenty occupants) and efficient sanitary fittings and their drainage. Every water closet or privy was to be properly connected with a sewer—if one was available, and no cesspools were permitted—unless they were unavoidable. The fact was that the sewerage of New York was still primitive like that of large cities elsewhere. There was widespread confusion about the effect of filth on health. While some doctors had come to believe that contagion was transmitted by specific bacteria, others held to the view that poor sanitary conditions produced a local atmospheric state that caused disease. A common nineteenth-century view was that quoted by the noted engineer Charles Haswell in his book *Sewerage and Sewage in the City of New York:* "we are practically saturating ourselves and everything about us, with deadly miasmatic emanation . . . the made and undrained land on which so many thousand of our homes are built, is packed with miasm . . . it comes to us on every breeze . . . we drink malarious water, cooled with malarious ice, and live and sleep in an atmosphere stifling with sewer gas."[6] The new act also prohibited the storage of combustible material and the keeping of livestock, and it required proper receptacles for garbage. The names and addresses of owners and agents were to be publicly displayed, all buildings were to be kept clean, health officers were to have free access, and the department was authorized to empty buildings that for medical or physical reasons were considered unfit for habitation.

For new dwellings there were additional requirements. A clear space of 10 feet was prescribed between the rear of a new building and any existing building, while a larger space was to be left between a new front building and an existing rear building on the same lot. Every habitable room was to be at least 8 feet high (unless in an attic) and was either to have a window or to connect with one that had or, if the room had an area of less than 100 square feet, was to be directly ventilated by a flue or air shaft. Halls on each floor were to be provided with windows. Water was to be available in the building or yard. Cellar floors were to be cemented, and each suite of rooms was to have at least one fireplace.

Violators were liable to fines and/or imprisonment and also to daily penalties. But although thousands of ventilating windows were put into existing rooms, hall staircases were lighted and aired, plumbing was improved, cellars were cleared, and buildings were cleaned, the final results were discouraging. While the *New York Times* could congratulate the outgoing Metropolitan Board of Health in 1869 on its "determined efforts to mitigate the horrors of the tenement houses,"[7] its own comments were less sanguine. "It must be borne in mind," its fourth and last report noted, "that the classes of people that are crowded into the most densely-populated houses and blocks are, with rare exceptions, so poor and ignorant, or so uncleanly in their habits, that they would breathe filth and sickness even in a prairie-cabin."[8] The limited potentialities of the board's reforms were later summed up by a sanitary inspector who sadly observed that "a mere technical compliance with the law of the State does not in all instances secure even a distant approximation to the conditions required by sanitary law, in regard to light and ventilation, while in many other respects it falls far short of meeting the real sanitary wants of the people. As long as the massing of huge tenement-houses on limited areas of ground is allowed, and those immense structures are packed like herrings with human beings, each contributing his or her quota of poisonous gas and effete animal matter to the confined atmosphere, the bills of mortality will continue to swell, notwithstanding the small transom windows, the roof-ventilator, and the sink-trap required by law."[9]

The same was true of new tenements. Although officers of the Board of Health optimistically described them as "all well ventilated, lighted and drained" and "models of what tenement houses should be,"[10] it was obvious that the application of the laws to the design of new buildings was even less effective than in the rehabilitation of the old. By the 1860s, the typical new tenement no longer was the front and rear house but had become a larger single building occupying up to two-thirds of the site. The restrictions of the 1867 act were intended to mitigate abuse of the earlier arrangement; ironically, when applied to the design that was then current, they extended and consolidated some of its worst features.

A 66-foot-long tenement on a 100-foot lot contained eight dark rooms on each floor. The new law required only a 10-foot yard and not even that if no adjoining building existed. And while it was forbidden to erect a front building too close to a rear building, there was nothing to prevent a rear building being erected against a front building. The resultant possibility was the "railroad" tenement, a 90-foot-long solid rectangular block of a building with twelve to sixteen rooms per floor, only four of them (at front and back) with direct light and air—a type just beginning to appear before the 1867 act sanctioned its legality. As with many restrictive laws, minimum standards soon became standard practice. Furthermore, even these were subject to discretionary interpretation; and while this was ostensibly the prerogative of the enlightened Board of Health, it devolved in practice upon the less praiseworthy Building Department.

The addition of the new tenement requirements to the existing bylaws had divided departmental responsibility: construction and fire prevention were under the jurisdiction of the Building Department; space and sanitary standards were the responsibility of the Board of Health. But whereas the former was set up to inspect plans and specifications (the submission of which had become compulsory in 1866) and subsequently to visit the works in progress, this was really outside the latter's capabilities. The Board of

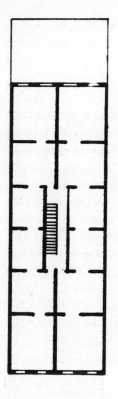

Typical railroad tenement house, ca. 1870, plan

Source: New York City, Health Department, *The Tenement House Problem in New York* (1887).

Health therefore concentrated on upgrading existing buildings, while the Building Department seemed to assume responsibility for the construction of new tenements. McGregor, however, attempting to dislodge his rival from its sphere of influence, disclaimed all obligation to enforce its ordinances, some of which he professed to oppose. The result was that the majority of the 1867 act's requirements were neither checked against a projected tenement's plans nor enforced while it was under construction—but after the building had been completed, it would be inspected by health officials, who could, if they liked, demand alterations. The outcome of this arrangement was obvious: few courts were willing to order substantial changes to property that had just been built with Building Department approval.

McGregor had been first appointed by the Republican mayor George Opdyke and had a reputation for probity. By 1870, when he was reappointed for a third term as building superintendent by the Tweed Ring mayor Oakey Hall, he had evidently learned to follow their example. A few weeks ago, editorialized the *Sun*, "we charged . . . and our charges have never been even denied, that he has connived for a long time at the grossest violations of the law providing for the safety of buildings in this city. We once more allege. . . . That for the last three years not one tenement house has been built in the city of New York in conformity with the law. That nearly every man building a tenement house within that time has paid from one hundred to five hundred dollars a house for the privilege of violating the law. That within the past three years over 5,000 [1107, according to Building Department records] tenement houses have been built, and that for the unlawful privileges accorded the builders over one million two hundred and fifty thousand dollars have been paid. And we cite, as an example, a case in which Andrew J. Kerwin was made to pay $1,400 for permission to build thirteen tenement houses in

Thirty-ninth street otherwise than as the law required. . . . In the face of all these reasons for sternly inquiring into Mr. McGregor's fitness for his position, Mayor Hall gives him a new lease of power! The general supposition is that he has done so to oblige Taxpayer Tweed, who is said to share in Mr. McGregor's illegal emoluments to the extent of $100,000 per annum."[11]

That these charges were closer to the truth than what the Board of Health inspectors reported is evidenced by the remarks of the president of the Real Estate Owners' Association speaking nine months later: "The laws regulating the erection of tenements in this city are a dead letter, on account of their impracticability. Not a single house in this city has been erected in conformity with those laws. Tenement property would not net four percent if those laws were complied with. They provide for permits to construct tenements otherwise than in conformity with the laws, if the permits are sanctioned by the Supreme Court. Every builder of a tenement house finds it to his advantage to obtain a permit as, by non-conformity, he saves about $3,000 in the expense of constructing a first-class tenement. We want laws made that can be observed, and do not want to be hampered by laws which are inoperative, and the evasion of which causes an outlay of money which we do not believe goes into the public treasury."[12] In 1868 several of the most eminent architects in the city had written to McGregor through the Citizens' Association deprecating the increase in the cost of low-income housing caused by what they considered to be unnecessary provisions in the new laws. They had also objected to his discretionary powers, the lack of on-site inspections, and the need to submit their designs for Building Department approval. The laws of 1871 and 1874 repealed some of the more stringent requirements, including those for fire prevention passed at the same time as the first tenement act, but did little to lessen the opportunity for graft.

The boom-and-bust pattern of building activity was once again repeated when construction declined after the panic of 1873. During the next five years real estate development gradually slowed down, for even tenements, generally considered to be a profitable investment, were hazardous when tenants could not pay their rent. By the end of the 1870s, however, business was getting back to normal, and reformers were again provoked into action.

The granting of home rule at the beginning of the decade had given the city control of its own administration. The fall of Tweed encouraged rectitude. In 1873 the Republican mayor William Havemeyer (who had helped depose Tweed but was later arraigned by the governor on a petition from the city for condoning corruption in his administration) appointed Charles Chandler to the Board of Health and Walter Adams to the Building Department. Chandler, an industrial chemist, had studied at Harvard and received his doctorate from Göttingen University. At the age of twenty he had been professor of chemistry at Union College, Schenectady, and from 1864, for 47 years, was professor (and, for most of that period, dean) at Columbia University. Before his appointment as president of the Board of Health, he had been employed to study some of the city's sanitary problems. Reappointed in 1877 for another six years by Mayor Smith Ely, his accomplishments during his ten years of office were varied and numerous, including the celebrated clearing of Washington Market, where, after cooperation had been refused by the police and public works departments, he and Stephen Smith, then one of the health commissioners, led an army of carts through the streets at night to pull down the stalls and remove the mess of putrid droppings.

Adams was less notable, having previously been McGregor's deputy. His integrity was also less unquestionable. Although the state committee that reported in 1876 on the city's departments found him to be an excellent administrator, the *New York Times* thought otherwise. "The great dark, towering tenement-houses, which offend the eye at almost every point," it wrote in 1877, "are witnesses, whether they stand or fall, of the mal-administration of a department which is continually imperilling not only the property, but the lives of the tens of thousands it is paid to protect."[13] When Adams was elected to Tammany Hall, the outcry forced him to forgo acceptance, and although he requested sick leave at the end of 1878, it was refused by the conscientious mayor, who replaced him by his deputy.

It was the usual story: the multiplication of jobs given as patronage, trained personnel shunned, violations of the law overlooked for bribes. Adam's withdrawal, it was claimed, occurred only because he was paid off by his successor, Henry Dudley, an architect himself and son of one of the best-known New York architects of the mid-century. Then followed the pattern established by the city inspector in the previous decade: first an abortive attempt to have the Building Department investigated by the city council, then by a grand jury, the abolition of the Building Department by the legislature in 1880, finally followed by Dudley's severance from Tammany protection and his job by a court judgment that upheld his removal from office.

But the Building Department's only legitimate concerns for new tenement buildings were their construction and fire precautions. Decisions on lot coverage, lighting, ventilation, and sanitation were the responsibility of the Board of Health. Unfortunately, up to August 1878, it did not even require the prior submission of plans. Chandler seems to have had three reasons for perpetuating this abdication of responsibility: it was outside his range of interest; he continued with his predecessor's assumption that the Building Department would do whatever was necessary; and he was apolitical at a time when the owners and occupants of tenements were major elements in political rivalry. What finally pushed him into action was the reform agitation during the winter of 1878.

The year before, the more recently formed State Charities Aid Association had joined the Association for Improving the Condition of the Poor in its concern for the housing needs of the poor. Its Committee on Out-Door Relief, afterward known as the Committee for the Elevation of the Poor in their Homes, collected information on model tenements from various sources and solicited further designs from notable local architects. It then invited a number of interested persons to meet with Alfred White of Brooklyn.

A partner in a family importing firm, then in his early thirties and involved in philanthropy, White was responsible for the first successful model tenements in the New York area, believing that it was "time to recognize that if the intelligent and wealthy portion of the community do not provide homes for the working classes, the want will be continually supplied by the less intelligent class and after the old fashion."[14] His first units, named the Home Buildings, were opened in February 1877 at the corner of Baltic and Hicks streets in Brooklyn. A second building was completed alongside them later in the year. He then purchased a 200-by-250-foot site in the adjoining block for the six-story Tower Buildings, which were set around a large quadrangle. Two rows of six- to nine-room houses along a grassy lane completed this development of 267 dwellings. The design of the apartment buildings was based on the British model tenements constructed in the previous decade for the Improved Industrial Dwellings Company under Sidney Waterlow. Open stairs at the front of the building led to small galleries serving two shallow three- or four-room apartments on either side. Although the first building had inner bedrooms, this defect was subsequently remedied, and all later rooms had outside windows. Each apartment had a water closet. Rents ranged from $6 to nearly $11 monthly and, with an initial return of 7½ percent on his investment, White's buildings became renowned both for their standard of accommodation (and tenantry, which was rigidly administered) and for their financial viability.

After pondering whether to set up its own model tenement company, the State Charities Aid Association decided to concentrate on obtaining administrative and legal reforms in collaboration with the Association for Improving the Condition of the Poor. Chandler was one of the latter's vice-presidents, while Carl Pfeiffer, his consulting architect at the Board of Health, was on the State Charities Aid Association's tenement committee—as were John Bowne, who had replaced Robert Hartley as executive secretary of the Association for Improving the Condition of the Poor, and two other of its senior officers, Henry Pellew and Willis James, at whose house a meeting was arranged early in 1879 to enlist the services of the city's clergy.

The outcome was a Sunday set aside for sermonizing on the evils of tenement life. Sickness, drunkenness, immorality, crime—these were summarized in a pamphlet circularized for the occasion. Seventy percent of the children under five who died had lived in the tenements; there were 6110 licensed plus 2000 unlicensed bars in the city, located largely among the tenements; the child who grew up with a drunken father and a debauched mother often ended up in a city jail. These themes were further developed at a crowded meeting organized by the State Charities Aid Association and held at Cooper Union, where prominent citizens such as Pierpont Morgan, Cyrus Field, Hamilton Fish, the young Cornelius Vanderbilt, and the octogenarian Peter Cooper (with his son, the mayor, presiding) heard a series of speakers reiterate the need for some sort of action and agreed to have a Committee of Nine prepare a bill for legislative approval.

Many experts thought that the law was already sufficiently stringent. The Association for Improving the Condition of the Poor, once again active in housing reform (inspecting tenements for itself and sending complaints to the Board of Health), observed in its 1878 annual report that the "health authorities of New York have labored earnestly to improve the tenement houses, and have accomplished much good. But their efforts in this direction are beset with many obstacles. *The existing laws are sufficiently broad to cover all the needs of the occasion....* if literally enforced [they] would abolish most of the remediable evils which affect the occupants of tenement houses.... [However] the owners of tenement-house property are a large wealthy class who exert a considerable political influence. It would be hazardous to assail their vested interests without the sustaining support of an aroused public sentiment. *Just here is where the battle is to be fought.*"[15] The *American Architect* agreed that what was wanted was not more legislation but more control: "The laws which regulate tenement and lodging houses are strict enough and definite enough to restrain the worst of their evils, if they could be adequately enforced, but the number of these houses is so enormous as to defy efficient inspection. Their owners shield themselves behind irresponsible agents, or are out of sight entirely, or plead poverty, and in various ways evade the law. Many are men of wealth, and of political influence of a kind against which it is difficult to contend in New York."[16]

In the fall of 1878, Chandler finally exerted his authority. Calling for the prior submission of plans from architects who seemingly had "not been aware of the actual features of the law,"[17] he upheld their rejection by Pfeiffer and refused building approval until their infringements were rectified. Thus almost six years after Chandler's appointment to the Board of Health and eleven years after its enactment, the 1867 law was finally enforced. The construction industry and public opinion had been temporarily suppressed by the panic of 1873; now both were resurgent. "The enormous value of the tenement house property of the city," Chandler had reported in 1876, "—probably $200,000,000—the high taxes, and the depressed condition of business, compel the Board to make haste slowly in urging radical and expensive changes in the construction of the tenement-houses, and it is doubtful if the majority of the existing houses, built upon our city lots, 25 feet by 100 feet, can be essentially modified in their plan."[18] With a tenement boom ahead, the truth of this last supposition was about to be tested.

4

The Competition

In December 1878 the *Plumber and Sanitary Engineer* announced a competition for the design of a model tenement. The magazine had been founded a year earlier by Henry Meyer, owner of a company dealing in water, gas, and steam supply fittings, who hoped to increase sales by popularizing the cause of good sanitation. As his managing editor he appointed the twenty-nine-year-old Charles Wingate, a Cooper Institute-trained sanitary engineer with literary ability who was also interested in reform. A relative of the secretary of the Association for Improving the Condition of the Poor, Wingate had helped prepare its annual reports and subsequently became a member of the State Charities Aid Association's tenement committee. The *Plumber and Sanitary Engineer* provided the occasion to couple philanthropy with publicity: "It being desirable to improve the condition of the tenement houses in this city, we have with that object in view united with Messrs. D. Willis James, F. B. Thurber, Henry E. Pellew, and Robert Gordon, in offering five hundred dollars ($500) as a premium for the best four designs for a house for workingmen, in which may be secured a proper distribution of light and pure air, with an arrangement of rooms that will yield a rental sufficient to pay a fair interest on the investment."[1]

The sponsors were active philanthropists. James, who, according to the reformer-clergyman Charles Parkhurst, loved everyone "from God down to the newsboy,"[2] was a businessman who throughout his life contributed quietly but abundantly to charity. In 1878 he was on the managing board of the Association for Improving the Condition of the Poor, as was Gordon. Pellew was from the British upper class and during his twelve-year residence in New York, through his middle age, helped coordinate the work of the various charitable organizations and to found the Charity Organization Society. Francis Thurber (who later gained prominence as the oldest law student in New York State) was a successful merchant.

The jury appointed to make the awards was equally distinguished and enthusiastic, including the president of the Board of Health himself, who welcomed the opportunity to obtain a model tenement plan. The four other judges were also men of repute. Robert Hatfield was the president of the New York chapter of the American Institute of Architects, and although he died just before the results were announced, he not only drew up the terms of the competition and arranged most of the preliminary details but also took an active part in assessing the entries. John Hall was the "Irishman with the golden mouth,"[3] who was Meyer's pastor at the Fifth Avenue Presbyterian Church. Henry Potter, proposed by Wingate, was then rector of Grace Church and later Episcopal bishop of New York and was noted for his involvement with the social needs of his parish. The fifth member of the jury of award, Robert Hoe, was of the third generation of a famous family that owned a press manufacturing firm on the Lower East Side, which had already built some housing for its workers. An art and book lover, he had been one of the founders of the Metropolitan Museum of Art. "A committee of award," commented the *American Architect*, "in whose judgment and equity everybody will have confidence."[4]

The competition was specifically intended to see what could be done with the single 25-by-100-foot lot. It was noted that the general problem of supplying satisfactory housing for the poor had been solved for large sites by White in Brooklyn, but that it was essential to provide a plan for building on the more congested New York lots. The need was to strike a balance between landlord and tenant: for the one, at least a 7 percent net return on his investment; for the other, protection from fire and molestation, as well as sufficient light, ventilation, seclusion, and sanitation, at a rent he could afford. "If each designer," concluded the *Plumber and Sanitary Engineer,* "will put himself in place of the owner, and strive to plan a sanitary building which will *bring in the most revenue,* he will not err."[5]

The response was unexpected, 190 designs being received, mostly from American architects but some from builders, civil engineers, plumbers, and "ladies," others from Canada, and even one from London, England. The following day the drawings were put on display at the Leavitt Art Rooms on Broadway, which for ten days, according to the *Tribune,*[6] were crowded with visitors. As the entries were not to be judged until after the exhibition closed, the public was left to make its own assessments.

The exercise was to divide up a 25-foot-wide and 90-foot-long rectangle enclosed on both sides so that all the internal parts appeared to open up to the exterior. The answer was to provide a court or well, and where this was placed determined the shape of the solution. The two most popular configurations were the internal side court block and the dumbbell. The first linked a front and rear house along one side of the lot. The second inserted a central connection between the front and rear houses, thus creating a small well on either side of the link. These two approaches could be varied by increasing the number of openings and decreasing their size, the first culminating in a building with one serrated side, the second in the legislated standard of a closed block punctured along its unwindowed sides with air shafts.

Although it stated that the internal side court was the best solution, the three plans commended and illustrated by the *American Architect* were all of the dumbbell type. Of these, "Octagon" and "Seven percent" had only eight rooms per floor, and therefore all the rooms faced onto the street, the yard, or the staircase courts. However, "Prüfet alles, das Beste behaltet," commended by the magazine for its "wonderfully ingenious plan" (and also by the *Tribune* for its "well ventilated and well lighted rooms"), had ten rooms per floor and solved the problem of the interior room by facing it onto a 2-foot-deep slot.

Generally the press canceled out each other's judgments.[7] Of the four designs favored by the *New York Times*, "I strive" and "Facimus" were rejected by the *American Architect*, the latter for having rooms with borrowed light and therefore not conforming to the competition conditions; "Oxygen," also approved by the *American Architect* as one of the most carefully studied plans, was dismissed by the *Tribune* as impracticable. (The fourth design listed by the *New York Times* was not described and went unmentioned in other journals.) The *Tribune* preferred two types of plans, the dumbbell and the side court block. Of the former it also illustrated "Prüfet alles, das Beste behaltet." The two examples selected from the second type were "Ben Travato" and "Number 36." The first left a 10-foot rear yard and had "a big well in a very small house," as the *American Architect* termed it. "Number 36" occupied all the site but had an internal court 70 feet long and 9 feet deep with all the plan elements, except two rooms at the front, facing onto it. Both plans contained twelve rooms per floor and covered about three-quarters of the area of the lot.

In summarizing the problem of providing housing for the poor, the *American Architect* emphasized some practical considerations. When the law permitted a building six stories high, it was "simply ridiculous" to propose anything lower; all plans with less than four suites to a floor were uneconomic; it was "sheer nonsense" to provide tenement dwellers with unfamiliar conveniences.

The two plans that appear to have been generally approved were the dumbbell type such as "Prüfet alles, das Beste behaltet" and the internal side court type such as "Ben Travato," which was designed by Chandler's consultant architect, Pfeiffer. Assuming five stories above ground level, the first had twenty of its bedrooms lighted and ventilated off two 50-foot-high courts 4 feet deep (with ten other bedrooms facing onto 2-foot-deep slots); the other had ten apartments containing 30 rooms, plus 10 toilets, lighted and ventilated off a 50-foot-high court that was 28 by 12 feet. Notwithstanding these limitations of the better entries, the competition was generally judged a success. The *American Architect* affirmed that "there is no question that the organizers of the scheme have been doing an excellent work and deserve the thanks, not only of the profession, but of the public at large." The *New York Times* observed that the fact that "a house which combines the advantages of health and, most especially decency, can be built for working people and their families becomes quite manifest from this exhibition." The *Tribune* predicted that the designs indicated "a marked advance in sanitary science. One cannot help feeling that the day is not far distant when working people can be lodged where they will be protected against fire, where they will not be overcrowded, and where they will have fresh air, pure light and domestic privacy." The competition judges were less enthusiastic.

The report of the committee of award was published in the *Plumber and Sanitary Engineer* at the beginning of March 1879.

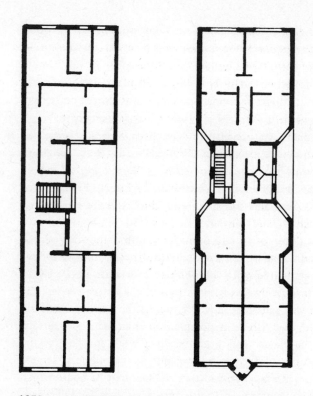

1879 tenement house competition entries "Ben Travato" (left) and "Prüfet alles, das Beste behaltet" (right) plans.

Source: *New York Tribune,* March 17, 1879.

Its preamble was direct and realistic: "The object of the competition was to demonstrate if it is possible to build a model house for workingmen on the existing city lot 25 × 100. . . . . [The] committee emphatically declare that in their view it is impossible to secure the requirements of physical and moral health within these narrow and arbitrary limits."[8] Then, not content with stating their conclusion that the problem could be solved only through statutory reform and declaring the competition void, the committee went on to award prizes to those plans that came "nearest" to fulfilling their aims.

In judging the plans, the committee eliminated all the submissions that had less than three or more than four families to a floor, the one being uneconomic, the other unhygienic, and set the number of rooms per suite at three or perhaps two if of adequate size. Like the *American Architect*, it also rejected too many conveniences, noting that even a kitchen sink or a water closet for one or two families was probably a luxury for the very poor. As for light and ventilation, a court opening onto the street was better than one enclosed, and one of ample size was better than several smaller shafts.

Having said this, the committee nevertheless awarded its four prizes to plans of the double house type with the staircase link. All showed twelve rooms per floor except the third-prize design, which occupied the same amount of area with ten rooms. All virtually ignored the fact that they had interior rooms and at most provided a shaft the thickness of the wall that in the first-prize winner's drawing was hopefully labeled "light and vent." This design, whose motto was "Light, air and health," was described by its thirty-two-year-old architect, James Ware (who had trained in the adjudicator Hatfield's office), as being excellently lighted and ventilated, a belief not shared by the *American Architect*, which had previously described it as a typical dumbbell plan with dark

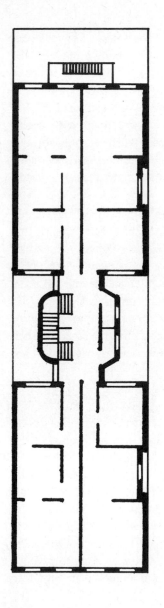

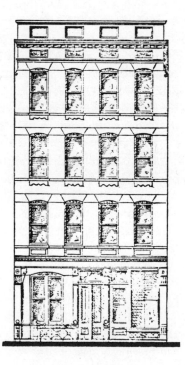

1879 tenement house competition, first prize winner, "Light, Air and Health," architect James E. Ware, plan and elevation

Source: *The Plumber and Sanitary Engineer*, March 1879.

interior rooms. However, even the architectural magazine was ambiguous in its judgment, as at the same time it described the almost identical fourth-prize-winning entry as a "double house on a good plan." The term "dumbbell" really described the type of plan generally used after 1887. Ware's design simply looked like two houses with an inset staircase link. The term, however, became popular after the 1879 competition (but, strangely, the *American Architect* critique of the entries continually referred to the "typical dumb-bell plan" as if it had been common before, though it was not).

The committee gave no reasons for its choice of first prize, and these can only be surmised. The open positioning of the staircase with its fireproof enclosure was a great advance from the dark interior flimsy stairway. The resultant elimination of interior corridors above the ground floor and the ease of access from dwellings to water closets, which were placed in the staircase link (although the second-prize winner kept his water closets in the yard), were also major improvements over the old hazards to morals and self-respect. The solution to the problems of light and ventilation, however, was largely illusory. In plan, the rationale of the dumbbell system appeared to be the ease of through ventilation and indirect lighting. A 33-foot-long suite of rooms with 9-foot-high ceilings and windows at each end looked in section as if the middle room might receive sufficient light and air for what was only a bedroom to be used at night. The illusion was in the functioning of the internal court. "[Holes] six or even ten feet square and fifty feet deep," the committee had stated in its report, or "long alley-way[s] five or six feet wide and extending to the top of a house are but poor substitutes for direct light and air, and usually only become receptacles for damp and dirt."[9] In the winning design, each pair of suites had to be ventilated through an internal court 50 feet in height (assuming a building of five stories, although the actual design contained only four), 120 square feet in area, and 5 feet across its narrowest distance. This internal court could not admit adequate light and air to the ten families that shared its volume. Of course, the committee had never said it could and regarded it merely as the best available compromise. In comparison with Ware's plan, the major internal court of "Prüfet Alles, das Beste behaltet" was only 4 feet deep; while the suites in "Ben Travato" shared a long dark passage, were small with ill-shaped rooms, had no potential means of cross ventilation, and ten families got from the internal court whatever light and ventilation they would ever receive.

The fact was as the committee had stated: it was impossible to house twenty families satisfactorily on a 25-by-100-foot lot. The committee had been unable to discover a design that solved its minimum requirements. Neither had the *New York Times*, the *Tribune,* nor the *American Architect,* but this did not prevent them all from publicizing their preferences as if they had. Before the competition awards were announced, everyone had assumed that something beneficial would come out of it. After the event, it was mainly the architects who continued to believe that some designs were better than others. This led the *Sanitarian* to remark that it was "not at all surprising that many of the exhibitors of the 186 rejected plans out of the 190 placed on exhibition should deem themselves to be equally entitled to the awards, seeing that it is now very generally conceded that the prizes were won by the most ingenious designs for dungeons. To have failed in such a contest is the greatest honor, and it is to be regretted that there are any among them still bent on advertising their wares."[10]

The architects were unabashed. The *Graphic* carried the plans and description of a design by Calvert Vaux, the noted codesigner of Central Park (and an entrant in the competition), in which every room had a window but suffered from other defects such as smallness and peculiarity of shape.[11] The *Tribune* extensively quoted a few architects including one who believed that the competition entry "Ben Travato" was a "nearly perfect design" and referred to his own plan for a tenement that presumably was of merit but was neither described nor illustrated.[12] Even the influential Richard Hunt, the first American Beaux-Arts-trained architect, who had previously designed the *Tribune* building itself, added his observation that one large court would have been better than three small ones. And at the fourteenth annual convention of the American Institute of Architects, its national secretary, A. J. Bloor, in a report ordered the previous year on the best method of solving the tenement house problem, condemned the winning designs for their dark middle room, "which is the horror of physicians and visitors among the poor, which has been so strenuously inveighed against by the Board of Health, and which, in practice, would have necessarily involved the official condemnation of the plans by the Building Department"; allowed that "no tenement-house ought to be built on a lot so ridiculously incongruous for the purpose"—then proposed to his fellow professionals that the problem could be solved by his own different (though equally defective) plan.[13] (Even as late as 1899 architects were still producing "model" tenements for 25-by-100-foot lots, such as the four-family, ten-rooms-per-floor design by Mary Gannon and Alice Hands, which was optimistically rendered with a porticoed, planted courtyard in the Italian style. These young architects had been members of the Ladies Health Protective Association's committee on tenement houses. In 1895 the *Tribune* reported that they had designed a six-story tenement between two fifteen-story buildings, which, the newspaper added, would normally shut out light and air—but not with their design. Un-

Tenement house, 1899, architects Mary Gannon and Alice Hands, plan and court
The sketch illustrates the architect's perennial capacity for self-deception. The tiny courtyard of the six-story building is rendered in a vaguely Italian style with the upper two floors merging into the sky.

Source: *Municipal Affairs*, March 1899.

fortunately, the secret of how it was done was never revealed.)[14]

By this time the editorial writers had perceived the futility of the exercise. "The [prizewinning] plans are on the whole ingeneously and compactly arranged," commented the *American Architect*, "and considering the restrictions of the case, may represent, apart from variations of detail, nearly the best thing that can be done. The question to which they lead is, How much is the best worth?"[15] "It is manifest," observed the *New York Times*, "that the able architects who so generally competed for these plans have not succeeded, and the inference, under all the circumstances, is that a light, healthy tenement-house, with good modern sanitary arrangements, cannot be constructed on an ordinary City lot and made to pay. Perhaps the gentlemen who offered the prizes really desired to demonstrate this to the public before proposing any other scheme."[16] The *Plumber and Sanitary Engineer* was quick to react to this criticism. In an editorial entitled "The object of our competition," it explained that "we had from the first, grave doubts of a satisfactory result being secured; but we thought that, pending such legislation, as sooner or later must be had, we might teach the single lot owner how he could build a better house than hitherto. . . . With very few exceptions, the houses erected within the past year are far from being equal to most of the plans received. . . . It was also hoped that by calling attention to the matter public sentiment would secure legislation that would restrict the placing of more than three families on a floor of a single house. . . . When owners of tenement houses to be hereafter erected on the single lot are forbidden by law to have rooms without outside light and adequate ventilation, the building of the single tenement will cease, except where they may secure higher rentals. Then, and not till then, will capitalists be able to erect houses in blocks or on large plots and find it profitable, which would be out of the question so long as single lot owners can continue to erect five-story buildings to accommodate from four to six families on a floor."[17]

The magazine's vindication of the virtue of its competition was upheld by the Association for Improving the Condition of the Poor, which commended its "good influence upon architects, builders, and the public generally,"[18] and by James Gallatin, whose job it was to get the new bill passed through Albany.[19] But by this time the magazine had forgotten its prizewinners. "The prime object of our late competition," it firmly declared, "was to demonstrate that such a dwelling was impossible."[20]

5

Chandler Moves

The announcement of the magazine's awards was followed by yet another public meeting at Cooper Union under the chairmanship of the president of the chamber of commerce, Samuel Babcock. This time it was attended not only by philanthropic citizens with their wives but also by many tenement dwellers who occupied the back of the hall and politely heard themselves described by the sanitary engineer George Waring as largely "ignorant and vicious persons."[1] For the last event of the evening the meeting was shown some forty competition plans by Chandler, who called for support in strengthening the law and its application by the Board of Health, which he claimed was hamstrung by the court of appeals.

The report of the Committee of Nine, which had been set up at the previous Cooper Union meeting, appeared soon afterward. Divided into two parts, the first dealt with legislative reform, the second with the establishment of two types of model tenements, one intended to be philanthropic, the other commercially self-supporting. While the former lapsed through lack of interest, the latter developed into the Improved Dwellings Association, with Bayard Cutting as president, Babcock as treasurer, and a board of directors that included some members of the Committee of Nine and some from the Sanitary Reform Society. Taking part in all three activities were Cutting, Henry Pellew, Willis James, Cornelius Vanderbilt, and Richard Auchmuty, a wealthy architect.

At a cost of $280,000, including $45,000 for land, 218 apartments and twelve stores were built in 1882 on a site 200 by 200 feet on First Avenue between 71st and 72nd streets. Designed by Vaux & Radford, those facing the avenue were on a superior shallow type of plan with a rear extension containing toilet and washing facilities; the others, of a modified dumbbell plan asymmetrically shaped to allow the courts to open to the rear, were in three houses along each of the streets. With coal lifts, ash chutes, laundry facilities, and free baths, rents initially ranged from $6.25 monthly for two rooms on the sixth floor to $15 monthly for four first-floor rooms. There was conflicting evidence as to the early economic record of these buildings, which were not demolished until 1960. Their agent told the *Real Estate Record* in 1886 that all the suites were rented, and he and the 1894 Tenement House Committee reported that a 5 percent dividend had been paid since its inception. Marcus Reynolds, writing in 1893, supported Cutting's statement to Jacob Riis that unforeseen expenditures had reduced its annual dividends to 4 percent. One factor in its early years may have been the isolation of the development, which was in a new neighborhood. Another, much smaller model tenement of 40 apartments and six stores had been previously erected in 1879 on Monroe Street on the Lower East Side by the Abner Chichester Estate. The estate's executors were not associated with the dedicated reformers but treated the building as one of their ordinary investments. Its plan was based on White's Brooklyn tenements, being two rooms deep on a lot 125 by 100 feet. Each apartment had its own toilet, but no gas or stoves were supplied, and the rents were somewhat more than those of the Improved Dwelling Association. The land cost $55,000, the building only $33,000 (the overall cost per unit being over one and a half times that of the First Avenue buildings), and the owners assumed a 7 percent return, though they did not account separately for their various holdings.

Whatever the economics of these ventures, they were exceptional at a time when the investment return from tenements was expected to be at least 10 percent. It was evidently impossible to provide an enlightened standard of accommodation and services at a competitive price. The main thrust of housing reform was therefore directed toward legislative controls that would force private enterprise to raise the quality of its offerings and at the same time, it was hoped, to lower its profits if the current rent levels were all that the majority of wage earners could afford. With the cooperation of Chandler and his legal advisor, a subcommittee of the Committee of Nine under Judge Charles Daly had drawn up a list of amendments to close the gaps in the existing law. While one of the more important provisions for licensing all tenements and their owners was rejected by the legislature, the bill, notwithstanding "the vigorous opposition of many landlords through the agency of their representatives at Albany,"[2] was speedily processed and passed into law in the early summer.

About the only improvement that the previous tenement act had brought was the school sink, a sewer-connected privy named from its use by the public school system. These ostensibly trapped and flushable closets were constructed of holed wooden boxes set over a masonry trench containing standing water that, theoretically, carried off the excrement when a plug was pulled by the janitor. In reality this was seldom done. Anyway the trench was usually blocked with ashes and garbage, and as the filth piled up and over the wooden tops, these improved conveniences proved as foul as the earlier cesspools, which were at least known to require periodic manual cleansing.

The new tenement act of 1879 was intended to be more productive than its predecessor.[3] Its strengthened building requirements set the permissible lot coverage at 65 percent and specified mini-

mum distances between front and rear houses and 10 feet from
the rear lot line (although there were still no limitations to height).
Bedrooms were to have windows, every occupant was to have 600
cubic feet of air, and each building a janitor. To implement these
regulations, the Board of Health was to be given an annual operating fund of $10,000 and a sanitary company of thirty police-
men seconded from the Police Department. Unfortunately, once
again, the apparently mandatory standards remained subject to
Board of Health discretionary interpretation. Here, commented
the *New York Times*, was the rub: "The poorer tenement-house
keepers are more or less in collusion with the rum-sellers and
petty politicians of each ward, and it is this class of men in the
Democratic ranks who obstruct all sanitary or reform legislation
in this City. These men, no doubt, in their influence on local politics and upon the Legislature, check and alarm the Board of
Health whenever it undertakes to carry out needed reforms. It is
a significant fact in this matter, that never till the movement for
tenement-house reform last Winter, did Prof. Chandler, President
of the Board of Health, venture to reject plans for tenement-
houses which contained dark bedrooms or the abuses of the old
system; he is too intelligent a sanitarian not to understand that
such features are inadmissible in properly-built tenement-houses,
but he no doubt feared the political influence which the landlords
could bring to bear on the Legislature. In this, both he and the
Board of Health have made a great mistake; nothing would make
this board so popular throughout the State as unrelenting vigor in
executing the sanitary laws against these abuses. The petty Democratic politicians of the City could do nothing against them in
Albany, if they had behind them the moral power of a great reform thoroughly carried out. The future welfare of the City, the
value of property, and thousands of human lives will now depend
on the courage which the Board of Health shows in executing the

new law. Let it not fail, as so many have done, from the timid inaction of our own authorities."[4]

From 1879 on, the Board of Health under Chandler inspected and approved all tenement plans prior to their construction, but these approached neither the spirit of the law or even the questionable standard of the *Plumber and Sanitary Engineer* competition winner even when the architect was James Ware himself. Chandler kept copies of the plans he received and pasted them in a series of scrapbooks.[5] From these it was obvious that the tenement house competition had no immediate impact on the architectural profession, which continued to follow standard commercial practice. A plan for a row of three tenement houses, signed by James Ware and submitted one year after his award, was made up of rectangular blocks with six internal rooms per floor ventilated off a "light well" 4 by 8 feet by four stories high. The typical, so-called double-decker plan, with two rows of rooms on either side of a stairway, contained 60 rooms on five floors and covered roughly three-quarters of the lot (not 65 percent as the law required). The staircase hall, which was to have windows at each floor level "unless sufficient light or ventilation is otherwise provided," gained its light and air through the roof and shared them with four internal bedrooms whose main windows, "having an opening of not less than twelve square feet, admitting light and air directly from the public street or the yard," often looked out only onto a 3-by-4-foot by 50-foot-high shaft of wood and plaster —even though the Board of Health itself limited this size to buildings of three stories or less and for a five-story building required a shaft 20 square feet in area (supplying "perhaps as much light and air as it is practicable to compel landlords to provide for their tenants in a crowded city").[6] The four inner rooms were ventilated through the four outside rooms; the front ones looked through the fire escape to the street below, while the rear ones

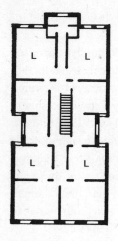

Tenement house, 1880, architect James E. Ware, plan
One set of living rooms is located off the light wells.

Source: *Ten Scrap Books of Tenement House Plans*, prepared for Professor C. F. Chandler (1879?-1883?).

faced over the outhouse to the backs of adjacent buildings.

Standards, however, were beginning to rise. In 1881 the first plumbing law was effected by the Sanitary Reform Society, an organization set up to continue the work of the Committee of Nine, which languished a few years later with the ill health of its president James Gallatin and then merged with the Association for Improving the Condition of the Poor. Requiring the registration of plumbers, it necessitated prior approval of projected installations by the Board of Health. By the mid-1880s other innovations were also becoming general through normal market demands. While the Board of Health was insisting that all inner rooms were to be ventilated by internal "light" shafts, another plan that was gaining commercial popularity utilized recessed brick party walls to create a shaft indentation that served up to 50 rooms from a slot 4 feet wide (but still did not reach the dark internal staircase). Of the last 100 tenement plans approved by Chandler, 26 were of this type (while only two were dumbbell in form).

This slow but steady change in ordinary tenement building standards continued through the 1880s, but without the benefit of Chandler's presence. In 1883, at the end of his second term as president of the Board of Health, his renomination by Mayor Franklin Edson was turned down by the Board of Aldermen, which also rejected a petition in his support signed by 3000 prominent citizens. The newspapers lamented the passing of a man of such "distinguished talent, practical capacity, fidelity to duty, and firmness united to modesty of character" who had lost his appointment "because he devoted himself to preserving the city's health and stood aloof from the deals and dickers upon which ward statesmen thrive."[7] Chandler himself thought that the manure merchants had pressed for his removal.[8] Whatever the major cause, it was likely that his recent involvement with tenement

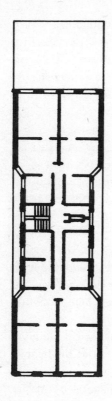

Typical tenement house, ca. 1884, plan

Source: New York City, Health Department, *The Tenement House Problem in New York* (1887).

house reform had not endeared him to his political masters. As his replacement, the factions in city government compromised with the appointment of the former Civil War general Alexander Shaler, who decreased the number of sanitary inspectors, increased the department's salary budget, and promoted the mayor's son.

In 1885 the state legislature, activated by reports of the city's insolvency, set up yet another Senate committee to investigate its administration. This included George Plunkitt of Tammany Hall, later immortalized by William Riordan, who quoted his views on "honest graft" and his own suggested epitaph: "George W. Plunkitt. He Seen His Opportunities, and He Took 'Em."[9] The committee did not investigate the building bureau of the Fire Department because of lack of time, but corruption seemed to be equally rampant among its inspectors, who were appointed through the patronage of the fire commissioners and not by the conscientious building superintendent. At the same time a grand jury indicted the Board of Health for not enforcing the law and thus permitting defective plumbing, leaking roofs, untrapped drains, and flooded cellars, which impaired the health of tenement occupants. "Are there not a number of cases on record in the Board where these things have gone on for months without being abated?" asked the Senate committee. "I know of some cases for weeks, not to say months," replied Shaler in giving evidence. "I know of cases where all sorts of excuses have been made by the owner—all sorts of influences have been brought to bear upon the officers of the Department to delay the expenditure of money necessary to make the changes. . . . When you say 'all sorts of influences,' what do you mean? . . . I mean personal, social and political, and religious and every other except financial."[10] Two years later, notwithstanding the protection of Governor David Hill, the upstate Democratic boss, Shaler was removed from office for accepting bribes in city militia armory site deals.

6

The Problem Solved

At the beginning of 1884, not quite a year after Chandler's removal from office, another wave of tenement reform was initiated by Felix Adler. Brought from Germany as a young child, Adler, the son of an eminent rabbi, had received his doctorate from Heidelberg University and then had gone to Cornell University as professor of Hebrew and Oriental literature. In 1876, at the age of twenty-four, he organized the Society for Ethical Culture in New York with the support of a group of influential persons who were disenchanted with the sectarianism and atrophy of established religions. First introduced to the hardships of tenement life when accompanying his mother on charitable visits, Adler broached the subject in his Sunday discourses, arguing from his platform at Chickering Hall on Fifth Avenue that the rich had a duty to share their wealth with the workers who helped make it. Appealing for philanthropic investment in decent housing as a means of improving the lives of the poor, he declaimed: "There is a call here for a great agitation, a mighty reform, a new abolition movement, a crusade against this new slavery. . . . Improve the homes and the grogshops will disappear. If we do not, their blood is upon our heads; if we do, the grateful mothers of these families will rain their blessings upon our heads."[1] The outcome of this agitation was the setting up of the State Tenement House Commission of 1884, with Adler as its main spokesman and Charles Wingate among its members.

Given its sample inspection of 968 tenement houses out of an estimated 26,000, the commission's figures could be projected to show that over a quarter of the approximately 5000 less than ten years old were classifiable as bad; of the remainder, two-thirds were bad; while those over thirty years old included one-seventh judged "very bad."[2] Thus, excluding the more expensive type of tenement house, about 14,000 buildings were envisaged as being substandard by the commission. Their twenty recommendations for improving this situation, however, were more concerned with administering the law than with setting new standards for builders to follow.

These proposals included: the redefinition of a tenement house to include those occupied by three families; the extension of all requirements for new buildings to old buildings when converted into tenements; a law making the filthy sanitary habits of tenants a punishable misdemeanor; a semiannual inspection of every tenement by the Board of Health; the registration of tenement owners' names and addresses with the Board of Health; the creation of a tenement house fund for the Board of Health (though it had legally had one since 1879); the submission of an annual report to the mayor by the Board of Health (this practice having ended under Chandler's administration); and the establishment of a permanent tenement house commission composed of the mayor and heads of various departments to meet annually and reassess the laws and their enforcement.

To improve the tenement environment, the commission proposed the razing of Mulberry Bend, the current slum core that stood a block away from the old Five Points, the electric lighting of tenement streets, and the provision of free public baths during the winter months.

Only four recommendations applied to buildings: that privy vaults be abolished, that water be supplied to every floor, that cellar floors be cemented, and that all rooms and halls have direct light and air—the latter two provisions being already required by law, and all of them being widely implemented by 1884. For, by this time, about one-half of all standard tenements were being constructed with the recessed brick party wall that made an open slot 35 feet long and 2 feet deep for the legally accepted admittance of "direct" light and air. A further evolution changed the straight flight of steps into a dogleg stair, faced it with two toilets for every four families, and placed them at the outside center of a plan that served fourteen rooms on each of five stories.

While the commission's report was submitted to the Senate in 1885—and shelved—another outcome of its activities, from the agitation of six years earlier, was a further block of model tenements, this time set amid the squalor of eastern Cherry Street. In his Chickering Hall lectures, Adler had envisaged a type of phalanstery with a common kitchen, art rooms, and playrooms. The building opened at the end of 1887 was six stories high and contained 108 two- and three-room suites. There were adequate lighting and ventilation from rear open courts, four suites set aside as a kindergarten, and a bricked-roof playground overlooking the East River. One house had hot and cold water in all apartments, while the others had cold water in the living room and hot water available free in the basement for baths and laundry. Every two families shared a water closet, which was heated as were the kindergarten and the main hall. The Tenement House Building Company, which had been formed to build this development, included Adler among its directors and was presided over by the wealthy banker Joseph Drexel and, on his death, the New York *Staats-Zeitung* proprietor Oswald Ottendorfer, both of whom had also been on the 1884 Tenement House Commission. Its rents were from $7 to $9 monthly for two rooms and from $10 to $14 monthly for three rooms, and dividends were limited to 4 percent, the surplus to be placed in a tenant fund. Unfortunately, the comparatively costly type of plan and construction, together with the forgoing of stores along the street, was insufficiently compensated for by a high occupancy rate and long tenancies. Furthermore, though Adler had continually insisted that the standards of the poor were superior to those of the dwellings they occupied and that it was only "squalid houses that make the squalid people,"[3] as poor Russian Jews filled the Cherry Street buildings, they threw their garbage out the windows, making the courts unsafe for children, put their stoves in the halls, used their living rooms as sweatshops, and brought in two or three lodgers to sleep on their bedroom floor.

The report of the 1884 Tenement House Commission remained dormant until the beginning of 1887, when the Sanitary Protective League, which had been set up two years earlier to alert the city to a potential epidemic of cholera, obtained a reading of its proposals in the Senate. This movement, organized by Charles Wingate and publicized by a series of his articles in the *Morning Journal* (researched over a period of two years by Gregory Weinstein, who claimed to have inspected, with another young man, almost every tenement house in Manhattan),[4] was aided by diverse organizations such as the Women's Conference, the Academy of Medicine, the Real Estate Exchange, and the Central Labor Union—but not by Adler and his friends, who apparently resented the interference. Welcomed as "the Tenement Commisioner of *The Morning Journal*," Wingate (with Samuel Gompers and Henry George) addressed a mass meeting of workingmen at Cooper Union, which passed a resolution condemning those "shameless and unscrupulous scoundrels" of "tenement-house landlords of the lowest grade"[5] who were trying to stop the current legislative reforms. In this they were supported by conservative real estate spokesmen who favored laws that codified general market practices and eliminated the substandard "unfair" competition of speculators. The agitation was successful, resulting in an amending act that incorporated most of the commission's recommendations (though the requirement for a water closet for every two families was modified the following year to one for every fifteen occupants with a minimum of one to a floor). These, in conjunction with a general building law revision of fire precautions passed in the same year, requiring that light and vent shafts be of fireproof construction, paved the way for the typical dumbbell tenement that became ubiquitous during the remainder of the century.[6]

The new law was administered by a new president of the Board of Health, James Bayles, who had replaced Shaler on his dismissal. Appointed by Peter Cooper's son-in-law Abram Hewitt (who with Tammany support had defeated Henry George and Theodore Roosevelt for the mayoralty), Bayles was a sanitary engineer and the author of a popular textbook on domestic plumbing. His interpretative regulations, requiring every building with more than four stories and containing more than twelve rooms on each to have light courts totaling 265 square feet (for twelve rooms, 215 square feet), and permitting a lot coverage of 78 percent, provided the final design determinants.

The solution for a standard five-story, fourteen-room-per-floor building was to pinch in the 25-by-85-foot plan at the staircase-toilet center, to increase the length of the slot formed by the party wall indentation to service five rooms on each side, and thus to produce the typical "improved" dumbbell silhouette, "superior in many respects to the one to which the prize was awarded in 1879." In these new plans, Bayles added, "the stairways are well lighted and ventilated . . . every room has a large

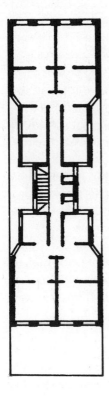

Typical dumbbell tenement house, 1887-1901, plan

Source: New York City, Health Department, *The Tenement House Problem in New York* (1887).

window opening directly upon a court sufficiently large to admit light to interior rooms, even on the lower floors . . . the water closet compartments are in a suitable and convenient place, removed as far as possible from the living rooms, and provided with special foul air ducts, as well as windows which furnish light from the large court . . . each apartment is provided with water, a kitchen sink and wash trays. . . . The halls are well lighted from the windows beside the stairs, and ventilation by louvred skylights above the roof is secured."[7] A tenement acceptable to enlightened opinion had been achieved through evolutionary legislation.

Belief in the success of the city's tenement reforms was shared by other, unbiased, observers. Reporting on tenements in Boston, a Massachusetts Institute of Technology civil engineering professor adversely compared them to those in New York City, where there had been "a constant advance in tenement-house designs, induced by a steady raising of the standard of requirements on the part of the Board of Health, until there has come to be about as much contrast between the best recent designs and the designs common ten or fifteen years ago, as there is between light and darkness."[8] The magazine *Building,* noting that the city had always pioneered practical solutions to urban problems, especially in the control of dwelling construction, referred to statistics showing that "in the large, modern tenement, with its well-lighted rooms, dry cellar and good plumbing, which is rapidly replacing the old 'rookery,' the death-rate is less than in portions of the city devoted to private residences."[9] "Already," wrote the *American Architect,* "thousands of people live in little city homes of two or three rooms, which are in every respect as well suited to family decency and health as apartments in the Fifth Avenue Hotel; and the number of such tenements ought to increase rapidly, and would do so, if as much eloquence could be expended in commending them as in the indiscriminate abuse of every kind of tenement-house."[10] The Board of Health concurred in this judgment, reporting in 1890 that everything was under control: "The plans on which tenement-houses are now built are in many particulars superior to the plan of a model tenement-house which was awarded first prize in the famous Plan Competition of 1879, although that plan at the time was generally regarded as too utopian ever to be equaled by tenement-houses erected by speculative builders in this city."[11] These were "not purely idealistic" plans, enthused Elgin Gould in his comprehensive survey of *The Housing of the Working People,* published in 1895 for the U.S. Department of Labor after years of research at home and abroad; "these plans have been followed out time and again in existing constructions." New York City's progress in tenement design was just "wonderful."[12]

7

Comparisons

By this time many of the buildings being built under the tenement acts could more properly be called apartments or, as they were then known, French flats. Ever since the Stuyvesant apartment house, designed by Richard Hunt, was completed at Eighteenth Street and Third Avenue in 1870 (it was demolished in 1956), this mode of household had become popular with tenants and profitable to landlords. By the mid-1880s, families protected under the tenement laws could be paying anything from $8 monthly for two rooms in a downtown slum, through $40 monthly for six rooms on 33rd Street, to over $450 monthly for a twenty-room suite in the newly completed Dakota apartments on Central Park West. This new way of living, supposedly brought on by the benefits of relegating the chore of upkeep to landlords and the shortage of servants (though the Dakota was abundantly supplied: its ratio between domestic and building staff and tenant was somewhere near 10:1), was reflected in the official statistics. Since 1875 a separate count of superior tenement houses had been kept, but the definition varied as the dividing line was maintained at $15,000 during a period of changing costs. In the second half of the 1870s roughly one-fifth of all legal tenements were listed as French flats, and of these about three-quarters were built between 40th and 86th Streets.

The residential growth of Manhattan had been mainly along its East Side. By 1880 this had been generally built up as far as 100th Street, while the West Side stopped at 59th Street on the southern edge of Central Park, with only the Grand Boulevard (later Broadway) serviced for building further north. Even though the elevated steam railroad had come into service in 1872 and by the end of the decade reached to 155th Street in Harlem along Ninth Avenue, the West Side suffered from difficult gradients, an exposed flank along the Hudson, and the lack of a recognizable focus. On the other side of the island, Lexington and Fifth avenues had become the fashionable center, the Third Avenue elevated ran to 129th Street, and between it and the East River was a mass of tenements.

Often proposed as a panacea for downtown overcrowding, the elevated had its fare levels fixed by the city's rapid transit commission. While the cost was ten cents up to 59th Street and fifteen cents beyond, half fares were provided for workers traveling during the morning and evening rush hours. Seventeen horse railroads and three omnibus lines charging a nickel each, made up the rest of New York's public transportation during this period. By the mid-1880s, over a quarter of a billion fares were purchased annually, 100 million of them on the elevated lines. The trip from the southern tip of Manhattan to 42nd Street took 23 minutes; up to 129th Street, 45 minutes. As downtown lots became scarcer and more expensive, speculators turned increasingly further uptown, especially to those areas east of Third Avenue and west of Eighth Avenue where land was plentiful and lots were cheap.

At the time of the Citizens' Association's sanitary survey in 1864, over half the tenements listed were located below Fourteenth Street. By the end of the century, these 9500 buildings had increased to 13,600 but represented only one-third of the total. At the same time, the number of low-cost buildings being constructed rapidly declined. In the first half of the decade following the 1879 act, the approximate ratio of tenements to flats built annually, in the Building Department's parlance, was 5:2; in the second half it was 2:7. Apartment houses were becoming the normal place of residence for all Manhattan families whether rich or poor.

The narrow, deep New York lot had been intended for the building of single-family houses with gardens. As long as the house was only two habitable rooms deep, there was no difficulty in arranging the plan, but as soon as a larger dwelling was required, the problem arose as to how to get light and air into the interior. Even in a private house such as that for a doctor on Fifth Avenue, designed by Bruce Price and illustrated in the *American Architect* in 1886, the staircase, two lower surgery rooms, the main-floor library, and an upper-floor bedroom faced onto a central side court, for the building was over 60 feet long and could not be lighted and ventilated entirely from front and rear.[1]

When apartments were built on a similar-sized lot, the more spacious the apartment, the more difficult it became to plan without internal shafts. For example, the plan illustrated in W. B. Tuthill's *The City Residence,* published in 1890, included a parlor, library, dining room, three bedrooms, bathroom, kitchen, and servant's room and was 25 feet wide and 80 feet deep. Inevitably the bedrooms were lighted and ventilated by two shafts each 30 square feet in area, while the servant's room shaft was 4½ by 4 feet.[2]

Similarly, the seven-story elevator apartment building at 57th Street and Ninth Avenue, designed by Albert Wagner around 1880, contained four suites per floor 90 feet in length and occupying a 75-foot frontage, with similar accommodation less the library. The consequence of this narrow width was that an inter-

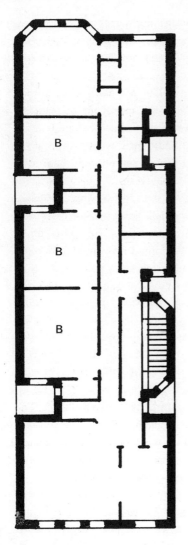

Model apartment house, 1890, plan
All the bedrooms are lighted and ventilated through shafts.
Source: W. B. Tuthill, *The City Residence* (1890).

nal shaft 85 square feet in area and under 4 feet at its narrowest depth lighted and ventilated seven stories, each with six bedrooms and two bathrooms, a total of 42 bedrooms and 14 bathrooms serviced by a slot 70 feet high.[3]

This use of shafts to light and ventilate bedrooms was common at the time. The suites in the five-story apartment building on 51st Street designed by Ralph Townsend and illustrated in the *Builder and Wood-Worker* in 1881 had their servant's room at the open rear overlooking the yard and their three family bedrooms clustered internally around a 3½-foot-deep slot.[4] The plans of the five-story apartment building at 52nd Street off Lexington Avenue designed by George Pelham around 1880 and marked "1st class flats" also had the servant's room at the back, while two family bedrooms and a bathroom on each floor were lighted and venti-lated off a 2-foot-deep slot.[5] Another five-story apartment build-ing of the same period designed by Andrew Spence for 244 East 79th Street had its three family bedrooms per suite also sharing a slot 2 feet deep, while the shaft labeled "light" to the servant's room was just under 2 feet square.[6] Thus, in relation to their rents and the standard of living of their occupants, the plans of these apartments were not generically different from those of tenements.

Neither rich nor poor had much natural light or ventilation. The difference was that whereas the living habits of middle-class ten-ants did not aggravate these conditions, those of the lower class did. Coughing and spitting accompanied closed windows; malnu-trition went with lack of sun; drunkenness and brutality with dark rooms and halls; forced overcrowding caused an accumula-tion of toilet excrement and garbage droppings that spread dis-ease; tenement dwellers had little concern for personal cleanliness and no baths. Between the time that the Association for Im-proving the Condition of the Poor closed down its tenement district bathhouse before the Civil War because it was not used by the local inhabitants and its opening of the People's Baths a generation later, the only popular way to get bathed was to wait until summer and use the free floating pools in the rivers.

Nor were tenements as well built as apartments. The most notorious example of what was known as "skin-building" became news when eight tenements, part of a development of 24 five-story units, 25 feet wide and 83 feet long, located on 62nd Street between Tenth and Eleventh avenues, collapsed during construction in 1885. Their speculative builder, Charles Buddensiek, one of the most prolific in the city, had used loam from his cellar excavations to mix in the mortar instead of sand, and when the foundations, poured in the winter, began to buckle in the spring, the whole superstructure of brickyard rejects and lumber waste bonded together with dry mud toppled to the ground, injuring a number of workmen and killing a German carpenter. On the *Tribune's* front page, eyewitnesses reported: "About 3 p.m. there was a sudden cessation of work, and the men throughout the buildings exchanged glances and uttered exclamations of alarm. A tremor like the motion of an earthquake was felt, the eight buildings began to totter, and in another second they tumbled into heaps of ruins. None of the men in or upon the houses had a chance to save themselves. There was a general sagging down the hill of the whole row, gradual at first, but rapid enough at the end. The creaking of timbers and the shouts of the frightened workmen were drowned in an instant by the terrific crash when the roof beams fell upon the mass of broken floors and walls in the cellars. A dense cloud of dust rose high in the air and spread far beyond the limits of the ruins, shutting them out of view for several minutes. The crash had been heard for a distance of half a mile. . . . Buddensiek had been standing in front of the third house of the row and had seen the rotten structures collapse. A brick had struck him on the foot and his face was white with fear when he limped to the middle of the unpaved street. One of his workmen, who also had narrowly escaped death, ran after him, shook his fist angrily and shouted: 'You ought to be hung for putting up such buildings'."[7]

Buddensiek was sentenced to ten years in prison, but expert witnesses testified at his trial that many other tenements were built no better. This opinion was supported by the report of an inspector from the Association for Improving the Condition of the Poor that, notwithstanding the plumbing act then in force, he had found holes as big as his fist in waste pipes of new buildings on 72nd Street;[8] and by Wingate's description of typical tenement construction where "the walls are thin and made of inferior brick, the mortar is mere sand, the plastering flakes off, the woodwork warps, the panels of the doors show streaks of light in them, and the window casings let in cold drafts of air. As for the plumbing, it is indescribably bad. . . . Traps evaporate or siphon out, and tenants will often put a cloth held down by a brick over the sink openings to keep out the stench."[9] On this type of investment, the owner hoped to make as much profit as he could.

The claim that tenement owners made an exorbitant profit was often heard. Over the years critics asserted that profits of up to 25 percent annually on the investment were common; the worse the property, the greater the return, especially if the widespread antipathy to blacks could be exploited. The early truth of this allegation (rejected by many owners who virtuously, and tactfully, proclaimed a 7 percent profit) was upheld by the *Real Estate Record*, which in 1871 noted that even ordinary housing rentals produced a 10 to 12 percent return on capital while apartment houses might be expected to net 25 to 35 percent. The subsequent pattern of this new type of real estate speculation, however, whose lucrative future was optimistically projected from the outstanding early success of the Stuyvesant apartments, included economic panics, vacant apartments, and mortgage foreclosures, which soon tempered the belief in easy pickings.

Nevertheless, when the Tenement House Building Company compared the expenses and earnings from its Cherry Street buildings with those that could have been expected from a typical tenement development, it concluded that an ordinary speculator would have erected 40 percent more suites for 25 percent less money by combining lower space standards with lower standards of construction.[10]

A supposedly typical financial statement drawn up by an architect was published in the *Real Estate Record* in 1885. His balance sheet for a downtown tenement investment listed: lot, $10,000; building, a five-story twenty-family "double-decker" (the name given to the plan with a central stairway and a line of rooms on either side), $14,000; rentals at $12 to $16 monthly, $3360; taxes, $360; janitor, $150; wear, tear, and hall gas, $200; vacancy loss, $250: annual income, $2400; investment, $24,000; return, 10 percent. The replacement of the first-floor front suites by stores would yield an extra 3 percent.[11] The problem of property depreciation was not recognized. As it turned out, it was, in fact, of no consequence. Speculative tenements lasted just as long as model ones and continually garnered their profits with each new influx of poor families. Furthermore, any decline in building value was to some extent offset by the overall appreciation of land in Manhattan.

The renting of stores, especially along the avenues, was an important factor in tenement economics. When Alfred White publicized his 7½ percent return from the first phase of his Home Buildings, he did not stress that 30 percent of the income from the property came from four stores—that the rent from a store was equal to four times that of an apartment.[12] The tenement owner who could convert his main-floor front into stores was fortunate; the one who could rent them to a liquor merchant with a "family" entrance off the stair hall was doubly so. Statistics of the period showed one saloon for every 110 men and women over fifteen years of age. Salvationist Ballington Booth counted 27 saloons along one side of three blocks in Cherry Street. Along one block of Water Street he counted 48 prostitutes.

Reformers had persistently pointed out for a generation that sexual promiscuity was unavoidable when men, women, boys, and girls, family and strangers, were crowded indiscriminately into dark rooms reached through dark halls. The maturing girl was faced with bitter alternatives. When Maggie grows into a comely young lady in Stephen Crane's novel, her brother tells her "Yeh've eader got t' go on d' toif er go t' work."[13] Her futile attempt to find pleasure and love ends in the river. Virtue was usually preferred, but it did not pay. As Jacob Riis wrote of a woman who had committed suicide rather than succumb, "the only living wages that were offered her were the wages of sin."[14] The girl who worked ten back-breaking hours for 60 cents a day returned home at night past the finery of her neighbor who earned twice that much by coupling with a man. While there were somewhere over 150,000 working females in the city and probably only 5000 prostitutes of varying involvement (of which not more than 1000 willingly traded the long, cheerless prospect of drudgery for gay company, bright lights, and pretty clothes), and while the reform movement of the 1890s had not yet forced the professionals out of the brothels into the tenements, the red-light district was in the slums and a constant provocation in the life of the poor.

The poor not only squandered their money on release through drink but also gambled it away in the excitement of playing "policy" number lotteries. At the same time their excess of expenditure (or shortage of income) forced them to live improperly in order to pay their rent. The nineteenth-century individualistic code feared the debilitating effect of indiscriminate charity and insisted upon a man giving money for value. Unfortunately, no matter how minimal their dwellings, many working-class families still found them too expensive. Riis, in *How the Other Half Lives*, tells of a typical tenant on Broome Street in the Lower East Side, a Jewish suspender maker who with his wife and eighteen-year-old daughter managed to earn about $6.25 weekly. His rent for two second-floor rooms was $10 monthly. By day the parlor was the workroom. At night the girl slept there on a bed, the three other children on the floor, while the parents used the small interior room. "For a wonder," wrote Riis, "there are no boarders," the family money being supplemented by the eldest boy, who, when employed, worked in a factory.[15] Whether his wage was too low or his rent too high—that is, whether he was exploited by his employer or his landlord—even the frugal worker-tenant found it difficult to meet his expenses. The solution was the paying lodger. The middle-class apartment building housed its single family per floor; each tenement story contained so many people as to add up to the densest population in the world. Every boatload of kinsfolk added its quota. Writing in 1882 on *The Problem of the Poor*, Helen Campbell quoted a tenant enumerating the occupants of a typical early "double-decker": "Now I'll tell you what I know about every one of those floors, and there's six with the basement. To begin with, there's four families to a floor. They're packed because they have to be. The men get little work and have nothing to pay for better rooms. The top floor has a family for every room, that is if you choose to call it a family. They're ragpickers mostly. Four men and three women live together in one of them and pay four dollars a month. Married? Oh, no! There's one widow on that floor. She has a back-room and takes seven boarders. I've seen the floor thick with them at night. . . . Just below is another widow that takes in servant girls out of employment for ten cents a night. . . . Next to her there's another rag-picker; bones and rags; he has four boys he employs, and one of the dark rooms where they sort is as bad as a slaughter-house. He's been complained of and forbidden to bring them in, but the Health Board can't come down every day so he don't mind. There's a washer-woman in front with four small children, and she has three men that lodge there and two boys eighteen and twenty. Yes, all in the one room and the closet back of it. . . . The next floor's the same. Four families on that and they all drink."[16]

While the building that Helen Campbell was visiting was probably one erected before the enforcement of the earlier tenement acts, the newer tenements were just as overcrowded notwithstanding the legal demand for 600 cubic feet of air per person. Riis tells of a visit to a typical later "double-decker" in which there were 43 families where there should have been 16. "In only one flat did we find a single family. In three there were two to each. In the other twelve each room had its own family living and sleeping there. They cooked, I suppose, at the one stove in the kitchen, which was the largest room. In one big bed we counted six persons, the parents and four children. Two of them lay crosswise at the foot of the bed, or there would not have been room."[17] The building Riis was describing was eighteen years old and had been built "upon the improved plan of 1879, with air shafts and all that." Unfortunately, unlike middle-class apartments, working-class tenements deteriorated rapidly, the inevitable result of tenant abuse and landlord neglect. Which came first was a matter of opinion. The buildings, Riis observed, "had made a fair start; they promised well. But the promise had not been kept. In their premature decay they were distinctly as bad as the worst. I had the curiosity to seek out the agent, the middleman, and ask him why they were so. He shrugged his shoulders. With such tenants nothing could be done, he said."[18]

A noted instance of the culpability of tenants had been recorded some years before when Henry Bergh wrote to the *New York Times* about his experiences as a model landlord. Having inherited some land at the upper end of Cherry and Water streets, he had erected ten five-story houses with only one suite on each floor. There was oilcloth in the entrances, gas-light in the halls, and water supplied to each dwelling. "For a while these houses were the abodes of a cleanly and respectable people, but the handwriting soon appeared literally upon their walls, that they must succumb to the inevitable dominion of dirt, destruction and disgrace. Their occupants destroyed the bannisters, defaced the walls, blew out the gas, instead of turning the faucets, and actually tore off the window shutters to make fire of. Their children exercised their skill in whittling all that their knives would cut, and upon the jambs and doors of the entrances they carved every conceivable figure which savage taste could invent."[19] Bergh's grievances were aired at the first Cooper Union meeting in 1879 and led to the arrangement that handed his property to the care of the same people who later took over the management of Gotham Court. Following the principles of Octavia Hill in London, the women who supervised the buildings maintained a constant interest in their tenants, and in return insisted on the weekly payment of rent, together with cleanliness and sobriety. The tenants apparently accepted the change with surprising readiness, and by the end of the year the buildings were redeemed. But with the loss of revenue from the corner store that was stopped from selling liquor, and with the constant expense of maintenance, the experiment was a financial failure, and the buildings were abandoned to revert to their original state.

The standard of tenants, the 1884 Tenement House Commission had affirmed, "is in advance of the condition of the houses which they occupy."[20] The constant influx of "wretched refuse," as the inscription on the newly completed Statue of Liberty put it,[21] which began to be swelled in the 1880s by persecuted Jews from eastern Europe and impoverished southern Italians, qualified this assertion. "As a tenant," observed the *Real Estate Record*, "the Italian can be called desirable only in the fact that he pays his rent always when due, and in all matters of money, no matter how small, he is most honorable. Further than this, he is very dirty and destructive, in time reducing a house to his own level, so that it is really fit for no other class of tenants. The Neopolitan may be considered as the most filthy, as he seems to have hardly a sense of decency at all, as a rule living in herds more than anything else, seemingly unconscious of filth or vermin."[22] Of 412 Italian families visited by the 1884 Tenement House Commission, 115 lived in dirty apartments. A similar proportion of Polish Jews had the same domiciliary habits. This constant refilling of the poorer class by new immigrants taking the place of those who had managed to rise in the economic hierarchy created a sense of immutability. "Scene after scene is the same," wrote Helen Campbell in 1891. "Rags, dirt, filth, wretchedness, the same figures, the same faces, the same old story of one room unfit for habitation yet inhabited by a dozen people, the same complaint of a ruinous rent exacted by the merciless landlord, the same shameful neglect of all sanitary precautions, rotten floors, oozing walls, vermin everywhere, broken windows, crazy staircases—this is the picture of the homes of hundreds of people in the tenement districts of New York.... An extreme case? If it only were,—but these are tenements built within a comparatively recent period, and thus nominally more comfortable than older dwellings."[23]

Into these households, the poor took their work. (However, one unpremeditated virtue of new tenement design was its inability to contain sweatshops. "In the apartments built nowadays, how is it?" asked the U. S. House of Representatives Committee on Manufactures in 1893. "In the apartments built nowadays," replied an expert witness, "the rooms are too small.")[24] The blight of the Irish, and later Italian, ragpickers was replaced in the latter part of the century by the Jewish sweatshops of the garment industry. First utilized during the Civil War, the system reached its apogee with the immigrant East European whose long hours of work at very low piece rates captured the market from his more conventional competitors. Rejecting the potential protection of labor laws and union solidarity, he avoided the discipline of factory employment so that he could work with his kinsfolk, rest on Saturday, and make as much money as his skill and stamina permitted. Lamentably, as his dexterity increased, his rate, figured to a tenth of a penny, was cut, and privation became the constant sum of his exertions (until he could save or borrow enough to exploit others).

Another trade that raised the rental value of tenements was cigar making, usually done by Bohemians. Prohibited by the state in 1884, the law was declared unconstitutional by the court of appeals after the Board of Health denied that it was a hazard to health. When officers of the state labor bureau tried to investigate conditions in these buildings, they were refused admittance. Reduced to collecting testimonies, they heard that "in busy seasons you can see any number of children employed in stripping and preparing tobacco; the number so employed would average more than twenty to a house and the ages would range from five to fourteen; they work from eleven to thirteen hours a day—sometimes more; they do not work as long hours as grown persons, but enough to kill them rapidly. . . . I have seen eight persons working in a small room . . . one of the eight was a little fellow, not more than nine years old, indescribably dirty and ragged; another was the grandmother, and both were stripping tobacco; such scenes are frequent; the stench, the filth, the utter wretchedness and seeming hopelessness."[25]

While such reports were considered by some to be exaggerated, the consumptive tailor in the sweatshop coughing sputum over his wares was a fact recognized at the end of the century by the federal government, which, noting the relationship between communicable diseases and tenement house manufacturing during the Spanish-American War, ordered all military clothing to be made in proper factories. "I see there a pale operator all absorbed in his work," wrote the poet Morris Rosenfeld. "Ever since I remember him, he has been sewing, and using up his strength. . . . And the tears fall in succession from daybreak until fall of night, and water the clothes, and enter into the seams."[26]

Underpaid, overcrowded, susceptible to sickness, drunkenness, immorality, and crime, trapped in the dirt of ignorance and neglect, the poor lived in housing that was not fundamentally different from that of other people but, in its minimal standard of accommodation, was at a level with their overall plight.

8

Interlude

James Bayles's presidency of the Board of Health only lasted two years. Mayor Hewitt proved to be too independent for Tammany boss Richard Croker's taste, and in 1888 he was defeated by the Democratic organization that ruled New York for the next six years. A plea by a delegation of physicians that Bayles be continued in office failed to move the new mayor, who replaced him by a man of dubious repute. The Board of Health then deteriorated into the usual patronage sinecure, but this transformation, which included William Prentice's resignation after twenty years as the board's lawyer and culminated in Cyrus Edson's appointment as sanitary superintendent, coincided with the act of 1892 that took away from the Board of Health its responsibilities for new tenement design and handed them over to a newly separated Building Department. Thus, during the next decade, the Board of Health legally limited its tenement activities to existing buildings, while the lighting, ventilation, plumbing, and drainage of new tenements, as well as their general structure, became the sole responsibility of the Building Department—though, with both departments firmly under Tammany control, the administrative result of this change was of no consequence. In this interlude between reform movements, a new personality came into prominence.

Jacob Riis was a Dane who had emigrated to the United States in 1870 at the age of twenty-one. Son of a schoolmaster, though trained as a carpenter, he landed in New York with little but a zest for life. Finding it impossible to obtain work in the city, he traveled around in search of a job, suffering much privation until he obtained employment as editor of a Brooklyn newspaper. Then in 1878, after a trip back home to marry his childhood sweetheart, Riis began his real career as a police reporter for twenty-one years, first with the *Tribune*, then with the *Evening Sun*.

His inquiries familiarized him with the dwellings of the poor, where much of the city's crime originated. The walk from his office on Mulberry Street to the Fulton Street ferry, on his way home to Brooklyn, took him past the worst of the slums along the "Bend" (now Columbus Park). He reported the sessions of the 1884 Tenement House Commission, where he first met Adler, and in 1888 attended a meeting at Chickering Hall, where he heard White ask an assembly of ministers, "How are these men and women to understand the love of God you speak of, when they see only the greed of men?" Riis had his text for a book; that winter he copyrighted the title *How the Other Half Lives*. "It was just a question," he wrote later in his autobiography, "whether a man would take seven per cent and save his soul, or twenty-five and lose it."[1]

Unsuccessful in finding a publisher, Riis tried to obtain church facilities to publicize what he had seen and, after initial difficulty in obtaining permission (which was refused even by his own congregation), was finally invited to give an illustrated talk at the Broadway Tabernacle. During the series of lectures that followed, he was heard by the editor of *Scribner's* magazine, who commissioned an article for the December 1889 issue. This article prompted Jeannette Gilder, editor of the *Critic*, to arrange for the publication of the book.

Written and published in 1890, *How the Other Half Lives* was an impassioned account of life as it was lived in the slums. For the first time the reformer appeared as a human being among others, neither compromised by excess money or conscience nor impersonalized within a philanthropic organization. Anecdote followed anecdote until a kaleidoscope of impressions formed an indictment of social degradation.

Riis was the first housing reformer to leave behind a sense of character and a body of eminently quotable writing. Yet he was limited in interest to a knowledge of those events in which he and his friends participated, and the evocative prose of his narrative often modified the past by omission and overemphasis. His later book *The Battle with the Slum* made no reference to such other reformers as Stephen Smith, Willis James, or even his direct contemporary Charles Wingate, and his early confidence in the inherent virtue of the Board of Health ensured that department immunity from criticism even when its good intentions paved the way to the "double-decker" hell that Riis abhorred. Nevertheless, his writing seethed with compassion. He describes nighttime, when a "sweet, human little baby despite its dirt and tatters . . . tumbles off the lowest step, rolls over once, clutches my leg with unconscious grip, and goes to sleep on the flagstones, its curly head pillowed on my boot." The children at school who repeat every morning in class "I must keep my skin clean / Wear clean clothes / Breathe pure air / And live in the sunlight"—then go back home, where "penury and poverty are wedded everywhere to dirt and disease." The suicide who left her message, "Weakness, sleeplessness, and yet obliged to work. My strength fails me. Sing at my coffin." The man who stood at the corner of Fifth Avenue and Fourteenth Street, "poor, and hungry, and ragged," stared at the passing carriages, then "sprang into the throng and slashed about him with a knife, blindly seeking to kill, to revenge."[2]

How the Other Half Lives excited sympathy, as Riis had hoped, and went through several editions, but it contained few proposals for improving the conditions it described other than appealing to the conscience of private enterprise. Included in a paragraph of miscellaneous suggestions was Adler's idea for rent control, but Riis had little confidence in the efficacy of the law, for "At best, it is apt to travel at a snail's pace, while the enemy it pursues is putting the best foot foremost."[3] (He later modified his viewpoint when Theodore Roosevelt was appointed president of the Board of Police in 1895.) His main enthusiasm was for rehabilitated and model tenements because "such is the leavening influence of a good deed in that dreary desert of sin and suffering, that the erection of a single good tenement has the power to change . . . the character of a whole bad block."[4]

One of these benefactors, Ellen Collins, who had a decade before converted a row of Water Street slums into model dwellings, wrote to Riis objecting to the bleak picture he had drawn. He replied that he had purposely done this to arouse the public conscience.[5] The fact was, however, that not all tenements were slums. Wingate, writing at the beginning of 1885, and using the death rate of their occupants as a standard, listed only 5 percent very bad and 10 percent bad, with 40 percent fair and 45 percent in good condition.[6] Later, perhaps with the more detailed knowledge gained through the survey that he had carried out as a basis for his articles in the *Morning Journal,* he modified these figures to 9, 24, 43, and 24 percent, respectively;[7] but even these proportions, set within a scale established against the criteria of excessive lot coverage, number of families, and deaths, meant that only one-third of the tenement stock, or 7000 buildings, were considered inferior by one expert's standards. While a member of the 1884 Tenement House Commission, Wingate had estimated that there were 24,000 tenement houses, of which 19,000 had more than one family per floor. The commission itself estimated 26,000 tenement houses and made no reference to French flats, although nearly 2000 had been built since their popularization a decade before; and from its sample survey it could be adduced that it considered 14,000 tenement houses to be below its unspecified standards.[8] This statistical difference between 7000 and 14,000—that is, between roughly one-third and two-thirds of the tenement stock—reflected the middle range of judgment of what constituted a slum. This differing interpretation of the facts was also evidenced by the 1887 reports of the Association for Improving the Condition of the Poor, which announced its withdrawal from tenement inspections, as these were merely "duplicating the work now so efficiently done"[9] by the Board of Health compared to that of the newly formed New York Sanitary Aid Society, which continued to discover "pestilential human rookeries, courts and alleys . . . reeking with poisonous and malodorous gases . . . dark and filthy passages swarming with vermin . . . dens in which thousands of human beings herd together."[10]

Yet even if, by the mid-1880s, half of all tenement houses were no longer suitable for occupancy, this was not completely disheartening, for only around 3000 had been built since the 1879 enforcement of the tenement acts, while 15,000, discounting changes in use, had existed for more than twenty years. The compilation of the 1884 Tenement House Commission's statistics showed that after ten years of habitation the ratio of good to bad varied little with extra use and the fact that only one-quarter of the newer buildings had deteriorated presaged success with the higher standards envisaged. Thus the problem, in modern terminology, was no longer new housing but the need for slum clearance and urban renewal. For by 1890 a tract of old tenement property had come into being that provided substandard housing for about half a million people. As the American and Northwest European moved to the more expensive flats uptown, this resevoir of cheap slums was filled by penniless new immigrants who, landing at Battery Park, traversed Broadway and Park Row to the Lower East Side, where they occupied the buildings that had been ravaged by their predecessors.

In 1893 a further wave of public indignation at the conditions in which these people lived was set off by the *Press* in a series of articles headed "New York Rents Must Come Down."[11] Thrown out of work by the depression and evicted by their landlords, their pitiful circumstances were portrayed by the newspaper, which showed that while each square foot of a Central Park apartment rented for 37 cents monthly, the owners of a downtown slum got 42 cents; and that included among the slum owners were Trinity Church and Ward McAllister, leader of New York's "Four Hundred" social set, author of *Society as I Have Found It* and sponsor of *the* Mrs. Astor.[12] The *Press* was righteously indignant: "Packed together like swine in the most thickly populated district on the face of the earth; paying outrageously high rents for outrageously mean quarters; oppressed on every hand by everybody, the denizens of our East Side live. It is a spectacle that should arouse the resentment of every honest man, and it is a spectacle which must incite the fear of every logical thinker. It is all wrong. It must be remedied."[13] The outcome was another tenement committee set up by a Republican state legislature, only too pleased to embarrass the city's Democratic incumbents. For even with the governorship under Tammany control, the combination of upstate Republican boss Thomas Platt and the New York establishment was irresistible; thus, when the Lexow committee's funds for investigating the Police Department were vetoed by Governor Roswell Flower, the cost of its operation was guaranteed by wealthy citizens spurred on by Charles Parkhurst's revelations.

This single-handed campaign against the Tammany organization by Parkhurst, who was pastor of the Madison Square Presbyterian

Church, had started in 1891 when he was elected president of the Society for the Prevention of Crime. Observing that much of the city's crime was supported by the Police Department itself, he inveighed against its corruption from his pulpit and, when rebuked by the grand jury for unfounded slander, personally collected evidence to substantiate his claims. Publicly presented with sworn affidavits, the grand jury was convinced, and a Cooper Union meeting was organized to demand reform. But the Police Department had a long-established practice in dishonesty that was not to be challenged easily. Counterattacking, it arrested the Society for the Prevention of Crime's own detective for extortion and attempted, unsuccessfully, to harass Parkhurst into submission. For two years the gathering of evidence continued, until in 1894 the Lexow committee was appointed. Guided by Parkhurst, it heard of promotions purchased, able-bodied men retired on pensions, and bribes received from poolrooms, policy shops, abortionists, and brothels.

Concurrently, the new tenement committee had met in May. With Richard Watson Gilder, a poet and editor of the *Century*, (and brother of Jeannette Gilder) as chairman and Edward Marshall, the Sunday editor of the *Press*, as secretary and executive officer, its other members were the sanitary superintendent of health Cyrus Edson, two lawyers Roger Foster and John Schuchman, civil engineer William Washington, architect George Post, and Solomon Moses of the United Hebrew Charities. Unlike the Drexel commission of ten years earlier, the Gilder committee devoted its investigation, not to a study of a cross sample of tenements as they had been built since their inception, but to all those buildings that were then considered to be slums. Thus it tacitly assumed that the new tenements generally were satisfactory, and this assumption was indirectly confirmed by its own observations. Asked to provide a list of the worst tenement houses in the city, the Board of Health enumerated 2425. Unsatisfied, the committee carried out its own examination and added 6809 more. These numbers can be compared to Wingate's assessment in 1887 of 7000, to show an increase that can be readily accounted for by a change in the legal definition of tenement and further years of physical wear. The erection of new buildings (which during the 1880s had been at a rate of around 1000 a year) was therefore not adding to the number of inadequate dwellings—but neither was it replacing them. The housing stock had simply expanded to include originally new units now from naught to sixty years old.

With its concentration on old buildings, the Gilder committee achieved little that affected new construction or its use. Its building recommendations, based on past offenses rather than current practices, and on the lowest rather than general usage, were ill considered and carelessly framed; thus they easily fell victim to lobbying in Albany, so that Gilder was repeatedly forced to modify his committee's proposals as they passed through the state legislature. For example, the committee condemned the use of wallpaper as a source of dirt and latent infection, and in the slum it certainly was, but unfortunately it was also a standard finish for better-class apartments. The reformers were in a dilemma because through the years they had vigorously resisted all attempts to differentiate between tenements and French flats in the belief that if the latter were exempted from the law, it would be impossible to define the former. Other interested groups had proposed a division by cost, by the number of apartments per floor, or by the inclusion of bathrooms, but each of these seemed to provide a loophole in enforcement. Given the situation that the law proposed by the committee to forbid the use of wallpaper would automatically prevent its use in middle-class buildings, it was easy to deride the committee's common sense. In this instance

The clause was modified to provide that all old paper first be removed and the wall or ceiling cleaned before new paper was applied, but this requirement was practically unenforceable.

The committee found that the "double decker," so called, is the one hopeless form of tenement-house construction. It began with the old New York dwelling altered over; and gradually a type was produced in some respects better and in some worse than the earlier forms of the narrow tenement. The double-decker cannot be well ventilated; it cannot be well lighted; it is not safe in case of fire. . . . Direct light is only possible for the rooms at the front and rear. The middle rooms must borrow what light they can from dark hallways, the shallow shafts and the front and rear rooms. Their air must pass through other rooms or the tiny shafts, and cannot but be contaminated before it reaches them. . . . These [buildings] permit an agglomeration of humanity which exists nowhere else, and which under a less rigorous code of health, a less keen watchfulness on the part of the authorities as to contagion, and firemen of less courage and efficiency, would create a state of affairs absolutely fatal to the public welfare."[14] Having made this comprehensive indictment of standard tenement design, the committee failed almost completely to correct its listed shortcomings.

The 1895 act that resulted from its report barred fat boiling in cellars (and the storage of rags) except in certain circumstances and at the same time improved some elements of fire prevention and fireproofing. The committee's attempt, however, to reduce the lot coverage of tenements closer to the prevailing statutory maximum of 65 percent virtually ended up legalizing the Board of Health's discretionary arrangement (75 percent instead of 78); the new law's antiovercrowding minimum requirement of 400 cubic feet per adult was one-third below that of 1879; and while it did require windows in every room and water closet compartment, it failed to define the "outer air" on which they were to open. Finally, declaring itself "a remedial statute," it stated it was, "to be construed liberally,"[15] thus permitting further inroads into the investigating committee's well-meaning if fuzzy intentions.

On the other hand, the Gilder committee, unlike its predecessor, looked outside the individual building and judged the environment as a whole. Its detailed study of four typical tenement blocks containing Italian, Bohemian, and Russian Jewish immigrants found serious neighborhood deficiencies. Parents wanted their children educated and seldom forced them to work before the legal age of fourteen, but the schools were "in the control of a grossly incompetent set of outside officials, at whose mercy the system is cramped and tortured into a low degree of educational efficiency."[16] Many children were being turned away through lack of space, and kindergartens were needed for those under the official entry age of eight. Extra parks were also required in densely populated areas where up to 500 persons lived on each acre of the Lower East Side. Another shortage was of bathing facilities. Of a quarter of a million tenement dwellers visited by the committee, only 306 had a bathtub at home. The rest could either use the bathhouse provided by the Association for Improving the Condition of the Poor or wait for the summer months when free floating baths numbering fifteen by the end of the 1880s permitted a certain amount of cleansing through obligatory bathing suits.

Summing up its environmental proposals, the committee asked for public drinking fountains and toilets, year-round bathhouses, electric lighting in the streets, and smooth pavements to minimize the accumulation of filth. To alleviate overcrowding, it advised pushing ahead immediately with the extension of rapid transit. To cut off the infiltration of prostitutes into family tenements, where they had been forced into concealment by the zeal of the

Parkhurst reformers, it demanded severe punishment. Two draft bills submitted by the committee to the legislature dealt with the provision of parks and playgrounds. The first required the creation of at least two small parks including playgrounds within the following three years, somewhere on the Lower East Side. The second required that new schools be provided with playgrounds and directed that others be built as quickly as possible for all those currently without. Finally, it made the demolition of unsanitary tenements feasible by providing compensation for their owners.

The act of 1866 had given the Metropolitan Board of Health the power to order the alteration or removal of any building that was considered dangerous to life or health. (It was under this act that Gotham Court was emptied, cleaned, and altered in 1871, and under the later act that it was demolished.) This, however, given the conditions of the time, was easier written than done except in unusual circumstances. The 1895 act was more detailed and specific. The Board of Health could condemn a building if it was itself, or made others, unfit for human habitation and was considered irremediable; the law would then determine compensation by a formula that provided for different situations. Together, these acts gave the city a moderate betterment program that happily coincided with the election of a reform administration.

The disclosures of the Lexow committee had led to a coalition that culminated in the defeat of the Tammany ex-mayor by a Fusion Republican, William Strong. (The Committee of Seventy, which organized the Fusion compaign, included an election plank on the establishment of adequate public baths and lavatories to promote cleanliness and increase public comfort. It was the custom for policemen to use the toilet facilities provided in saloons, where they might be found when absent from their duties.) The resultant change in the administration led to the appointments in

1895 of George Waring as commissioner of street cleaning and Theodore Roosevelt as president of the Board of Police. For the first time the streets in the tenement districts were liberated from the garbage and ordure that had seemingly been an intrinsic part of their environment. Parading with his uniformed "white wings," putting, as he said, "a man instead of a voter behind every broom," Waring's Augean achievement brought the Lower East Side up to the standard of other, richer areas. Equally effective in his purging of the Police Department and the enforcement of the law, Roosevelt quickly fulfilled his earlier promise to Riis by closing down the tramp-infested police station lodging rooms, where in his indigent immigrant days Riis had been robbed and his dog clubbed to death. This efficiency did not necessarily bring affection. Waring was notoriously tactless; Roosevelt applied the law literally, believing that if it was wrong, it should be changed and not that its implementation should be moderated. Such punctiliousness in an imperfect world provoked antagonism and tempered the popularity of reform government.

The new superintendent of buildings, Stevenson Constable, was also disliked for adhering to the rules with a slow haughtiness more appropriate to a civic guardian that a public servant. As one architect put it, it was as difficult for a person to see him "as to see the President of the United States."[17] His predecessor, Thomas Brady, had been considered "a most honorable official"[18] in the Lexow committee's hearings, and when Mayor Strong began looking for his replacement, 500 persons including the notable architects McKim, Mead & White, and Carrère & Hastings, together with such organizations as the New York chapter of the American Institute of Architects, had asked for the retention of this "upright, clean official" who had "won in an unusual degree the confidence and regard of real estate owners, architects and builders."[19] The following month a group of tenements on the

Lower East Side collapsed during construction killing five persons; and while a coroner's jury headed by the architect Ernest Flagg exonerated Brady, who was "seriously hampered by the character and incompetency of many of the men employed in the Department,"[20] and attached all blame to the responsible inspector, Brady was forced to resign. Thus the new 1895 law was administered by the new superintendent.

"The people living in the western end of Delancey-st.," reported the *Tribune*, "are looking wonderingly at a building that is fast reaching completion, and they can hardly believe it to be a tenement-house. It is No. 28, and here S. W. Korn is building a house under the new tenement law, and in comparison with the rookeries around it is almost a palace. There will be no living rooms below ground, and no sliding down our cellar door. There the ground floor is one long room, to be used as a store, with the staircase for the upper floors—there are five of them—winding through the center of the house, adding to the ventilation greatly.... Another great thing in this new house—and in the future they will all have to be built on the same plan—is that the airshaft only starts from the first floor. This in the first place prevents the shaft from being a chimney for a fire suddenly to leap from the cellar to the roof; and secondly, it is an important item in preventing illness. At the Department of Buildings Superintendent Stevenson Constable told a *Tribune* reporter that he hoped that in a short time there would be a great improvement in all the tenement houses. 'All new houses will have to be built in strict accordance with the present law,' he said, 'and without doubt the condition of the poor will be much ameliorated. These new buildings mean ventilation and the saving of thousands of children's lives.' "[21]

If Constable was arrogantly optimistic about the erection of new tenements, Riis was unpretentiously so when it came to pulling down the old. The Gilder committee's demand for the elimination of rear houses and unsanitary tenements derived from its belief that these caused the city's high death rate, for "it is a well-known fact that human dwellings, by prolonged occupation, become so saturated with the bodily emanations of those who have lived in them, sick and well, as to be less healthy than newer houses."[22] (The report continued: "It has often been proposed to construct hospitals of flimsy and inexpensive material, after the manner of a temporary shelter, and destroy them by fire every few years.") Riis, appointed general agent of the Council of Confederated Good Government Clubs in the spring of 1896—a position he held for one year—and made responsible for the implementation of the betterment program, heartily concurred with the need for pulling down as many slums as possible. People do not always realize, grumbled the *American Architect*, that sanitary regulations "must, at present, be very lax, for the reason that, if the tenants are ordered out of houses unfit for habitation, they have no other place to go; and until good houses are provided by those able to build them, the rookeries must be endured, or the people who live in them will have to camp in the streets."[23] This argument, while attractive to Tammany Hall, failed to impress Riis. "I had no stomach for abstract discussions of social wrongs," he later wrote. "I wanted to right those of them that I could reach."[24]

In a society where free enterprise was being brought within acceptable bounds by regulatory legislation, individual hardship always initially accompanied the imposition of higher standards. No one had expected the abolition of child labor to be accompanied by a mandatory rise in adult incomes to make up for the family's financial loss. Some reformers did see the wider implications of their actions: Adler, for example, had already pointed out that the indirect result of new laws such as the 1881 plumbing act had been to "legislate the poor out of the better houses"[25]

because higher costs were reflected by higher rents; but his recommended limited-dividend housing on publicly owned land to
act competitively against private rentals was a countermeasure
that was politically unthinkable at that time.

With so much to be immediately improved, reformers generally
had little concern for any harmful side effects that their actions
might cause. Each had his own pet project and became aware of
potential interactions usually only when they affected his own
pursuits. Riis never paralyzed himself with philosophical qualms.
When the popular press printed cartoons of homeless men shiver-
ing at a police lodging house door closed by order of police president Theodore Roosevelt, his mentor was unrepentant: "decency
had to begin there, or not at all."[26] However, when Parkhurst's
crusade drove the prostitutes from their brothels, Riis was quick
to object that this would push them into the tenements.

Nevertheless, the ad hoc reformer could not afford to weaken
in his aims. Riis, virtually single-handed, took fourteen years to
get the teeming slum of Mulberry Bend converted into a park.
The 1887 small parks act had provided for the expenditure of a
million dollars annually to lay out parks in the densely populated
areas below 155th Street, but by the time of the 1894 Tenement
House Committee, only three had been initiated and none completed. With Riis on the citizens' committee that was appointed
to locate two further parks required by the new act, the sites
were selected in three weeks. At the same time he drew up a list
of tenements (including Gotham Court) whose existence was a
threat to the city's health. "Conceive, if you can," Riis wrote
later in his autobiography, "the state of mind of a man to whom
a dark, overcrowded tenement has ever been as a personal affront,
now suddenly finding himself commissioned with letters of
marque and reprisal, as it were, to seize and destroy the enemy
wherever found, not one at a time, but by blocks and battalions

in the laying out of parks. I fed fat my ancient grudge and grew good humor enough to last me for a dozen years in those two. They were the years when, in spite of hard work, I began to grow stout, and honestly, I think it was tearing down tenements that did it."[27]

While Riis was enjoying himself demolishing slums, the most successful of the nineteenth-century model tenement movements was being organized. Resulting from a two-day conference called by the Association for Improving the Condition of the Poor to consider the advisability of building improved dwellings for the poor (but not, according to Elgin Gould, for the lowest division of society that included "the drunkard, the incorrigible, the criminal, the immoral, the lazy and shiftless," who should be rounded up in public lodging houses under police supervision, the sexes separated, and the children institutionalized),[28] an Improved Housing Council had been set up in 1896 under Gilder's chairmanship. Its executive committee, which included Samuel Babcock and Fulton Cutting (his brother being vice-chairman), invited architects to submit plans for a competition where the only prize would be the building commission.

Its detailed rules listed the inadequacies of standard tenements: their internal courts excluded light and air while conducting fire, heat, noise, and smells; planning and construction were uneconomical, with a quarter of the lot being occupied by nonrentable elements; the public areas, containing the toilets, were poorly lighted; the apartments, half of which faced to the rear, were inflexible and had bedrooms that could be reached only through other rooms or outside corridors.

The competition sponsors wanted plans for a 200-by-400-foot block site that generally covered only 70 percent of the land and contained 55 percent as clear rentable space; that divided the block into separate sections, each with its own enclosed fireproof staircase lighted with its halls at each floor; that had courts of 900 square feet or more giving cross ventilation to all apartments; that provided all rooms with a window to the outer air so that the majority of apartments had at least one window overlooking a street; that permitted the direct access of living rooms from halls, and bedrooms from living rooms; and that gave each family a toilet and an average space of 400 square feet.[29]

Compared to the profuse entry for the 1879 *Plumber and Sanitary Engineer* competition, the result was disappointing: only 28 plans were received, of which merely a few observed all the conditions. Of the three designs recommended by a three-man jury consisting of Gould, a member of the Association for Improving the Condition of the Poor, and a Boston architect, one was by the earlier prizewinning architect James Ware, and another by Ernest Flagg, who was then making a reputation as an authority on improved tenement planning. Born in Brooklyn, trained at the Ecole des Beaux-Arts and later noted as the designer of the 47-story Singer Building, Flagg was one of the few who differed from the typical architect who, as the *Real Estate Record* noted, "had very small concern for any of the social problems that have come from time to time within the range of his professional activity. . . . Indeed, left to himself the architect apparently would continue to the end of time planning buildings, careless of their sanitary condition, so long as clients were satisfied with them. . . . Year after year, the profession has been busy erecting tenements and flats which have recently been characterized . . . as 'the worst curse whichever afflicted any great community.' . . . Doctors, politicians and philanthropists have all addressed themselves to the problem of improving the character of the tenement accommodations in this city, and the reforms, such as they are, that have been effected in the last twenty-five years are due to their labors and to the thought and discussion which those labors have promoted. The

architect has held himself aloof from the work and his chief lament
has been that the conditions of modern life in a city like New
York, and the requirements of clients are inimical to truly artistic
work, meaning by artistic work close copying of the architecture
of other centuries and other societies."[30]

Flagg's approach to the problem, outlined in an article on "The
New York tenement-house evil and its cure," published in *Scribner's* magazine in 1894, was that it was simply impossible to design a satisfactory building on a 25-by-100-foot lot. His prizewinning scheme for a city block was based on a 100-foot-wide rectangular hollow plan divided by fire walls into four sections, each
containing three apartments per floor, reached by corner staircases set in at the angles of a large interior court. Shortly afterward
when, following on from the Improved Housing Council, the City
and Suburban Homes Company was incorporated, these plans were
adapted to a nineteen-lot site, at 68th and 69th streets between Amsterdam and West End avenues, given by the widow of Alfred Corn-
ing Clark in exchange for shares. The six-story buildings, opened in
1898, contained 373 apartments, each with its own toilet. There
were free spray baths, and the halls and stairways were heated.

The next City and Suburban Homes Company project, the First
Avenue Estate at 64th Street between First Avenue and Avenue
A, was based on Ware's prizewinning scheme and was more sophisticated in plan and services. Completed from 1900 on, each apartment had hot water, steam heat, gas fixtures and range, and basement storage. There were dumbwaiters and chutes, showers and
tubs, even a special room for baby carriages. Also six stories high
and based on a similar plan dimension, its design was better organized than that of Flagg and more sensible in its layout. As the first
Tenement House Department report later wryly remarked, "It is
interesting and significant that the same architects who for many
years turned out nothing but one 'dumb-bell' plan after another

are now the leaders in planning the best and most desirable types of houses . . . and many of them often excused themselves by saying they had to plan what their clients wanted to build."[31]

The City and Suburban Homes Company was presided over by Elgin Gould until his death in 1915. Canadian born, he had received his doctorate in political science from Johns Hopkins University during the same period as Woodrow Wilson. His definitive survey, *The Housing of the Working People*, published as the eighth special report of the U. S. Commissioner of Labor in 1895, was based on research carried out in the United States and Europe between 1887 and 1892. Like most of his contemporaries, Gould rejected the evolving European practice of municipalities assuming authority to provide their own working-class housing as being unsuitable to American conditions and advocated minimum-standard laws supplemented by housing supplied by private enterprise for limited profit. This attitude was summed up by Edward Marshall when he observed that "during the existence of the present unstable and ofttimes corrupt system of American municipal government it would probably be unwise to advocate the city construction or city management of dwellings for the poor,"[32] a point of view that was soon to be reinforced by the publications of the muckrakers. The business-oriented *Real Estate Record*, perhaps beginning to believe that working-class housing was no longer a suitable private investment, or merely being ironic, commented: "What the [1894] Tenement House Commission should do is to convert itself into a municipal government reform association, and when they have got an administration that can be trusted, secure to it power to build improved dwellings."[33] In the meantime, the City and Suburban Homes Company was set up as a limited-dividend corporation annually paying its stockholders a 4 percent dividend before World War I, by which time it owned nearly 3000 apartments.

The Clark Estate added 373 model tenement units to the few hundred that had resulted from the reform agitation of the 1880s. Another 610 on 41st and 42nd streets off Tenth Avenue were sponsored and designed by Flagg himself, supported by the capitalist Ogden Mills. The First Avenue Estate initially supplied a further 869. Thus, by the end of the century, altruistic landlords had built about 2000 dwelling *units*, accommodating not more than 10,000 persons. In the same period since the first enforcement of the tenement acts, approximately 20,000 *buildings* containing three-quarters of a million persons had resulted from the ordinary investment of private enterprise conforming more or less to existing nineteenth-century law. It was evident that if any significant impact on housing standards was going to be made, it would come, not from the example of enlightened capitalism, but from the enforcement of regulatory legislation.

9

The Problem Restated

In his report on *The Housing of the Working People*, Elgin Gould had rejected the view stated by British philanthropist Sydney Waterlow that "it would not have been right to build down to the lowest class, because in so doing his company would have been obliged to construct a class of tenements which, it is to be hoped, no one at the end of a few years would be satisfied with."[1] This dissimilarity of outlook reflected the difference between the comparatively closed society of Britain, gradually raising standards of its poorest citizens through a century of evolutionary reforms, and the open, immigrant society of the United States continuously absorbing the indigent of Europe. The former could assume a constant rate of improvement that would render a low-standard building obsolete long before the end of its normal life. The latter envisaged a constant high level of need by a recurring influx of similar groups. In practice, the more depressed condition of the British working class compared to its American counterpart meant that even with its higher ideals it reached only the same level of accomplishment, as evidenced by the similar buildings produced in London by Waterlow and in Brooklyn by White. All improved tenement builders tried to find a balance between the standard set by the market and that believed by those in authority to be best for the occupant's soul—that is, neither too low to sever him from society nor too high to let him forget his place. Recognizing the gap between the tenant's known mode of behavior and the quality of his new habitation, the philanthropic landlord developed a system of paternalistic control originated by John Ruskin's associate Octavia Hill. The City and Suburban Homes Company excluded the "incorrigible" and employed Blanche Geary to educate the rest through weekly visits.

Gould's rejection of Waterlow's reasoning was ill considered: there was more than one cause of changing standards. While, no doubt, the imported domiciliary habits of the incoming tenants remained constant, there being little difference in background quality between the Irishman's cabin of the 1840s and the East European Jewish hovel of the 1880s, the conditions acceptable to the American community were themselves susceptible to change. That which was tolerated at the beginning of the century (such as corporal punishment) was rejected as time passed by. Though the Jewish or Italian immigrant was no better than his Irish or German predecessor, the old rookeries provided for the latter were no longer acceptable to advancing public sensibility. Housing reformers who twenty years earlier had considered the imposition of a 4-by-3-foot shaft a major success, now found their actions considered little less than sinful. For by the time of the 1894 Tenement House Committee, Hartley of the Association for Improving the Condition of the Poor was long since dead; Pellew, now living in Washington, was in his sixties; Chandler was fifty-eight; Wingate, who had retired to the congenial atmosphere of Twilight Park in the Catskill Mountains, Riis, and Adler were in their forties; Lawrence Veiller was twenty-two. A new generation had arrived.

A City College graduate, Veiller had joined the Charity Organization Society in 1892. The society, incorporated ten years earlier, had been initiated by Josephine Shaw Lowell of the State Board of Charities to coordinate and augment the activities of the city's charitable organizations. Dedicated to giving the poor a fair chance in life through social reform plus induced self-dependence (and support where this failed through no fault of one's own), its organization included both headquarter policy committees and district caseworkers, with whom Veiller worked on the Lower East Side during the economic depression of 1893. Convinced that better housing was the key to social improvement, Veiller began his career as a housing reformer.

After working as a plan examiner in the Building Department under the reform superintendent Stevenson Constable, Veiller returned to the Charity Organization Society, where on his own initiative he drew up a memorandum outlining a course of continuing action to raise the standard of tenement building. Initially offered to and declined by the Association for Improving the Condition of the Poor and the State Charities Aid Association, Veiller's memorandum was taken up by the Charity Organization Society itself, which under the auspices of its president, Robert de Forest, called a conference to discuss the problem toward the end of 1898. After pointing out that the Greater New York Charter authorized the municipal assembly to appoint a committee of experts to revise the city's building laws, Veiller contrasted this potentiality with the fact that the departments of building and health seldom enforced the existing laws; that buildings were designed by architects for a $15 to $25 fee and were constructed with used materials and supervised by subcontractors themselves; and that if left unchecked, the state legislature was apt to pass further laws in the interest of those speculators who were busily tearing down three-story tenements and building six-story ones in their place. What was needed, Veiller argued, was a permanent organization to assure the enforcement of existing laws, oppose retrogressive legislation, propose remedial legislation, and gain expertise in the whole field of tenement housing. The conference concurred. Veiller was appointed secretary to a committee chaired by a lawyer, Frederick Holls, which included Gilder, Adler, Gould, Riis, architects George Post, Ernest Flagg, and Phelps Stokes, de Forest, Charity Organization Society general secretary Edward Devine, Constant Andrews of the Association for Improving the Condition of the Poor, and another lawyer John Vinton Dahlgren, who died and was replaced by Andrew Carnegie.

On January 1, 1898, Manhattan, Brooklyn, the Bronx, Queens, and Staten Island were amalgamated into Greater New York under a municipal assembly consisting of a council and a board of aldermen. Its charter authorized the establishment of a commission to prepare a new building code for the new metropolis. This was to be formed of experts, but there were too many to include with every interested group claiming essential expertise. The original resolution had proposed a lawyer, architect, mason, carpenter, ironworker, plumber, and civil engineer. At the commission's winter public hearings on its consitution (held before the creation of the Charity Organization Society tenement house committee), Devine stated that his society had no specific recommendations for the amendment of the building laws but wanted a just and competent body presumably in accord with a substitute resolution requesting the inclusion of architects, engineers, lawyers, and city representatives from the building, health, and fire departments. The city answered with a commission made up of five members of the Building Department, three builders, an iron contractor-engineer, an architect, and a corporation counsel. For by this time the Tammany Democrats had once more been returned to power (on the campaign slogan of "To hell with reform"), and Brady was back as president of a Building Department that was again "honeycombed with corruption. Instead of being a machine for the impartial enforcement of the law, it is an agency for the oppression of all who do not know how to gain indulgences by the judicious payment of tribute, or who will not purchase favors by means which the self-respecting man and the good citizen shun as they would the infection of leprosy."[2]

Furious at the city council's snub, Veiller's committee made another attempt to add an architect, an engineer, and a representative from the 1894 Tenement House Committee and, when this failed, took the dispute to Albany. Two bills were proposed: the first, withdrawing the right of the municipal assembly to revise the building laws and restoring this power to the state legislature, where it had previously been lodged; the second, establishing a commission of eleven specified representative members to serve without pay. Both bills failed. Accepting that the municipal assembly had the authority to supplement existing tenement laws (though not to alter them), the Charity Organization Society committee spent the following months preparing a list of suggestions, which were debated by a special conference held in May 1899 and attended by reformers and social workers such as Lillian Wald of the Nurses Settlement, James Reynolds of the University Settlement, and Mary Simkhovitch of Friendly Aid House. The outcome was a brief containing fifteen suggested amendments to existing tenement law.

The publication of these proposed ordinances in June 1899 was well received and officially approved by the New York chapter of the American Institute of Architects, the Architectural League of New York City, the Association for Improving the Condition of the Poor, the Children's Aid Society, and the settlements. The *New York Times*, noting that the demand for a 6-foot-wide, 150-square-foot air shaft was tantamount to abolishing 25-foot-wide tenements, commended the Charity Organization Society committee on its realistic approach. Veiller hedged. In replying to the *New York Times*, he denied that the enlarged air shaft would make single-lot tenements obsolete; it would only reduce the num-

ber of rooms per floor from fourteen to twelve and an investor's
return from 10 to 8 percent. The *New York Times* was disgusted
at such apparent chicanery. "If, on account of the huge interests
arrayed against them," it editorialized, "they choose to pretend
that 'with some modifications,' such tenements can be built," they
would no longer be able to count on its support.[3] Illustrating their
contention that a single-lot tenement would still be feasible, the
Charity Organization Society committee published a four-family,
twelve-room-per-floor plan with the enlarged court, but its arrangement was tortuous, and its bedrooms were all only 6½ feet
wide, showing single beds end to end where couples were expected
to sleep.[4]

By this time there were other problems. Ten weeks after the executive of the committee had put forward its recommendations
to the municipal building code commission, the latter had presented its own proposals to the municipal assembly. In its report,
the commission stated that it had incorporated most of the Charity Organization Society's amendments; in fact, it had simply ignored them. At a public hearing, Veiller (and many others, including the former building superintendent, McGregor) spoke out
against the new code, but all counterarguments were brushed
aside, and it was passed in the fall of 1899. It is a "credit to our
own city and a model for other cities to copy," complimented the
Real Estate Record;[5] the only opposition was from a lot of cranks,
observed one of its correspondents.[6]

Frustrated by municipal politics, Veiller moved to arouse public opinion. Working sixteen hours a day for months on end, he
set up a tenement exhibition, the first of its kind. Held on Fifth
Avenue at 37th Street during two weeks in February 1900, it was
opened by Governor Theodore Roosevelt and viewed by 10,000
persons. Costing $10,000, its models, photos (over 1000), maps,

charts, diagrams and tables were arranged in five large rooms on two floors. One set of illustrations showed bad housing conditions in the city, especially the results of narrow air shafts, contrasting with model tenements in the United States and Europe. Another portrayed typical workingmen's homes in 40 American cities. Poverty and disease maps pinpointed their breeding places with black dot markers, while a cardboard model of a 200-by-400-foot block at Chrystie, Forsyth, Canal, and Bayard streets alongside the Bowery on the Lower East Side showed its 39 tenement houses, with 605 apartments containing 2781 persons (or over 1500 to the acre), including 466 children under five years of age. There were 441 dark rooms and 635 rooms lighted from shafts, 264 water closets but not one bath. Other parts of the exhibition showed lodging houses and the interrelationship of social amenities such as playgrounds, parks, recreation piers, baths, and libraries. Also on display were prizewinning plans from a model tenement competition organized by the Charity Organization Society committee and judged by Bayard Cutting, Gould, Wald, Alice Lincoln, who was an improved-tenement manager from Boston, Stokes, and William Mead from McKim, Mead & White. From designs submitted by 170 architects for model plans on 50-, 75-, and 100-foot frontages, fourteen were commended and twelve highly commended, the first prize of $500 going to Thomas Short of New York for a plan based on a 50-foot unit paired on a 100-foot lot. (The competition also called for a model plan for a 25-foot lot, but although the *18th Annual Report* of the Charity Organization Society stated that the prize for the best plan in this category was awarded to the French architect G. F. Sebille, of Paris, this was not mentioned in Veiller's account of the competition published in the *American Architect*.) To complement the exhibition, through the evenings of the second week lectures were given on various aspects of tenement living, starting with S. A. Knopf on "the tenements and tuberculosis" and ending with "the tenement house problem and the way out" by Riis.

The private developer was not convinced. Replying to criticism from Flagg in the *Real Estate Record*, one of the largest tenement owners, Peter Herter, commented: "Mr. Flagg says in effect that all these men for all these years have been working, so to speak, willfully, or, as it were, in the air, making plans just to suit them- selves, or, perhaps, as Mr. Flagg would put it, making plans just to see how unsanitary and uncomfortable tenement houses can be. . . . No, our architects and builders have not been dealing with an imaginary problem, but one that contains a great many hard fac- tors, all of which have demanded consideration. They have had to deal with financial conditions, with the prices of lots, the value of money, the tastes of tenants, the desires and requirements of ten- ants, the several laws, the different municipal departments, and so forth. The pressure of all of these factors has gone to make our tenement houses just what they are to-day. So to speak, these are the forces that have created the tenement house and controlled its evolution."[7] Veiller thought otherwise and was not to be thwarted, and this time his success was complete. "Tell me what you want," promised Governor Roosevelt, "and I will help you get it."[8]

The Charity Organization Society decided that the most prom- ising method of attaining their ends was to establish a new state commission. Preparing a bill to this effect, they submitted it to Albany. Builders, speculators, and Tammany Democrats com- bined to stave off the reformers by delaying the passing of the bill so that it could fall under Mayor Robert Van Wyck's veto, but at the last moment they were foiled by Veiller. Changing the application of the bill from New York City alone to cities of the first class, including Buffalo, he was able to bypass Mayor Van Wyck and have the bill ratified by Governor Roosevelt. So in the spring of 1900 a commission of sixteen, with de Forest as chairman and Veiller as secretary, and including five other members of the Charity Organization Society plus Alfred White, began a year's inquiry into every aspect of tenement living.

Its plan of action, drawn up by Veiller and approved by the commission, was to study: the results of the four legislative and four private investigations carried out during the previous half century, beginning with the 1842 report of City Inspector John Griscom; the practices of speculative builders who put up tenements for sale and not for investment; tenement conditions in major American and European cities; the nonenforcement of existing laws in new construction; all tenement fires within a two-year period; tenement fire escapes; and prostitution and policy playing. Its findings formed the major part of the definitive two-volume (nearly 1000-page) survey *The Tenement House Problem*, edited by de Forest and Veiller and published at the end of 1903, by which time de Forest had been appointed New York's first tenement house commissioner and Veiller had become his executive deputy.

In its inspection of tenement buildings, the commission of 1900 concentrated on those under construction, "the evils" of existing tenements being "so generally well known" as not to warrant undue reinforcement.[9] Of 650 multiple-dwelling buildings being erected in Manhattan, it found that just over one-half were standard tenements rather than apartment houses, and it limited its investigation to these. The results confirmed popular impressions. Only 15 buildings out of 333 did not violate the law in some respect. That tenement builders evaded the more arduous fire-prevention ordinances with the aid of the Building Department's interpretation of the law was commonly known—and overlooked because of the potential extra cost entailed; fire escapes were also omitted, the commission found, due to "the pride of the architect and the owner, who dislike seeing cheap iron balconies upon the front of their buildings."[10] It was less generally realized that after a generation of legislation over one-quarter of all new buildings covered more than the mandatory maximum 75 percent of the lot, and some still left less than the minimum 10-foot yard.[11] Confronted by the commission, the Building Department president Brady first disagreed with its findings, then denied everything, and finally blamed his subordinates. "The shifting of official responsibility," commented one of his colleagues, "is quite a science."[12]

By this time the provision of at least one water closet for every two families and windows in every room was standard practice, but tenements remained far from comfortable. Reporting on their experiences, a group of College Settlement workers who rented a suite in a newly completed tenement on Orchard Street told the commission: "We remained in the house seven months. We feel that they were well spent, but we have no desire to continue the experiment. We found many difficulties in the way of comfortable living. Though the houses were new, the odors soon became insufferable, and the air from the shaft . . . became so foul that we could not sleep in the rooms opening on it without feeling we were taking a great risk. The stairs were usually so dirty that it was unpleasant to use them, and clothing was constantly being soiled with the contact. But how could this be helped? There was the traffic of twenty-two families."[13] The gas fixtures were so cheaply made that there was continuous leakage, drafts rattled the badly fitting doors and windows, the rooms were soiled with spattered paint and plaster. Who was responsible?

In a chapter on "The Speculative Building of Tenement Houses," Veiller laid the blame on the middlemen who, as the *Commercial Advertiser* put it, "inflate prices by every trick, device, scheme, practice, that is known to the business."[14] The building owner, often an immigrant himself who by hard work and stinting had saved up a capital of $5000 to $15,000, was only third in the line of those who profited from the operation. Initially the land was purchased and held by what was known as a building loan operator, who loaned it to a builder in rows of three to twelve lots at a 10 percent markup and a repayment interest of 5½ to 6 percent. A further substantial loan of cash from the building loan operator enabled the builder, who usually had little capital of his own, to pay off his subcontractors (or "lumpers" as they were called), who worked at a flat rate with supplied materials. Toward the end of the six months that it took to erect the building, the builder obtained a permanent long-term mortgage with which to pay off his loans of land and cash, and he proceeded to sell the building at a further $1500 profit. The final owner therefore bought his property for $40,500—$3500 more than the original cost of land and construction, of which $2000 profit (plus $1000 interest) had gone to the building loan operator for his role as entrepreneur.

To force the operator out of business, the commission could have promoted either municipal or model tenements. The former were inconceivable. No large city, it argued, could provide homes for all its working population. Who, then, would benefit other than those with "influence"? And even they would trade better housing for loss of independence. That which might work in Europe was unacceptable in New York, where reformers could envisage the administration stacking municipal tenements with voters ensuring continuing political support. On the other hand, notwithstanding Gould's insistence that all model tenements made a profit, which "ought and doubtless will satisfy a large class of investors,"[15] they too continued to exert little influence on the supply of tenements, and the commission was left to counter existing deficiencies by modifying the law.

Its major achievement through the Tenement House Act of 1901 was in opening up the inner courts.[16] Bypassing the problem of the 25-foot-wide building, which, although "necessarily inferior in light and air to one built upon a larger lot," was "sanitary and should not be prohibited,"[17] the commission rendered it economically obsolete by its requirement for greater open space. For a six-story building (the maximum nonfireproof height enacted by a subsequent amendment, though the commission first set a limit of five stories or 57 feet), 60-foot-high inner courts had to be at least 12 feet to the lot line or 24 feet wall to wall and 24 feet in length, while outer courts had to be 6 feet from the lot line or 12 feet wing to wing. The minimum yard for this height was 12 feet, the lot coverage 70 percent. Other requirements were for shafts and staircase halls to be fireproofed and a separate water closet for each family, though this was a provision that was already common. Also included were penalties against prostitutes and the owners of those tenements where they were known to live, who were liable to fines of $1000.

But the other most significant change was in the act's administration. Pointing out that lack of enforcement of the various tenement laws was due largely to the division of responsibility between the health, building, fire, and police departments of the city, the commission recommended the establishment of a single, separate Tenement House Department. This new department was to consist of three bureaus: one for the approval of new construction, one for the inspection of completed buildings, and one for the maintenance of records for every tenement house in the city. All plans and specifications were to be approved prior to construction, and all new tenement houses had to be certified before they could be occupied. After completion, all tenements with an average rental below $25 monthly were to be inspected at least once monthly. (Miscalculating the character of its proponents,

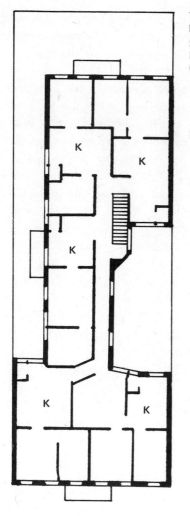

Typical six-story new-law tenement house, ca. 1905, plan

Source: New York City, Tenement House Department, *2nd Report* (1905).

the *American Architect* sardonically commented that the new department would merely "strengthen Tammany Hall by placing at its disposal a new and plentiful crop of 'plums,' in the shape of salaried positions and opportunities for extortion.")[18]

At the beginning of 1901 the tenement house bill was submitted to Albany, where it was passed with near unanimity by both branches of the legislature after the Republican governor, Benjamin Odell (who had succeeded Roosevelt on his election to vice-president) had announced that he was "in thorough sympathy with [its] object and purposes."[19] One of the act's provisions permitted plans submitted before April 10 to conform to the old law if excavation was begun before June 1 and the first tier of beams set within another two months. In the six weeks between the bill's publication and its approval, clients raced their architects to take advantage of the concession. The winner was architect Michael Bernstein who filed 53 plans for 76 buildings, 38 of which had been used previously. When many of these were subsequently disqualified for not relating to their actual sites, Bernstein replied that surveyors seldom agreed on their dimensions and that, anyway, an architect was much like an author who constantly improved his book until it finally went to press.[20]

The establishment of a Tenement House Department was a separate enactment incorporated into the new Greater New York charter and was scheduled to be effective from January 1, 1902.[21] The new tenement law came into operation during a Tammany administration, but that year a further round of reform centered on the Police Department, which had previously been condemned by yet another state legislative committee. Conforming to tradition, the chief of police William Devery, known for his iron rule and such sayings as "touchin' on an' appertainin' to that, there's nothin' doin'," was ousted by the abolition of his office. A Committee of Fifteen, including Felix Adler, Jacob Schiff, and, as secretary, the Columbia University professor and economist Edwin Seligman, was set up with the encouragement of Bishop Potter to investigate the red-light districts and their protection by the police. It found that young girls were being seduced and "sold" to procurers at $25 a head; and in a limited survey it obtained evidence that over 300 apartments were being used for prostitution. In an attempt to forestall the committee's report, Tammany boss Croker appointed his own committee of five but was outmaneuvered by the district attorney, William Travers Jerome, who personally led surprise raids against gambling and disorderly houses. Switching tactics, Tammany disbanded its investigating committee and reappointed Devery as "deputy" police commissioner. But the reformers were aroused, and the Fusion candidate Seth Low won the mayoralty in a landslide. Taking office in 1902, he appointed de Forest first commissioner of the new Tenement House Department, and he in turn brought in Veiller as his deputy. The era of the "old-law" tenement house was over.

II

It is economically unprofitable now, it has been
economically impossible for many years past, to
provide a large part of the population of this State
with decent homes according to American
standards of living.

New York State Reconstruction Commission, 1920

10

The Rule of Veiller

Seth Low's reform administration lasted two years, during which time the former Brooklyn mayor and president of Columbia University continued his career of enlightened public service. The Tenement House Department exemplified this approach. In their brief term of office as the commissioners responsible for the housing conditions of over 2 million persons who lived in the tenement houses of the new city of Greater New York, Robert de Forest and Lawrence Veiller claimed that "in place of the non-enforcement of the laws in new buildings in the past, every new tenement house now conforms to the law in every detail; the existing houses are being frequently and systematically inspected, foul cellars have had the accumulated filth of years removed, defective and unsanitary plumbing which had apparently existed for long periods has been remedied, houses unfit for human habitation have been vacated, hundreds of houses have been radically reconstructed and improved, light has been let into dark rooms, vile yard privies and privy sinks have been removed, and the whole sanitary condition of the city raised to a higher standard."[1] "If there is any department in the city government which has made its promises good and deserved well of the people of the city," commented the *Real Estate Record*, "it is the Tenement House Department."[2]

Veiller's mastery of the use of restrictive legislation, backed by influential support for his standards, allowed him to dominate the activities of the real estate and building interests. Reminiscing in his old age (he lived until 1959), Veiller recalled, "I was standing on the floor of the Senate one day when a man came over to see me and said, 'Mr. Vie-ay.' [His name was pronounced Vay-ay.] I said, 'Yes, you want to see me, sir?' He said, 'I am Samuel Strassburger. I am a builder and I want some changes in this damn Tenement House law. I went to see Governor Odell and he referred me to Senator Stranahan—the Chairman of the Cities Committee [1899-1902]—I explained what I wanted and he said to see you, so here I am.' We adjourned from the Senate floor to one of the adjoining lobbies and I asked him what were the changes he wanted in the law and what was troubling him. He told me. I promptly replied, 'You can't have it.' He said, 'Well, you act as if you were the Legislature.' I said, 'Oh, no, but just the same you can't have it.' 'Well,' he said, 'I guess you are the Legislature in this matter. I saw Odell and he sent me to Stranahan and Stranahan sent me to you, and you say I can't have it.' "[3]

Year after year, both in and out of office, Veiller continued to say "You can't have it." Besides the ineffective annual attempts to weaken the requirements of the 1901 law, three major efforts were made to break its comprehensiveness. Each one failed. The new century refused to return to the laissez-faire of the previous one. The original act was amended to accommodate certain less stringent requirements for the smaller tenement houses in the outer boroughs, but when in 1903 the Brooklyn builders made a concerted effort to have major changes approved by the legislature, they were stopped by an outburst of public censure. Three hundred delegates opposing the offending bill marched in double file two blocks long from a special train to the state Capitol. "No member can support it," summed up the *Evening Post*, "without writing himself down an enemy of civilization."[4] The political inviolability of the housing reformers was seen in Governor Benjamin Odell's retreat from tacit encouragement of certain amendments to his final pronouncement that he would veto any measure that attempted to undermine its effectiveness. As the *Real Estate Record* pointed out, the 1901 Tenement House Act was not just a set of building laws but the embodiment "of an attempt to raise the standard of living. It is part of a wholesome social ideal. Fundamentally it cannot be disassociated from the work of our churches, colleges, schools and other institutions which have for their aim, the betterment of people."[5]

Two of the major tests of the act's constitutionality were initiated while de Forest and Veiller headed the Tenement House Department. One was based on that part of the law which required the upgrading of existing tenements, including the replacement of old-type sanitary facilities by sewered water closets. Determined to quash such improvements, which cost up to $1000 a building,[6] the United Real Estate Owners' Association looked around for an ideal plaintiff to test their case in court. Their choice was a poor, respectable widow named Katie Moeschen. The argument was that having once been required to substitute a sewered sink for a vaulted privy fifteen years earlier, she deserved compensation from the state if it wished to legislate any further change. The jury, to whom the case was referred by a Tammany judge wishing to offend neither his district supporters nor his legal superiors, rejected the argument, and its judgment was upheld three years later by the U. S. Supreme Court. The principle thus established was that property standards could be retroactively updated by law.

The second test, known as the Grimmer case, began in 1901 and ended in 1912. The plans for an apartment house had been filed with the Building Department shortly after the enactment of

the new law. Turned down for not complying with its requirements, they were modified and resubmitted and approved as an
apartment hotel, whereupon the owner erected the building as
previously planned. The Tenement House Department declared
its occupancy illegal. At first the courts upheld its ruling, but in
1912 an upstate judge on the court of appeals ruled that by definition of the 1899 building code an apartment could be differen-
tiated from a tenement if it contained its own kitchen, bath, and
toilet. Veiller, who by this time had returned to the Charity Organization Society as director of its Department for the Improvement
of Social Conditions, moved to protect his legislation. With the
draft of a bill clarifying the accepted definition of a tenement
building, he briefed the Democratic Senate majority leader (later
U. S. Senator) Robert Wagner, who within 24 hours had guided
the bill through the legislature. At this point fate intervened. The
Assembly speaker, whose signature was required, had left for the
weekend and was snowed under in a train in northern New York.
Taking advantage of this respite, hundreds of landlords crowded
Wagner's doorstep through Sunday, while others assailed Governor
John Dix with protesting letters and telegrams. Both men wavered,
and a postponement was declared while hearings were held, but
finally the reformers prevailed, and the bill to include all multiple
dwellings was signed ten days later. New York City being what it
was, the Grimmer building remained occupied as an apartment
house.

The third major attempt to disable the Tenement House Department was more involved and circuitous. In March 1911, more than
140, mainly female, employees died in a fire at the Triangle Shirt
Waist Company factory. The resultant public outcry against prevailing working conditions and the lack of safety precautions caused
the enactment of factory laws that added to the inspection of
buildings by existing government departments. Building owners,

harassed by inspectors from the city's building, tenement house, fire, police, and health departments, the state's labor department, and the water, gas, and electricity companies, demanded that all inspection be unified. This was generally considered reasonable; the only question being debated by the summer of 1914 was not whether inspection responsibilities should be grouped together, but whether these should be centralized in an expanded city building department or delegated to the building bureaus in the five boroughs. The state investigating commission proposed a central authority; a mayor's committee, which included Veiller and Alfred White, suggested leaving it to the city's Board of Estimate to decide; and in the legislature a bill introduced by the senator from Brooklyn, Charles Lockwood, moved for decentralization (which would reduce the authority of the Fusion party mayor). During the months of open discussion, the housing reformers had appeared indifferent, while the press had supported any rationalization of bureaucracy. The introduction of the bill, however, made it clear that a general grouping of inspection responsibilities would divest the Tenement House Department of its authority. Once again Veiller acted. When the legislature opened its hearings, representatives of the city's reform administration, the City Club, and charitable organizations ranged themselves against the real estate interests and architectural profession. The newspapers, alerted, came out against the bill if it meant disabling the Tenement House Department. Notwithstanding the mounting opposition, the bill was passed by the legislature, only to be vetoed by Mayor John Mitchel, who refused to permit any meddling with "one of the most important measures for the protection of public health ever enacted."[7] The bill's supporters demanded an early veto so that it might be overridden, but Mitchel deferred action until the legislature had adjourned. The following year a compromise was reached that set borough supervision under a central Board of Standards and Appeals but excluded the Tenement House Department from its provisions.

Fifteen years had passed since Veiller had served as its deputy commissioner. Seth Low's short-lived reform administration had foundered on the public's reaction to an excessive probity that made itself felt in such acts as closing beer halls on Sundays (election night saw prostitutes celebrating in the streets); and with Tammany under its new boss Charles Murphy (the discredited Richard Croker having retired to the United Kingdom as a gentleman of leisure), George McClellan was elected mayor. Son of the Union general who had been dismissed by President Lincoln and later ran against him for the presidency, McClellan had previously served as a Democratic congressman and afterward became professor of economic history at Princeton University. Although he subsequently quarreled with Tammany, his initial appointments were dictated largely by Murphy and included that of Thomas Crain as tenement house commissioner.

Leaving the city administration, Veiller became secretary to the City Club, a nonpartisan group desiring a businesslike municipal government. From this position, which he held for four years, he pressed for better traffic regulation, relief from pushcart congestion, a four-year mayoralty term instead of two, the expansion of the rapid-transit system, and the control of franchises. At the same time Veiller continued to serve on the tenement house committee of the Charity Organization Society. Through the year 1904 he watched the disintegration of the department he had created and, when official counteraction was declined, proceeded by himself to gather evidence of incompetence and corruption. Initially reluctant to censure a Tammany nominee, Mayor McClellan was persuaded to do so by a trip with Veiller through the sewage of the slums and by the threat of exposure of Crain's reversion to the venerable practice of supporting party followers out of public funds. Forced to resign (but subsequently appointed a judge who heard the abortive manslaughter charge against the Triangle Shirt Waist Company owners), Crain was replaced by Edmond Butler—an "honest, intelligent man of high ideals," according to Veiller[8] —who served as commissioner until 1909. The next mayor, the Brooklyn civic reformer and antigraft justice William Gaynor, who served from 1910 to his death in 1913, first interviewed Veiller for the post and then appointed John Murphy, the secretary of the Citizens' Union, another "honest" man though "not brilliant."[9] Thus from mid-1905 through the reform administration of John Mitchel that ended in 1917, the Tenement House Department was comparatively principled and efficient. This favorable atmosphere reflected a wider public conscience, which during this time manifested itself in the social criticism of the muckrakers.

Beside his major involvements in defense of the tenement house law, Veiller counseled Commissioner Butler on how to cope with the excessive accumulation of violations (123,000 by the end of his term in office);[10] and largely wrote *For You* in conjunction with Commissioner Murphy (a pamphlet issued by the Charity Organization Society and Tenement House Department advising tenants on their needs and responsibilities—"Plants cannot grow in the dark, neither can children. . . . When you rent a flat make sure that all the rooms are light and have plenty of air").[11] His manipulation of New York's tenement legislation, however, came to an abrupt end in 1917, when he resigned from the tenement house committee of the Charity Organization Society.

With limited construction accompanied by the predisposition of tenants to spend their rent on services and equipment rather than on space, realtors in Brooklyn desired to profit from the conversion into single-floor apartments of houses that had outlived their spaciousness of former times. To achieve this end economically, they requested the right to provide vertical shafts to ventilate internal bathrooms. The mere mention of "the unspeakable airshaft" with its fire hazard was sufficient to raise Veiller's ire. The Charity Organization Society committee nonetheless reached a compromise with the Brooklyn interests and approved a scheme where only the middle bathroom had a shaft while the top had a skylight and the bottom a window. Veiller quit. "I for one," he declared publicly, "do not care to devote my time to working with a committee which gives more attention to the interests of those dealing in real estate and financing houses than to the welfare of the great mass of people of New York City who are unable to protect themselves."[12] His resignation came ten days after the American entry into World War I.

While the bill was signed into law by Governor Charles Whitman, rising construction costs, coupled with the necessary loss of rentable floor area, rendered conversions unprofitable. (Eight years later a more lenient bill was approved by the legislature but vetoed by Governor Alfred Smith.) But at a time of widespread government intervention in the economies of the world, Veiller's belief in regulated laissez-faire seemed to belong to another age. In his reminiscences he recalled that whereas Mayor Low had considered him "radical" at the turn of the century, social workers later thought him "conservative and reactionary."[13] In 1901 Veiller had made a generation of reformers look like compromising amateurs; by 1917 his faith in private enterprise had estranged him in turn from another generation of reformers who believed that the still-existent housing problem could be solved only through government initiative. Veiller's impact on New York's dwelling standards was nevertheless remarkable and was preserved in the continuing nomenclature of "old-law" and "new-law" tenements. The former were very slowly altered or demolished; the latter were built to a standard that sufficed for more than a quarter of a century. His claim, however, that the poor would thereby benefit subsequently proved to be largely illusory.

11

The Filter Clogs

The main mass of tenement houses in the nineteenth century had been built directly for the lower-income groups. The legislation of higher standards for housing raised not only its quality but also its cost and therefore its rent. The result was that the direct supply of housing to the lower-income group virtually ceased at a time when immigration was still climbing toward its peak. While in the first years of the twentieth century the momentum of prevailing entrepreneural practices continued the erection of lower-rental dwellings so that in 1905 more than one-third of all new construction could still be labeled "tenements" (with 55.6 "flats," 3.5 percent "elevator flats," and 3.6 percent "apartment houses"),[1] the end of the decade saw the development of upper Manhattan to satisfy the tastes of larger incomes. That higher standards required higher rents had been perceived by Felix Adler twenty years before; it was reiterated by Jacob Riis in his lament that tenement house reform was tending "to make it impossible for anyone not able to pay $75 to live on Manhattan Island."[2] By the end of 1910, 116,950 new-law apartments had been built.[3] In the same period the population of Manhattan increased by roughly 435,000. At the prevailing average of over four rooms to an apartment, and allowing for demolition and use change, there had been a sufficient number of dwellings built to house the new population. Unfortunately, while

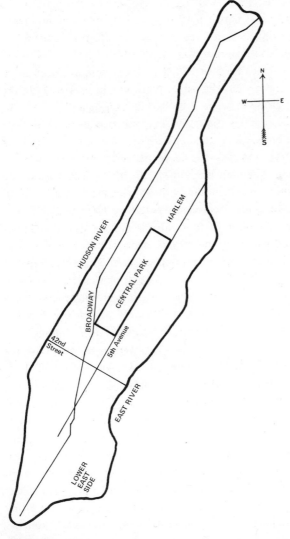

Manhattan, map

the housing generally was middle class, the new population was not, for in the years between 1901 and 1910, half a million more immigrants landed in Manhattan.[4] Veiller's reforms therefore cut off the supply of low-rental housing at a time when it was still in demand. In its place he substituted the hope that as better buildings rendered others less desirable, these would pass down to the lower-income groups.

The great surge of immigration that reached its peak in 1907 was largely from southern and eastern Europe. Encouraged by a government trying to clear the depressed countryside of its excessive population, 9 million Italians left during the first years of the twentieth century at an annual rate that before World War I reached one emigrant for every 50 inhabitants. Often illiterate and mostly unskilled, over 2 million of these people crossed into the United States. They came with the lowest proportion of women and children and had the highest proportion of those who returned.[5] More refugee than emigrant, their contemporaries the East European Jews came only to stay, seeking a new life in the promised land. By the end of the century, the Lower East Side was "a seething human sea fed by streams, streamlets, and rills of immigration flowing from all the Yiddish-speaking centers of Europe. Hardly a block but shelters Jews from every nook and corner of Russia, Poland, Galicia, Hungary, Roumania; Lithuanian Jews, Volhynian Jews, south Russian Jews, Besserabian Jews; Jews crowded out of the 'pale of Jewish settlement'; Russified Jews expelled from Moscow, St. Petersburg, Kieff, or Saratoff; Jewish runaways from justice; Jewish refugees from crying political and economical injustice; people torn from a hard-gained foothold in life and from deep-rooted attachments by the caprice of intolerance or the wiles of demagoguery—innocent scapegoats of a guilty Government for its outraged populace to misspend its blind fury upon; students shut out of the Russian universities and come to these shores in quest of learning; artisans, merchants, teachers, rabbis, artists, beggars—all come in search of fortune."[6] By the time the Russian czar was shot by Soviet revolutionaries, there were almost one and a half million Jews in New York City.[7] These new Americans had little to spend on rent.

The housing stock, graded by usage into lower, middle, and upper rental levels, was therefore being extended at its center while being filled through its base. For this filtering upward of people or filtering downward of apartments to materialize, either rents would have to go down, or incomes would have to go up. As it turned out, neither event succeeded in taking place at a time or in a manner that might have been predicted.

At the turn of the century in his book *The New Metropolis,* Idell Zeisloft had divided Manhattan's residents into seven economic classes. At the top there were 10,000 persons in families with an income of over $100,000 a year; at the bottom were a million poor, of which 7000,000 were "submerged" below a tolerable existence.[8] For this 38 percent of Manhattan's population, Veiller's reforms were only palliative, being limited mainly to the insertion of partition windows to lighten internal rooms and the replacement of school sinks by water closets (though by 1914 the Charity Organization Society tenement house committee was claiming that they had been made into "decent dwelling places").[9] This considerable task was virtually completed by 1915, but that same year saw over 100,000 other violations still on the department's records; and within the same period less than a dozen old-law buildings were upgraded into new-law tenements.[10]

While workers in the early years of the century earned from a laborer's low of about $8 weekly to a bricklayer's high of $32, very few even when fully employed could afford a rent of more than $25 monthly.[11] In a study of living standards in 1907, Caroline Goodyear of the Charity Organization Society declared that

$20 a week was the lowest income on which a couple with three children could fend for themselves, and that $4 per room per month was the minimum rent at which decency could be maintained.[12] Other authorities regarded $16 a week as a sufficient wage but conceded that a dwelling rented at $13 monthly would probably consist of three small rooms, including one without a window, would share a toilet and have no bath, and would require an extra amount to be paid for kerosene lighting and for coal for heat and cooking.[13] Even at the upper rental limits for the working class, the choice was between an unserviced five-room old-law apartment and a three-room new-law apartment with bath and steam heating but no space for contributing lodgers, who were an important source of income to workers who paid higher rents.[14] In the first years of the century, the level of real earnings remained constant. Yet, although workers typically earned too little to pay for standard new-law apartments, it was evident that they occupied some of them, because otherwise no displacement of the population would have taken place. That they were able to do so derived from the urge for betterment and the availability of some new-law apartments in the lower-rental range.

A "greenhorn" immigrant would work for a pittance while he found his place in the way of life of his more settled compatriots, like the impoverished talmudic scholar in Abraham Cahan's novel who worked his way through the garment trade to become the tycoon David Levinsky.[15] His rise from rags to riches was obviously exceptional, but push, hard work, and thrift were everyday attributes that brought increasing prosperity. Developing expertise commanded higher earnings; frugal living allowed a worker to put aside money that later gave him the choice of where to live. The free schools and City College (which had a 75 percent Jewish enrollment at the time)[16] Americanized the children, who encouraged their parents to move into more tolerable surroundings where a seemingly better life could be maintained.

Their new home might be a new-law tenement in the Lower East Side, further along the edges of Manhattan, or in the Bronx or Brooklyn. Wherever it was, its standard would be relative to their purchasing capacity. Not all new-law tenements were of a superior quality. Ordinary investors were not going to put high-class buildings in low-class neighborhoods. Like those built in the nineteenth century new-law tenements ranged from the $25,000-a-year suites off Central Park (at 998 Fifth Avenue, designed by McKim, Mead & White)[17] to the six-story walk-ups filling in the Lower East Side. Whether the latter were significantly better than their predecessors was a question variously answered. Notwithstanding Veiller's declaration that the new law heralded a new era in housing, the improvements in lighting, ventilation, sanitary facilities, and fire prevention still left much to be desired. A visiting British expert found the new law's standards "infinitely too low,"[18] and a subsequent British government paper declared that "only in a very limited and strictly relative sense would this type of house be now described as an unqualified success,"[19] as stated in Veiller's first departmental report. Twenty-three years later, a Tenement House Department observation that many of the buildings erected during this period had "considerably deteriorated"[20] was a reflection on both the prevailing standards and their lack of implementation.

It was habitual for reformers to blame all shortcomings on corrupt administrations as, for example, when a Charity Organization Society report of the 1930s declared that the Tenement House Department had been ineffective except under the Fusion mayoralties of Seth Low and John Mitchel,[21] overlooking the fact that Edmond Butler, who served as commissioner from 1905 to 1909, was considered both intelligent and honest and that his successor, John Murphy, who served from 1910 to 1917, was appointed, not by Mitchel, but by his Democratic predecessor, Mayor William Gaynor. The Tammany appointee who followed

Veiller might have been corrupt, but he had held his position for only eighteen months. However, he made a useful scapegoat. Butler described in 1906 how the tenement building business had "largely fallen into the hands of a class of men (building on speculation, not for investment) not trained to the business, who are therefore incapable of detecting transgressions of the law in the construction of their buildings, and are at the mercy of unscrupulous and incompetent architects and contractors. . . . On account of the unfitness of so many builders, a practice had grown up among the builders of employing Inspectors of the Department (nominally after office hours) to superintend or advise in regard to the construction of the buildings. The effect of such a practice, in itself a violation of the law, was deplorable."[22]

Contemporary eyewitness accounts supported this view that the old problems lingered on under the new law. In the *Evening Post* a social worker in an article on "Daily life in a model tenement" observed that while its entrance hall was lined with mosaic and the front door was plate glass, the plumbing was defective, and there was often no water (the hot water constantly being thoughtlessly left to run or used up in free baths for curious visitors).[23] If cheap new-law tenements were just as questionable as their old-law predecessors, so was their use by equally unsophisticated immigrants. In the *University Settlement Studies Quarterly*, a description of a year's residence in an Italian-occupied new-law tenement chronicled its downfall. As soon as it was completed and rented, the building with its light rooms, sanitary plumbing, and individual toilets was sold to an Italian couple who lived with their five children at the back of the store and leased the remainder to a countrywoman for a guaranteed fixed annual income of $6000. In a year, the plumbing was destroyed "more through ignorance than malice," the woodwork and plaster were split by nails, and wood was chopped on the floors until ceilings opened up cracks through which water from the broken pipes leaked (when it was running). The well-lighted halls made excellent playgrounds for the children to escape from their elders, one family of four adults and two children in a three-room apartment having seven lodgers who slept on mattresses that were rolled up during the day. On one occasion, a young boarder set up an ornate brass bedstead in his rented space, piled it high with bedding trimmed with lace, curtained it off from the ceiling, and consummated his marriage with his imported bride (after which she was set to sewing pants fourteen hours a day, seven days a week).[24]

This overcrowding of tenements that were too expensive for normal occupancy gave the Lower East Side an even higher density than that lamented by the Tenement House Committee of 1894. Then, an area below Fourteenth Street with a density of 986 persons per acre had been portrayed as one of the most crowded spots on earth, far surpassing its nearest rival in Bombay. By 1910 there were 30 Manhattan blocks that approached the maximum density of 1300 to the acre permitted by building and tenement house statutes; and the population on the East Side below Fourteenth Street had increased by 175,000 in the intervening fifteen years.[25]

Mounting concern over the effects of this situation in 1907 brought together a group of social workers including such settlement leaders as Lillian Wald and Mary Simkhovitch in a Committee on Congestion of Population in New York, with Benjamin Marsh as its secretary. The following spring an exhibition supported by the Tenement House Department, the Charity Organization Society, the Association for Improving the Condition of the Poor, the City and Suburban Homes Company, and other welfare and reform agencies was organized in the Museum of Natural History. The outcome of the interest it evoked was the establishment of an official New York City Commission on Congestion of Population by the incoming mayor, William Gaynor, which, also with Marsh as secretary, made its report in 1911.

In its list of fourteen causes of congestion, it contended that the development of lower Manhattan as the center of employment raised the price of peripheral land and put it beyond the means of those who lived there if they were to conform to socially acceptable standards. Of nearly half a million factory workers in Manhattan in 1906, two-thirds worked below Twentieth Street, where the clothing trades were concentrated. To obtain "a good standard of housing for unskilled wage earners," the commission argued, "the maximum value of land should not exceed 50 cents per square foot."[26] The earlier report of the private congestion committee had used $1 per square foot as a standard and had noted that of 2609 blocks in Manhattan, only 42 fell within this category.[27] The assessment map gave the East Side land values as averaging between $4 and $16.[28] Part of the solution that the commission proposed was a policy of decentralization based on European precedents where municipalities and private enterprise would collaborate in housing metropolitan emigrants in new garden cities linked by rapid transit. The aim had to be to find other employment, and the commission advocated farm schools and instruction in gardening; for even if, as it pointed out, the growth of the metropolitan region had been ordered by a city plan so that the outlying boroughs could have prepared land for low-priced housing, and rapid transit had been extended as a public service rather than for profit, the poorly paid worker was still tied to his central location by his long hours at his place of work and by the clannishness of his life at home. Working sixteen hours a day, the worker had to use his time making money, not spending it riding subways. And if the Lower East Side was a physical slum, it was a social haven to many of its inhabitants, with their workshops within walking distance of meals supplied by local carts that utilized local talents and satisfied local customs, with a rich community life and a steady stream of hometown lodgers to help pay the rent.

The commission's report was lengthy and panoramic, being a compilation of thirteen committee studies on subjects ranging through neighborhood issues such as parks and crime to larger problems of wages and immigration. One of its proposals was that the property tax based on an equal charge against land and building assessments should be changed so that only one-third came from the building and two-thirds from the land, thereby penalizing its nonuse and encouraging development. By 1909, however, the apartment vacancy rate in Manhattan stood at over 7.5 percent,[29] and while some of the old-law apartments were probably uninhabitable, the 7000 empty new-law apartments were only lacking tenants who could afford them. For one negative factor that the report showed by omission was that congestion was not caused by a shortage of housing; the deadlock came from the tenant's shortage of rent.

Seemingly, as wages did not go up, rents should have gone down. Paradoxically, they went up instead. The comparatively higher cost of new-law apartments was reflected in their higher rents. For those to whom rent was not a critical expense, an upward move was a matter of preference. As the apartments that were vacated were taken over by those with lower incomes, the ratio between wages and rent began to diminish this element of choice. The $20-a-week garment worker might spend more than $20 a month on rent, but only if he gave up trying to save or if he cut down on other necessities. The outcome might have been a situation where a layer of apartments remained vacant just above the reach of the average worker's range. The landlord would then have had to take his loss in either empty rooms or lower rents. Unfortunately for the tenant, it did not work out that way.

At the turn of the century, the extension of a public service uptown that encouraged the development of elevator apartments (previously dependent on their own electric generating plants), and the promise of improved public transit (including the subway to 145th Street and Broadway, which opened in 1904), together with the normal inducements of the city to expand to the north, caused the overbuilding of the Upper West Side. The speculation in land and buildings that followed the initiation of this movement led to an upward spiral of values.

A similar situation arose on the Lower East Side, but there the speculation was not mainly in land and new buildings but in the ownership of old-law tenements. The enactment of the new tenement standards had initially affected real estate holdings by depreciating old-law tenements; but the shock of reform soon passed, and when amendatory legislation had removed some of the most expensive requirements for updating existing property, a new demand for it arose. The 25-foot tenement became an excellent investment for several reasons. It had a larger proportion of rentable space than its successor; it had potentially cheaper accommodation, having been relatively cheap to build; it was in great demand by workers and immigrants; it required a smaller down payment by the purchaser as a percentage of its lower value and was therefore within the means of such common investors as merchants and professionals (who were now unable to afford the larger new apartment buildings virtually required under the new law); and, being considered a good investment by realtors, it was easily financed, sometimes for 100 percent of its value with as many as four mortgages. During 1903-1905 almost every tenement building had been sold at least once and sometimes several times at a profit. "Phenomenal,"[30] recorded a real estate operator afterward. "In sections thickly populated, such as Mulberry St., Mott St., Elizabeth St., etc.," wrote a contemporary, "I really think that it is possible to raise the rent as high as a man likes to do."[31]

At this time the value of property was thought to be constant. As a Columbia University economist observed in 1915, "It is notorious that depreciation funds are seldom provided for the buildings in New York, dependence being placed upon the increase in land values to counterbalance the decrease in building values through wear and tear."[32] Obviously, the person who bought property at an inflated price and was required to invest more capital or raise a higher mortgage than that already held was forced to raise its rents to meet its increased cost of financing. Unfortunately, the tenant who occupied the same rooms under successive owners could hardly be expected to appreciate that the capital profit made by one landlord when selling the property had to be collected by the next landlord through an increase in the rent.

The outcome was often like what happened to Samuel Cohen, who bought a double tenement house of 40 apartments and raised the rents an average of $4 a month to cover his increased mortgage repayments. Living in one of the ground-floor apartments, he was jeered at by his tenants, who broke his windows before the police could be called. Abusive notices were posted around the neighborhood in English and Yiddish, mud and garbage were thrown at his buildings, and he was forced to ask for police protection to walk through the streets. Finally the court ordered his rebellious tenants to be evicted, and the bailiffs moved in to pile their belongings on the sidewalk, where they waited in a summer thunderstorm to be carted away.[33] Cohen was not a profiteer and had done nothing wrong, but he was receiving in calumny what his predecessor had gathered in profit. His neighboring owners, seeing that he was now receiving more than they did for similar accommodation, proceeded to raise their rents to match.

Similarly, while some landlords improved their properties and consequently raised their rents to provide a reasonable return on their investment, others simply increased sympathetically without any compensating benefits. By 1907 a University Settlement worker had recorded an average of $3 or 20 percent increase on *un*improved property.[34] The rent ceiling of old-law tenements was to be reached only when a new apartment became a viable financial alternative. In the meantime, the mass of people were at the mercy of their suppliers.

The public demand for old-law tenements had been intensified by a building slowdown, stemming from entrepreneurial uncertainty and disgruntlement over the reform movement, coinciding with increased immigration. The Lower East Side overflowed northward into East Harlem and pushed older inhabitants into the West Side, causing renewed speculation there. The spectacular building activity of 1905-1907, which added 70,000 apartments to Manhattan, thus met the downtown shortage of tenements with an uptown provision of flats. Faced with the phenomenon of rising downtown rents notwithstanding extensive uptown construction, the Charity Organization Society could propose only that until the decentralization of industry would draw workers off Manhattan and so reduce their market demand, immigration should be restricted and rapid transit improved.[35] The filtering process was proving far too slow to help the every-multiplying poor.

As the increased rents of old-law tenements provided with new facilities or larger mortgages tended to raise the rent of all old-law tenements, the construction of higher-standard dwellings also initially tended to raise the rents of all lower-standard units. Downtown landlords, seeing their tenants face the choice between their $20-a-month rent and a $35-a-month apartment uptown, were encouraged to raise their rents by the amount that would still keep their offering within tolerable limits. In this they were helped by their uptown colleagues. During the three boom years, over 1000 new apartment buildings were planned for the West Side between 110th and 155th streets on land previously inflated by speculation.[36] The resulting high rents and consequent vacancies might have prompted a reduction in rents, but this, as a general solution, would have acknowledged the imprudence of the investment or even the inevitability of bankruptcy. Instead, rent-free periods were offered to those who acquired leases in the belief or hope that the inevitable interplay between supply and demand would sooner or (not much) later again turn to the landlord's advantage. In West Harlem, rather than wait for this to happen, the empty apartments were filled by opening them up to blacks.

Unlike the immigrant European who found employment in the manufacturing industries, the job opportunities for blacks were limited mainly to menial help. The uptown move of the rich and their facilities, as well as the building of Pennsylvania Station and the surrounding redevelopment of the major existing black neighborhood (together with the demolition of other tenements for the new Grand Central Station and the Williamsburg, Manhattan, and Queensboro bridge approaches, all constructed during the first decade), made West Harlem an alternate location for the black community. Recognizing the opportunity to exploit potentially depressed real estate values, a young black, Philip Payton, set up as a realtor with "Management of Colored Tenements a Specialty." By 1904, at the age of twenty-four, he was able to found the Afro-American Realty Company with a subscribed capital of an estimated $100,000, which, although it went bankrupt four years later, popularized Harlem as the center of the black community.[37] Initially both sides were pleased. For the first time in their lives, the tenants were being offered decent accommodation (though the disproportion between the rent and their income necessarily led to overcrowding). The landlords, for their part, were able to buy up property cheaply by frightening away middle-class whites and then to obtain increased rents from a section of the community that was accustomed to being cheated. They were further able to enhance their profits by withdrawing the maintenance and services that such high-quality buildings required, though this was later to cause Harlem to deteriorate to the physical level of the Lower East Side. Built as a low-income area, the Lower East Side survived as a slum during a period of rising standards; Harlem was a middle-income residential development that was reduced to a slum by overuse and neglect. In the early part of the century, however, it gave "an impression of spaciousness, of cleanliness, of prosperity, of success." As a contemporary noted, "Beside Little Italy and the Ghetto, Harlem shines."[38] Nevertheless, when hard times came, Harlem suffered with the Lower East Side. Before overbuilding could force down rents, an economic depression brought down wages.

The panic of 1907 appeared in New York with the collapse of the Knickerbocker Trust Company and was resolved with the help of a group of bankers led by J. P. Morgan. Its aftermath of unsettled economic conditions threw one-third of New York's labor force out of work. Landlords who had sustained high rents through necessity, prudence, or greed reacted to the plight of the unemployed by insistence on their payment. Faced with mass evictions, strike agitators organized tenants to demand lower rents and obtain legal assistance. In such encounters on the Lower East Side, usually both protagonists were Jews, while the administration was Irish; thus, when a neighborhood organizer circumvented a ban on meetings by driving a peddler's wagon up East Broadway with a Yiddish sign urging people to demand cheaper rents and a cartload of orators extolling socialism, Patrolman Duffy, who could not understand a word that was being said, was forced to arrest him for reckless driving. Later, when, with red petticoats fluttering in support from tenement windows, an intimidating throng of 5000 tenants gathered outside the hall where landlords were debating this threat to their livelihood, it was violently dispersed.

"Rent strikers badly clubbed in fierce riots," reported the *World;* "Marshals ready to oust 600 families."[39]

This winter of unemployment followed the first successful strike in the garment industry when 1500 workmen won union recognition and four hours off their 59-hour week. The setback of the year of depression was followed in the fall of 1909 by the first great strike of women in American history when a mass meeting of waistmakers at the Cooper Union vowed: "If I turn traitor to the cause I now pledge, may this hand wither from the arm I now raise." Though little was gained, it set the scene for the following summer when the International Ladies' Garment Workers' Union, having survived internal clashes between its anarchist and socialist factions, celebrated its newfound strength by renting Madison Square Garden for a mass rally that brought 75,000 cloakmakers out on strike. Settlement came through the auspices of the Ethical Culture Society and was negotiated by Felix Adler's brother-in-law, Louis Brandeis, who evolved the "protocols of peace" that established the principle of labor-management consultation.[40] The outcome of this show of labor muscle was shorter hours and higher wages. In terms of housing this meant that although the Lower East Side remained a desirable location for the factory population, a move uptown or into Brooklyn or the Bronx now became a viable alternative. Previous poverty had kept a proportion of the newer apartments empty; by 1909 both new and old buildings had a vacancy rate of over 7 percent. With better times, the newer apartments began to be filled; to hold their own in the resultant competition, the older apartment owners were forced to lower their rents. Thus, paradoxically, whereas the shortage of money had previously permitted low rents to be raised toward those that were simply out of the workers' reach, an increase in incomes forced low rents down until a reasonable market choice ensued between lower and higher standard alternatives. The work-

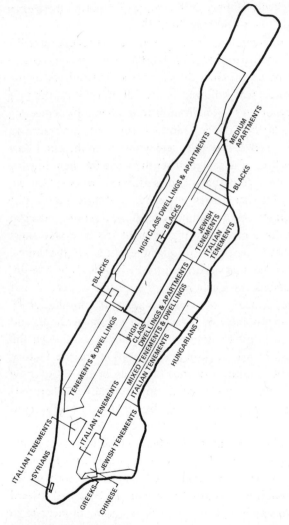

Residential districts, 1912, map
Source: *Real Estate Record and Builders' Guide*, May 11, 1912.

ing class family that had been unable to afford a new-law apartment rent had been forced to pay more for an old-law tenement or shift for itself. When tenement rents dropped by about $1.50 a room monthly to their prespeculative level, these families were free to use their extra purchasing capacity on better accommodation if they so desired.[41] The result was that while continued immigration maintained the level of occupancy of old-law apartments, by 1916 the vacancy rate of new-law apartments had been more than halved.

The overbuilding of moderate rental accommodation had occurred during a period of straitened circumstances. It might have been expected that when prosperity returned, a new round of building would occur. As the *Real Estate Record* pointed out at the beginning of 1911, the need was for walk-up flats.[42] What was built, however, were elevator apartments. Once again, instead of providing directly for the economic group that needed housing most, the industry built for the next-higher income level. Before the panic of 1907, the average room cost of a new apartment was about $500; between 1910 and 1916 it was $950.[43] The difference resulted from type and location, the latter being fireproof elevator apartments, nine stories on cross streets and twelve stories on the avenues, in uptown neighborhoods for upper-middle-income families. Then, as this wealthier taste was satisfied, entrepreneural interest in housing declined. Between 1910 and 1916, the annual construction of multiple-dwelling units in Manhattan fell from 9344 (compared to 29,465 in 1906) to a pre-World War I figure of 5021 (the lowest being 4125 during the minor depression of 1914). Of the 1916 total, less than 5 percent was built below Fourteenth Street and over 50 percent above 155th Street.[44]

The belief that social and financial interests might normally be compatible was based on the simplistic assumption that the fulfillment of community needs would satisfy the investor's primary ambition, which was to use his money as profitably as possible. Events proved otherwise. For the real estate entrepreneur, housing was only one of a number of potentially profitable types of development. If it was temporarily unprofitable, he could invest his services elsewhere. Notwithstanding what reformers asserted, his actions were not bound by any moral precepts. The fact that he supplied a public necessity did not make him a public servant any more than it did those who supplied other goods or services that might be considered essential in an industrialized society. The turn-of-the-century consolidation of New York as a financial and industrial center brought with it the need for more office buildings, apartment hotels, expensive residences east of Central Park, department stores along Fifth Avenue, and loft space for the factories that followed their retail outlets uptown. (This move nearly ruined them by jostling immigrant workers against the carriage trade, until a "Save New York" movement brought zoning ordinances that protected residential and business areas. The infiltration of factories and the uncontrolled height and bulk of offices, including the 52-story Woolworth Tower, so compromised investments that land assessments south of 40th Street declined by an estimated $120 million. "It is too big a city, the social and economic interests involved are too great to permit the continuance of the *laissez faire* methods of earlier days," declared the City Building Districts and Restrictions Commission.)[45]

The real estate entrepreneur could involve himself with the type of building currently most profitable; and if he wished to remain in housing, he could limit his involvement to the price range of his choice. The 1905-1907 apartment building boom was induced by the speculation in old-law tenements and the high rents that ensued. The 1910-1916 decline was predicated on a reverse movement of rents that made the competitive offering of middle-standard housing a questionable venture in Manhattan. By World War

I, the building up of Manhattan was almost completed. Although there were still some 2000 vacant lots in the borough, the construction of new lower-rental units in the established, older areas generally required the demolition of existing buildings. To replace low-rental units by other low-, or even (if environmentally feasible) middle-, rental units was financially venturesome when similar accommodation at a reduced rate could be supplied on unsullied cheap virgin peripheral land at an extra weekly cost of less than a dollar carfare and a few hours of traveling. Thus, for example, in 1912, out of 300 old-law tenement houses that were demolished in New York City, only 72 were replaced by new-law buildings compared to the 1885 built during that year.[46] The eventuality was a centrifugal movement of Greater New York's population. In 1905, 54 percent of its inhabitants lived within four miles of City Hall (that is, north to Central Park and south to Prospect Park in Brooklyn), and over half of these people lived in Manhattan. By 1915 this inner area only contained 40 percent of the population, and the borough of Manhattan was receiving less than one-quarter of the city's new apartment units.[47] In the resultant spread into the Bronx, Brooklyn, and Queens (connected to Manhattan by the Queensboro Bridge in 1909 and by the Long Island Railroad the following year), the measure of entrepreneurial effort was financial return, not the establishment of a desirable social fabric.

Similarly, while the laissez-faire advocate might believe in the equity of a law of supply and demand, it was often one-sided with a necessity like housing. Those who demanded had little influence over supply; those who supplied could exploit demand. Although food, rent, and clothing, in descending order, were the major household budget items, food and clothing were purchased in more or less numerous and offsetting transactions, while rent was a lump sum that fell due every month. By 1916, while continuing immigration had kept the old-law vacancy rate steady, a rising standard of living had more than halved the number of empty new-law apartments. The American entry into World War I in the spring of 1917 initially countered the movement through the mobilization of family heads and the doubling up of households; but the cessation of immigration coupled with high wages for war work began to empty the old downtown slums and fill the newer uptown buildings.

At this point, the economic seesaw was again overbalanced by the application of profit maximization. The ensuing shortage of uptown apartments produced a 10 percent rise in rents and thereby encouraged the elevation of the whole rental scale.[48] Admittedly, other prices rose even faster. According to the National Industrial Board, the New York cost of living rose 65 percent between 1914 and 1919, while rents rose only 20 percent.[49] And rising rents, like other living cost components, were not only contributory to, but also dependent on, other inflationary price movements, so that the cost of extra services formed part of any rent increases. Nevertheless, it could be seen that some of the extra rent was being demanded because it could be obtained. This was only just, the landlords countered: did any tenant offer to pay more rent when conditions were reversed?

Caught by the inflationary upturn of prices to match wages, families were forced back to their old habitations. A survey carried out for the federal government to ascertain the availability of accommodation for war workers found that, out of over half a million Manhattan apartments, there were only 3923 vacant that rented monthly for $50 or less.[50] At the same time, the virtual cessation of domestic construction during the war, which was counted as an act of patriotism at a time when materials, labor, and money invested in war industries and government liberty loans were scarce and expensive, resulted in the completion of only 850 apartments during the two years 1918 and 1919. Returning veterans, reestablishing households, filled the remaining vacancies and further encouraged rents to rise.

The grade of dwelling that private enterprise had supplied for the use of nineteenth-century immigrants had been rejected by the rising standards of housing reform, which had served the community rather than the poor by preventing private enterprise from reaching down to this level. The early years of the twentieth century up to the end of World War I saw 150,000 apartments built in Manhattan to a more acceptable standard, but in the circumstances these did not benefit the incoming and continuing lower-income groups. Of the more than 400,000 old-law tenement suites that existed at the turn of the century (the census then having been inaccurate), about 390,000 still remained.[51] Most of these, twenty years older, were as crowded as ever. Immigration, depression, and war had nullified the assumption that upward movement of tenants to better housing would empty, and provoke the replacement of, substandard buildings. As a later tenement house commissioner philosophized, "It may take a long period of time [to bring about the elimination of the old-law tenement] but in the scheme of the universe, 50 or 100 years is a very short space after all."[52] In the meantime, the filter had backed up, and the slums were once again filling to capacity.

Stick and Carrot

The attempt to exploit shortages was, of course, not unfamiliar to a country that had enacted laws during the Revolutionary War against the many speculators who took advantage of the nation's difficulties. In World War I, the government used various devices to restrain profiteering, as it was then popularly known, including the imposition of a substantial excess profits tax. The postwar debate over whether or not profiteering existed in housing brought on a multiplicity of investigations. John Hylan, who defeated the incumbent reformer John Mitchel and served as mayor for two terms until 1925, established a Mayor's Committee on Taxation and Rent Profiteering under Nathan Hirsch, a renegade realtor. This was supplemented by the Committee on General Welfare of the Board of Aldermen. Concurrently, the new governor, Alfred Smith, appointed a housing committee as part of his Reconstruction Commission, and the legislature formed its own Joint Legislative Committee on Housing. At the beginning of 1920 a state of emergency was declared.

With the vacancy rate in Manhattan dropping from 3 percent in 1919 to 0.6 percent in 1920 and even less in the city at large,[1] it was generally agreed that this time high rents were caused mainly by a housing shortage. Although the Mayor's Committee suggested that much of the increase in rents was, as in 1902-1903, due to frequent sales and speculation and estimated that only one in ten landlords was directly profiteering from the lack of accommodation, the Joint Legislative Committee condemned "leasters" who never sowed but always reaped, and an interviewee in the *Real Estate Record* observed that while the lack of new buildings and the temporary excess of demand over supply obviously contributed to rising rents, this was "simply the working out of a natural law."[2] (Office rents also skyrocketed, and users attacked "soulless skindicates" who were in the business for "what the traffic will bear.")[3] As to why there was a housing shortage, most authorities agreed: the cutback in private building during 1918-1919, the lack of investment money, and uncertainty over the trend of inflation.

The second year of war had seen the secretary of the treasury appeal for the cessation of all unnecessary construction, the Capital Issues Committee restrict the granting of credit to the building industry, and the Labor Department and War Industries Board first direct men and materials into war industries and then control private building through the use of permits. Although the Treasury Department withdrew its credit restrictions four months after the end of the war and a general building boom ensued, residential construction remained abnormal: the national dwelling starts for 1919 were 74 percent of the prewar decade average; for 1920, only 58 percent.[4] There was general agreement that few people with capital would invest it in housing because of its relative uncertainty and unprofitableness. Potential major financial sources such as savings banks and life insurance companies had placed large sums in Liberty Loan Bonds so that although the 1919 legislature amended the banking law to permit savings banks to make building loans, and the Joint Legislative Committee in 1921 suggested compelling insurance companies to set aside a larger percentage of their funds for this purpose, no further significant investment occurred. Life insurance companies operating in New York State at that time had roughly $2 billion or nearly one-third of their assets in mortgage loans at generally 5½ percent interest, but these were limited to 60 percent of the building cost to guard against a subsequent deflation of values.[5] Private investors looked for larger returns to compensate for tax deductions.

Although a federal income tax had first been imposed during the Civil War, it was not until the Sixteenth Amendment was passed in 1913 that it became a permanent source of revenue. In that year the basic rate was set at 1 percent, with surtax ranging from 1 to 6 percent; five years later the basic rate was 6 to 12 percent, and surtax could be as high as 65 percent. The choice for an investor faced with the unpredictable prospects of postwar conditions was between safe 5 percent untaxed government bonds, industrial securities that (at a time when American exports were in great demand by devastated European countries) might yield as high as 9 percent, and 6 percent mortgages that could drop to a 2 to 3 percent return after federal and state taxation.[6] With the price of labor and materials making the cost of housing prohibitive, any attempt to raise interest rates was impracticable. Just before the war the average cost of a Manhattan apartment room had been less than $1000; immediately after the war it averaged $1330.[7] As the Merchants' Association of New York's special committee on housing observed, a new world price level had come into existence.

In the five years between 1915 and 1920, both wages and the cost-of-living index had doubled, so that workers were no better off than before, even though their earnings (in U. S. industry) averaged more than $30 a week.[8] The Merchants' Association committee assumed that workers were receiving a higher share of industrial profits without contributing greater productivity, thus forcing material prices to rise. The Joint Legislative Committee believed the cause to be price fixing. Ironically, it was the federal government itself that had brought certain industries together during the war so as to eliminate unproductive competition and establish uniform prices for negotiated cost plus fixed percentage profit contracts. After the war such industries continued to cooperate in spite of the antitrust laws. The Joint Legislative Committee, under the guidance of the famous New York lawyer Samuel Untermyer, asked for its powers to be enlarged to tackle these combinations. When potentially self-incriminating members of manufacturing organizations such as those for cement and steel evaded investigation by staying outside New York State, Untermyer pressed the legislature to request help from the Congress, and the first prosecution in a federal court took place against sand and gravel dealers at the end of 1920. That year building costs peaked.

Concurrently, real estate taxes also mounted, rising 27 percent between 1915 and 1920; but when rents rose 38 percent in the city (compared to 49 percent in Chicago and 108 percent in Detroit), landlords were abused as "leeches" and "gougers."[9] Housing had become an emotional, yet safe, issue on which politicians could compete in expounding self-righteous homilies. Newspapers such as the *World*, which published 28 articles on the housing shortage during the summer of 1920, kept readers informed—or inflamed (though the major news of late September was the anarchist bombing on Wall Street that killed 38 persons in the lunchtime crowd). Public reaction had to be kept under control. When the East Side League began to organize tenants, providing half a dozen "This house is on strike" signs printed in red in English and Yiddish for a dollar annual dues, it and similar groups were investigated by the district attorney. "If this poisonous virus is not removed," commented Judge Aaron Levy, "these people will be able to lead this great mob of people into anarchy, riot and revolt."[10]

In their rearguard action against this overwhelming public censure, real estate operators could only plead that they too were human and entitled to fair play. The situation was more ambiguous than it appeared, for as the Charity Organization Society tenement house committee secretary (and ex-tenement house commissioner) John Murphy wrote in the September 1919 issue of the *National Municipal Revue*, "were it not for the fact that a housing shortage is testified to by so many unimpeachable authorities, one might be pardoned for doubting its existence."[11] Comparing the housing stock of Manhattan in 1910 and 1919, a Columbia University professor of social legislation, Samuel McCune Lindsay, argued that while 49,515 apartments had been constructed during this period and only 23,094 demolished or converted to other uses, leaving a net increase of 26,421 that could house over 100,000, the population had in fact *decreased* by 47,439, so that in 1920 there was room for 150,000 persons more than in 1910.[12] On the other hand, Murphy's claim that accommodation for 100,000 persons lay empty because it was of too low a quality to be tolerated by a more affluent tenantry was not borne out by the official vacancy rate, which dropped the following year to 0.18 percent. Evidently, while the population had gone down, the number of households had gone up. The change could have been due to uncrowding, a decreasing family size, increased veteran marriages, or the young or previously dependent setting up their own households, a possibility made feasible by a rising standard of living and changing social attitudes. Such demographic explanations, however, were of little interest to those involved. The landlord had a sellers' market and no incentive to change it. For those who were not landlords, two problems existed: how to moderate the existing imbalance, which permitted profiteering; and how to restore equilibrium by encouraging construction.

Initially, the most-favored solution for encouraging construction was by making mortgage holdings more profitable. Reporting in the summer of 1919, the Merchants' Association housing committee (which was chaired by a member of the architectural firm of McKim, Mead & White, and whose representation included investors, insurance companies, and bankers, some of whom also served on the housing committee of the State Reconstruction Commission) proposed that taxes should be waived on the interest of up to $40,000 of mortgage investment. Although both state party platforms in the 1920 elections supported this proposal, which was also recommended by the U.S. Senate Committee on Reconstruction and Production, it had two major flaws. First, the exemption would have to cover both old and new mortgages, as otherwise it would result merely in the transfer of existing investments; and second, it needed the remission of a federal tax that required the approval of an unwilling Congress.

While the Joint Legislative Committee also included mortgage interest tax exemption in its 1920 report, its initial proposals, adopted at a special session of the 1919 legislature, attempted to encourage the large-scale supply of money rather than small private investors. It urged the state's representatives in Congress to press for the federal tax exemption of the recently enacted New York Land Bank bonds, then at a disadvantage relative to untaxed government securities, and the passage of a Home Loans Bill that would extend this source of mortgaging from farms to urban housing. It also appealed to loan institutions, together with unions and chambers of commerce, to aid in the construction of dwellings; and it passed a law permitting savings banks to make building loans. Its other actions included the modification of the tenement house law to permit the conversion of four-story dwellings and two minor amendments to the landlord-tenant laws. When none of these had any effect, the next legislature gave up trying to stimulate building and concentrated on constraining landlords.

Under American constitutional law, the literal application of such provisions as those in the Fourteenth Amendment that "No State shall make or enforce any law which shall abridge the privileges or immunities of citizens of the United States; nor shall any State deprive any person of life, liberty, or property without due process of law" was often tempered by what was known as the police power of a state that defended the health, morals, and welfare of its citizens. In 1919 the Congress itself had imposed rent controls in Washington. The following year, designating the shortage of housing a hazard to health and morals, New York State followed suit. Opposition to this move was confined to real estate operators. The State Reconstruction Commission housing commitee report, tabled in March 1919, pointed out that it was inconsistent to urge capitalists to build houses while threatening to take away their incentive. Nevertheless, "warehouses throughout the city" were "filled to overflowing with the furniture of families that have been dispossessed," the Mayor's Committee on Rent Profiteering had heard over 40,000 cases during the year, and while from "all parts of the city came tales of leaking roofs, lack of water or gas, leaking pipes, stairs that are rotten and shaky,"[13] dilapidated apartments were full of tenants who could not complain for fear of eviction. Notwithstanding the New York Association of Real Estate Boards representative's assertion at an Albany meeting of the Assembly Committee on Cities and Taxation that "If you seek to hamper real estate men any more you will be confronted by a cessation of building altogether,"[14] rent-restricting bills were introduced into the legislature. The next hearing, according to the *Real Estate Record*, "resembled the convocation of the Constituent Assembly in Petrograd following the overthrow of the Kerensky regime."[15] The opposition was to no avail, and on April 1, 1920, the rent bills were signed into law. As they applied only to existing premises, it was hoped that they would not discourage new construction.

There were twelve clauses to the rent laws, two of which were approved at a slightly later date. Their intent was to protect established tenants and to ensure that rents were not raised arbitrarily. It was made a misdemeanor for a landlord to harass a tenant, who had to be proved objectionable before being dispossessed, a proceeding that could be delayed six months; and though an annual 25 percent increase in rent was a permissible maximum, tenants might still refuse to pay it if they could show it to be unjust. What constituted a "reasonable rent" was to occupy the courts for the next six years. Within a year, 100,000 rent disputes were awaiting trial by jury, and over $10 million in rent was held in trust by the courts pending their decisions.[16]

The first judge to attempt to provide general guidelines for the calculation of a socially acceptable rental standard was from the appellate division of the supreme court in Brooklyn. His method was to calculate the gross rental; allow for operating expenses, vacancies, unpaid rents, and building depreciation at 2 percent a year (this being considered normal for tax returns); and thereby obtain the net rental by these deductions. The next step was to establish the fair market value of the property. If the net rental did not exceed 10 percent of the property value, then the rent was not unreasonable compared to other current investments.

Unfortunately, other justices had other solutions. Some did not allow for depreciation (presumably on the basis that the rise in land value compensated for the decline in building value. By 1916, fire insurance companies had realized that buildings could actually *increase* in value because of the rising costs of replacement); some tied repairs to the building value and did not deduct them as

Housing bills, 1920, "Another Czar Dethroned"
Source: *The World*, September 25, 1920.

operating expenses; others allowed a return on the owner's investment alone, recognizing that most of the building capital was held
in mortgage. When a Manhattan court took this view, arguing that
the existing market value of a property was based on excessive
rents and therefore any percentages related to it would automatically lead to further profiteering, the governor was asked to inter-
vene, and he requested clarification from both the Joint Legislative Committee and the Mayor's Committee.

The Real Estate Board of New York added its own reasons
for rising rents. These included: the costs of improved social services such as education and hospitals, plus the $10 million subsi-
dy required to maintain a five-cent carfare, which had doubled
taxes in fifteen years; higher standards in building services and
maintenance demanded by administrators and reformers; and the
national immigration policy (then under review) whereby "Europe
has sent her feeble and incompetent people here so that 34 percent of the inmates of our public and criminal institutions are ali-
ens whose maintenance must be paid for by the tenant."[17]

In the case of a pre-World War I (that is preinflation) building,
the difference between a return based on the landlord's original
equity and that based on the property's current value was considerable, the first favoring the tenant, the second, the landlord.
Furthermore, there was doubt as to what constituted a fair return. First mortgages produced up to 8 percent, and it was felt
that a landlord should be compensated at least for his annoyances. The Manhattan appeal court compromised: 8 percent was
ruled a fair return, but this was to be based on the property's assessed value (which was made synonymous with its actual value
by enactment of the 1922 legislature). This generalized method
of calculation remained in use until 1926, when the state court of
appeals declared that each case of rent adjustment was dependent
on its own particular circumstances, but by then times had

changed, and the average annual rent increase had dropped from nearly 16 percent (1918-1919) to 0.4.[18]

Another factor that was widely held to discourage investment in housing was its high cost of construction. Even the City and Suburban Homes Company, which limited its annual profit to 5 percent, found that it would have to charge $14 a room monthly on a Brooklyn site, when twenty years earlier it was averaging $4 and its current average was $8.63.[19] Employers blamed strikes and higher wages; the unions pointed to price fixing and higher profits. To increase the supply of building materials and to make them more competitive, the Joint Legislative Committee proposed petitioning Congress to embargo shipments overseas and to legislate the priority of their domestic distribution after food and fuel. Just before he became secretary of commerce in the Harding administration, Herbert Hoover, a mining engineer by profession and first president of the Federated American Engineering Societies, had initiated a study by a committee of seventeen engineers of unproductiveness in six major industries.[20] The two greatest deficiencies of the building industry, the committee reported, were inefficient management and inhibiting unions. There were too many small, unstable, and incompetent firms, poorly equipped and haphazardly utilized. The lack of planning and the acceptance of seasonal employment produced an average working year of only 190 days, which was further decreased by frequent lockouts and strikes. As for the operatives, their output was restricted by limiting apprenticeship, rejecting laborsaving devices, quashing incentive by demanding uniform wages, and reducing the weekly hours of work. Yet once again, while the committee emphasized its belief that the cost of labor and materials had to be lowered before a revival of building was possible, it had no specific recommendations to ease the national housing shortage.

By then it had become apparent that rent controls and exhortations did nothing to increase the supply of housing. This had been evident to the housing committee of the State Reconstruction Commission, whose membership was made up largely of progressive professionals. Appointed in January 1919, the main committee was chaired by a Buffalo lawyer, but it included Felix Adler, now close to seventy years old, and had for its secretary an architect, Clarence Stein, who was active in the City Club. Associated with this committee of ten were two advisory groups, one for upstate New York, the other for the city, with representation from loaning institutions, limited-dividend corporations, the National Urban League (the black organization founded in 1910), and the Charity Organization Society, architects such as Robert Kohn and Frederick Ackerman, builders including Alexander Bing, social workers, and city planners. Reporting in March 1920, the committee concurred with the general view that there was a housing shortage due to the temporary cessation of private building, the shortage of materials, labor difficulties, and the lack of investment; but these, it insisted, were not the real problem; "It is economically unprofitable now, it has been economically impossible for many years past to provide a large part of the population of this State with decent homes according to American standards of living. Decent homes and wholesome environments in which to bring up children cost more than most workers can afford."[21] While the committee's statement that private enterprise had never built housing for low-wage earners was patently untrue, and it was only a half-truth that most workers had never attained an "American" standard of living, the inference being that this standard was independent of time and taste, it was certainly true that the supply of new low-rental housing had been brought to an end by the conditions prevailing after World War I. What you want,

chided a Title Guarantee and Trust Company official, is "an apartment which now costs $30 for a man who can only pay $20."[22]
(Three years later a Bronx builder was refused a half-million-dol-
lar loan by the company because his workers were considered to
be demanding unreasonable wages.)

To some the solution seemed obvious. When the mayor of
Newark told a mass meeting in New York during the spring of
1919 that his city had erected 400 tents to aid the homeless, he
was countered by the president of the Tenants' Union with a proposal for building millions of small homes on Long Island. The
advocacy of municipal housing was a natural development of wartime policies. As chairman of the Council of National Defense's
Committee on Labor, Health and Welfare, the doughty American Federation of Labor leader Samuel Gompers had appointed
a subcommittee on housing early in 1917 to study whether a
housing shortage would impede wartime industrial expansion. His
advisers reported that it would. Furthermore, it was evident that
private enterprise would be unable to cope with national demands
and that responsibility for meeting these needs should be assumed
by government. A few months later another committee chaired
by Otto Eidlitz, a builder who subsequently presided over the
United States Housing Corporation, reinforced the need for a federal housing authority. Thus more than a year after war had been
declared against Germany, Congress began appropriating $75 mil-
lion for workers to be housed by the Emergency Fleet Corporation of the Shipping Board and a further $100 million to be ad-
ministered by the United States Housing Corporation, which was
set up by the Department of Labor's Bureau of Industrial Housing and Transportation. One hundred and nine days later the war
was over.

The two federal agencies were responsible for roughly 15,000
dwellings. The United States Housing Corporation, under the gen-

eral management of Burt Fenner of the architectural office of McKim, Mead & White, and including the wealthy housing expert Phelps Stokes and the landscape architect Frederick Law Olmsted, Jr., provided a complete service of design, construction, and management. The Emergency Fleet Corporation, with an architectural staff headed by Robert Kohn and including Frederick Ackerman and Henry Wright, maintained strict overall controls but cooperated with private developers and shipbuilding companies.[23] Both imposed a social and architectural imprint on a building type that had previously derived from market practices. The effect was twofold, showing that housing could be made tasteful and humane and that government could bring together the expertise to build it. Government housing had become a possible alternative to the free enterprise supply (or lack of supply) of low-rental dwellings.

Before joining the Emergency Fleet Corporation, Ackerman had been sent to England by Charles Whitaker, the editor of the American Institute of Architects' *Journal*, to gather information on wartime housing. His articles praising English achievements under the garden city architect Raymond Unwin were printed in the magazine during the fall and winter of 1917-1918 and were then included in a book entitled *The Housing Problem in War and Peace*. The following year Edith Elmer Wood published *The Housing of the Unskilled Wage Earner*, in which she described the origins of government housing in the United States, beginning in 1909 with the Massachusetts Homestead Commission, which had, during its ten years of operation, produced twelve frame houses on a seven-acre tract. Her foreign examples from Europe, Latin America, and Australasia were more impressive. Recognizing social objections, her counterarguments were that although housing was a state responsibility, the federal government could implement a housing loan act; that while class legislation was unconstitutional and the concept of a working class alien to the American way of life, a classification based on a family's annual income could determine its right to be helped through the police power of a state; that a government's provision of housing to low-wage earners would be neither charitable, pauperizing, nor socialistic but a non-profit-making process, giving workers a fair deal; and that times had changed since state and municipal governments had been too corrupt to administer such a program, a charge previously made by Jacob Riis and Lawrence Veiller among others. (The civil service might have improved since the formation of the Municipal Civil Service Commission, but the New York State commission that investigated the municipal commission in 1914-1915 itself reportedly hired friends and relatives as stenographers and inspectors.)

In New York this municipal housing movement was propounded not only by Socialist aldermen and assemblymen but also by the Democratic governor and mayor and by the Fusionist leaders in the city council. Alfred Smith, who had grown up in the slums alongside the Brooklyn Bridge, had been elected to the Assembly through Tammany boss Charles Murphy, but his subsequent elevation to governor in 1919 and his following three terms of office (he lost in the 1920 Republican landslide) until his presidential nomination in 1928, proved him both a progressive and a capable politician. Fiorello LaGuardia, elected president of the Board of Aldermen in a Tammany upset, had been a Republican congressman before World War I and returned to the House of Representatives for the decade 1923-1933. The city council, however, remained Democratic, while both houses of the legislature were controlled by the Republicans. When Manhattan Borough President Henry Curran, also elected as a Fusionist in 1919, proposed a special session to amend the state constitution after the corporation counsel had ruled that the city did not have the legal authority to build its own housing, Tenement House Commissioner

Mann rejected it as an acceptable solution. While his friend, Mayor Hylan, announced that a municipal housing program could start at the beginning of 1922 if the first legislative approval for a constitutional amendment was given at the proposed extraordinary session, the only bills submitted by Mann were to permit the city to raise mortgage funds for private builders and to give them the benefit of property tax exemption, an idea that seems to have come from real estate interests. Although Smith hesitated over calling together the legislature because of the anomalous position of the Socialist assemblymen who had previously been expelled, he wanted legislation to immediately provide new housing and to establish a long-range program. Ignoring the call for municipal housing and turning down the request for a mortgage bank, the legislature adopted the proposal to exempt new construction from local property taxation. The first major attempt to introduce housing as a public service had foundered against a set of beliefs that considered any such act to savor of bolshevism.

With municipal housing as one of the election planks in the Democratic party platform of that year, Smith was defeated by the Republican candidate, and he returned to the trucking industry, this time as chairman of the board. By 1923, when he was once again installed in Albany, the postwar furor over the housing shortage had died down, and a continuing Republican legislature (except for the Senate in his first session) made government housing legislation impractical.

To equalize the market competition between the rents of existing dwellings and those that might be built in a period of inflated costs, the proposal was to exempt from taxation until 1932 most residential buildings completed within a two-year period (except those with less than four stories above a ground floor used for other purposes). The calculated saving would correspond to a 20 percent reduction of the income required to meet a normal investment return and so put new construction on an equal footing with existing buildings. Although the enabling act was passed and signed by Governor Smith in the fall, its use by the city was delayed while attempts were made to limit the statute so that moderately priced dwellings would be favored. The mayor argued that unless the concessions were carefully framed, they would merely accrue to builders and owners, a prediction that was later confirmed by the State Commission of Housing and Regional Planning. The compromise reached at the beginning of 1921 was to encourage larger moderately priced apartments by limiting the tax exemption to $1000 a room and up to $5000 a dwelling. The immediate result was a burst of building activity. In 1921 in Manhattan, 1392 apartments were completed; the figures for 1922-1924 were 5316, 6306, and 11,156.

These apartments, however, were at the higher rental levels even though in 1923 the city placed a further limitation of $15,000 per apartment building. As the tenement house commissioner pointed out in his 1925 report on the current housing situation, builders could see no future in other than modern apartments with heat and hot water and extra material comforts that required more than $15 to $20 a room monthly rent to give suitable return on their investment.[24] Furthermore, while the building boom created employment during a depression and so mitigated labor unrest, it also encouraged wage demands that perpetuated the inflated costs that were themselves a major cause of the earlier housing stoppage. Builders were not interested in producing low- or even moderate-rental dwellings but desired to continue their prewar activity of satisfying the upper-income market. Consequently the savings from tax exemptions were not passed on to tenants, who were anyway of a class that had no need of financial support, but were simply accepted by investors as an inducement to build what they wished. State, city, and professional reports agreed that although tax exemptions had aided suburban homeowners (11,350 units in 1920, 55,990 in 1922, mainly in Brooklyn and Queens), it had done nothing to help the less than wealthy tenant. Even the $15,000 building ceiling failed to divert investment into low-rental dwellings, leading the State Commission of Housing and Regional Planning to declare that "In the light of this after-experience it now seems that tax exemption might better have been withdrawn from apartment building construction entirely, or extended in full under such restrictions as to make it applicable only to buildings in which rents did not exceed a maximum fixed by ordinance."[25]

There were only two low-rental projects built in this period. The Phelps-Stokes Fund opened its buildings on East 97th Street in March 1923. The following year the Metropolitan Life Insurance Company completed 2125 apartments in Long Island City. Its interest in housing had been aroused by Samuel Untermyer of the Joint Legislative Committee, who used it to persuade Governor Nathan Miller to sign as a temporary expedient an amendment to the insurance law permitting insurance companies to construct low-rental housing, against the advice of real estate interests that considered such investment too speculative. Known as the $100 million Metropolitan Life bill (though only $6 million had been pledged), it was utilized by that company alone. Its aim was to pare down costs by rationalized administration and construction with bulk purchasing, the mechanization of site operations, organized delivery, and the support of labor. (Labor was envisaged in the preparation of the bill as choosing to work efficiently below the prevailing wage scale in exchange for preference in renting apartments. As it turned out, there were 331 building operatives among the original 2125 tenant families.) With land a fraction of its cost in Manhattan, rents were still $9 a room monthly including heat and hot water. More than 6000 applications were received while the buildings were under construction, and finally 10,000 applicants were unable to be accommodated. The five-story buildings costing $7.5 million were designed by Andrew Thomas in association with Everett Waid and were completed in the summer of 1924. Preference was given to families with children whose annual income did not exceed $4000. When the ground had been broken for the project, reveille played, and the flag raised, the seven-year-old daughter of the field captain stepped out from a descending steam shovel hopper carrying a bronze spade and said: "The children of New York want me to thank you ever so much for these beautiful homes. Now we needn't be shut up anymore in the dark old tenements where we haven't any place to play; but we will come here to live in sunshine and see the wonderful garden and the flowers all day."[26] Many thought that a new era in corporative public concern had begun: "If this project proves successful it seems bound to have . . . a revolutionary effect on city housing," editorialized the *Real Estate Record*.[27] By the time its success was evident, however, the general housing shortage had ended, and a period of economic depression and war was to pass before another such development took place.

Initially the greater supply of high-rental apartments gave little comfort to the majority of workers. Although the vacancy rate for new-law apartments in Manhattan went from 0.18 to 1.09 percent between 1921 and 1924, the old-law vacancy rate reached only 0.48. Testimony to the Commission of Housing and Regional Planning in the fall of 1923 observed that one vacancy on 29th Street had ten applicants, five of whom had been waiting for two years; other tenements vacated ten years previously as unfit for habitation were now occupied; and a Columbia University professor of public health reported an increase in infant mortality and the general death rate. One hundred thousand families were doubled up, a former city health commissioner asserted, while thousands on the Lower East Side lived four persons to a room.[28] A decade after Jacob Riis's death, conditions were reverting to nineteenth-century squalor.

The Commission of Housing and Regional Planning had been set up by the state legislature in May 1923 to study housing conditions and requirements and to plan for them in cooperation with local and federal authorities; to collect and distribute information; to assist in the preparation of legislation and regulations for housing, zoning, and planning; and particularly to study methods for lowering rents through savings in construction and planning. Organized in August 1923 under the chairmanship of Clarence Stein, its first specific task was to determine whether the housing emergency still remained and, if so, to make proposals on how to cope with it. Its conclusion was that the emergency laws should be extended for two years, pending a comprehensive study of the overall problem (though at the same time the Charity Organization Society tenement house committee was congratulating itself that the housing crisis had passed without resort to state aid).[29] In the meantime it recommended the extension of state credit through the State Land Bank and permission for cities to engage in public housing.

Its second report studied the impact of tax exemption. Like the Mayor's Committee on Housing, headed by Tenement House Commissioner Mann, which claimed that exemption from taxation merely allowed real estate developers to gather extra profits, Stein's commission observed that it had as yet brought no direct benefit to the tenant and aided only home builders or possibly those who bought a house from a builder. Yet both reports accepted the developers' argument that the tax exemption law had broken the building deadlock and that any apartment building would finally benefit the lower-income groups. The commission's recommended solution, therefore, was to extend the tax exemption law but to further restrict it to favor low-priced or low-rental dwellings. Its subsequent reports developed this approach. The fact was that by 1926 the stimulation of the building industry *had* affected the lower-income market; the general vacancy rate had more than trebled in the preceding year. The filtering process was working.

An upward movement of real wages during the first half of the 1920s, especially among garment workers,[30] and the effect of the 1924 Immigration Act, which limited the annual entry of foreigners to 2 percent of the 1890 ethnic populations (effectively diminishing the influx of eastern and southern Europeans), had so lessened the demand for old-law tenements that as one real estate operator put it, "We haven't tenants enough to go round."[31] There were, the tenement house commissioner had insisted in 1924, "a great many mechanics and laborers whose income would justify a greater expenditure for rent but who prefer to live in the housing now under investigation because of the cheaper rent rather than seek increased comfort and facilities at an increased outlay."[32] Events seemingly proved his observation just. General prosperity under the Coolidge administration, a borough population that decreased 18 percent during the decade, and a building boom emptied the lowest class of housing. In 1925 the Manhattan vacancy rate for old-law tenements was 1.9 percent, in 1926 it was 4.65, and in 1927 it was 7.14. A consolidating middle class was raising its standard of living through the marketing practices of private enterprise.

At the same time, however, the social distance between old-law and new-law tenements was widening. The state commission's reports during 1926 again exposed conditions of disrepair, congestion, sickness, immorality, and demoralization (paralleled by inefficiency in the Tenement House Department) and noted that of the 23 tenements condemned by the 1884 Tenement House Commission for covering 100 percent of an inner block site, 14 were still occupied.[33] This increasing gap between lower- and middle-income groups was reflected in Manhattan rents: a cold-water flat rented at from $4 a room monthly, any heated apartment ranged from $11 up, while new construction started at $20.[34] Relatively stable construction costs[35] and a continued high level of output did subsequently cause rents to fall, but the lowest rents would not drop below their economic floor. Unfortunately, there were still many families that could not afford this minimum rent, which was being asked for a standard of accommodation that could no longer be tolerated by society at large.

Restrictive legislation had stopped the inadequate solutions of the nineteenth century, but it had been unable to generate adequate solutions for the twentieth century. As the Commission of Housing and Regional Planning pointed out, the rents that the poor could afford were too low to buy a decent product from private enterprise. "The housing of the lower income groups in new construction," it observed, "is not profitable ... some supplemental organization must function in a field which business enterprise does not and cannot enter."[36] However, while the commission narrowed its interest to new construction, the point was that the poor could not afford any reasonable housing, whether it was new or secondhand. The idea of upgrading old housing had been promoted in 1920 by the Joint Legislative Committee on Housing and the State Reconstruction Commission, which together had sponsored a competition for the remodeling of a tenement block on the Lower East Side. Though there were "many good suggestions" among the 42 plans received (including knocking down the middle sections of alternate dumbbell tenements to open up interior courts), and though $4000 was awarded in prizes, no "complete solution was found in any one plan, nor did any single plan provide a combination of good housing and low alteration cost that would make an investment for a whole block practical at the present time."[37]

Thus, as the filtering process operated, two resultant problems were perceived: there were still families who were simply too poor to rent the apartments at the bottom of the acceptable housing stock; and as housing fell below the acceptable standard, there was no orderly system of pulling it down. As the *New York Times* remarked, "In their growth the commercial districts have been chiefly cutting their way through the first-class residence districts of other days . . . it is the old, unsanitary firetrap tenements that are the slowest of all buildings in the city to yield before the wreckers."[38] The first new-law (post-1901) apartments in Manhattan were demolished in 1917, and there was a steady number of these better-class units torn down from 1924 on.[39] Entrepreneurs obviously were not interested in continuing the logic of the filtering process by replacing units as they became obsolete. At the same time political opinion did not allow the government to do this itself. Two problems therefore seemed to require solutions: how to reduce the cost of privately produced new housing to a minimum for those who could not afford acceptable existing housing on the open market even when its aging had decreased its price; and what to do with the emptying slums that were at the center of a burgeoning metropolis.

To provide low-cost housing that even the poorest could afford, the Commission of Housing and Regional Planning looked to see if economies could be achieved through regional planning and greater factory and site efficiency with the standardization of parts, quantity production, and mechanization. However, the architect Grosvenor Atterbury, who had been involved with prefabrication since the turn of the century and with the support of the Russell Sage Foundation had developed a hollow-core con-

crete-panel system that was incorporated in the housing at Forest
Hills Gardens in Queens, calculated that while building represented
63 percent of the cost of a project, it constituted only 50 percent
of the normal selling price; and with only two-thirds of this
amount susceptible to reduction, a saving of one-third would reduce the rent by only $1 per room per month. The commission
further argued that as the cost of financing made up over one-half
of the running expense of an apartment building (with amortization 16.6, taxes 10.4, and maintenance 18.3 percent), and as second mortgages ranged upward from 11 percent, any reasonable
saving would have to derive from a lowering of market rates to
the first-mortgage level of 6 percent. Unfortunately, while "financial institutes should recognize a social responsibility" to provide
such funds, there was no "ground for real hopes" that they ever
would.[40] The commission therefore proposed a State Housing
Bank to aid in financing projects, the formation of limited-dividend companies to develop buildings, and a State Housing Board
to advise on and approve projects and supervise their erection.

The rallying call was back to "philanthropy and five percent,"
though now it was six. "The greed of capital that wrought the evil
must itself undo it,"[41] Riis had written a generation before. Developers were being asked to tear down the slums and rehouse
their occupants with the blessing of the state. Government was
going to do its part by bringing down the cost of money; private
enterprise would reciprocate by cutting down its profits. That this
solution was being seriously proposed was a reflection of the
times and its personalities. The commission's chairman, the architect Clarence Stein, was concurrently involved with the design of
Sunnyside Gardens in Queens for the limited-dividend corporation
headed by the socially conscious Alexander Bing. Business was
booming under a "Keep cool with Coolidge" administration.
Governor Smith was eager to try any cure. "This whole question

has been investigated, and re-investigated," he told the legislature when transmitting the commission's proposals, "and investigated all over again until there are in existence today official records on file in the Capitol at Albany sufficiently large to fill volumes of books. One outstanding fact still remains . . . that the construction of certain types of homes for wage earners of small income is unprofitable under the existing system. All the investigations disclose the undisputed fact that the building of homes has in the past been looked upon as an enterprise conducted like any other business in which the element of speculative profit has been the compelling force. Until this situation is changed it will be impossible to rebuild the tenement areas which continue throughout the years to be a menace to the health and the morals of the country."[42] Legislators were not yet ready for direct government intervention to solve the problem of rehousing the remaining poor. Instead they were offering to go into partnership with the city's entrepreneurs.

13

Reluctant Partners

Unlike earlier suggestions for increasing the supply of low-rental housing, Governor Alfred Smith's plan was specifically to encourage the replacement of substandard tenements through slum clearance and direct renewal with the lowest-cost housing that then seemed feasible. Having reached its peak in the years before World War I, the population of Manhattan was now decreasing. The hope that the northward growth of business would take care of the deteriorating property that lay in its path faded when the midtown leapfrog development climaxed in the 1920s with the erection of the Empire State Building at 34th Street and Fifth Avenue. A large pocket of slums now remained between the old and new commercial centers. While real estate interests generally supported the idea of limited-dividend companies rebuilding slums, which were undesirable both as homes and as investments, they were against the idea of government low-interest loans, which were contrary to their principles of private enterprise. In this they were joined by Lawrence Veiller, who equally abhorred any kind of tenant subsidy.

In 1910, seven years before Veiller had withdrawn from New York's housing reform movement, he had founded the National Housing Association with the support of the Russell Sage Foundation. As its secretary and director and with Robert de Forest again president, he organized its annual conferences, published their proceedings, and edited its magazine *Housing Betterment,* which he largely wrote himself after 1916. His other writings during this decade included books on housing law and reform methods. These activities in housing, zoning, and planning molded American specialist opinion and furthered restrictive legislation throughout the nation. At the same time, when more positive action was suggested (or in Veiller's view, threatened), he used the association's facilities to condemn and deride government intervention. His arguments were largely moralistic stemming from the middle-class reformer's belief that the deserving poor did not want charity. This precept, laid down in the previous century by the Association for Improving the Condition of the Poor, was applied to subsidized housing by the Charity Organization Society's general director, Lawson Purdy. If, he wrote, "the rents are in fact less than some would pay for the accommodation, then the tenants favored by limited [dividend] rents must in some manner be selected out of the community. If the basis for their selection is their financial status, their inability to pay any more rent, then the persons thus favored are the recipients of charitable relief, however disguised. They enter a special class to which most self-supporting persons will not desire to belong. If certain persons overcome their natural and proper reluctance to be the recipients of special favors from their wealthier fellow-citizens, they have overcome something in themselves to their own detriment. Some part of their self-respect is gone. The very persons sought to be benefited are those who are damaged."[1]

If, added Veiller, one embarked on a program of state socialism, why not subsidize food and clothing, or even cars and theater tickets? Such concessions as tax exemptions or special mortgage rates that were limited to one group of persons, who consequently paid less rent than would normally be required on the open market, indirectly supplemented incomes. To this extent what was saved on rent might be used on luxuries such as a "radio, talking machines, player pianos, furs, diamonds, the movies."[2] The reality was that while many poor people might use what little money they had unwisely according to middle-class standards, the effective public conscience was not prepared to let them live in conspicuous slums. On the other hand, taxpayers were unwilling to raise them to their own (hard-earned) standard of living. The political compromise was therefore to replace slum dwellers with marginal members of the middle class. As Veiller argued, a statutory rent of $12.50 a room would not benefit the 70 percent of New York's population that, according to State Housing Commission chairman Clarence Stein, could afford no more than $40 monthly. Stein himself, when commissioned with Henry Wright by the entrepreneur Alexander Bing in 1924 to design a pilot project for the first American garden city as a limited-dividend enterprise, produced a design for a group of tenants with a median income of $60 a week. The land cost of this development, Sunnyside Gardens in Queens, close to the Metropolitan Life Insurance Company apartments, was 50 cents a square foot; on the Lower East Side it was over $6.[3] It was obvious to its critics that limited-dividend housing could not be occupied by those it was supposed to rehouse.

Enticed by rumors that John D. Rockefeller, the Metropolitan Life Insurance Company, and others were ready to invest $100 million in such a venture, the legislature was unimpressed by Veiller's arguments. Being Republican, however, as it was during most of Smith's Democratic governorship, it rejected both proposals for government financing. In May 1926 the emasculated State Housing Law was signed without recourse to a public hearing. "The mountain labored and brought forth a mouse," commented a real estate observer. "A mustard plaster plan that will not cure our civic cancer," said Norman Thomas, the Socialist leader.[4] Events proved them right.

The new act replaced the Commission of Housing and Regional Planning by the State Board of Housing, and the architect Clarence Stein by Darwin James, president of the East River Savings Bank and a Republican associate in the philanthropies of Alfred White. In addition to the duties of its predecessor, the board was instructed to promote cooperatives and limited-dividend corporations based on such models as the City and Suburban Homes Company, which by that time owned over 3000 units and was averaging a 5 percent dividend.[5] The purpose of the new law was to encourage tenants to rent or buy their dwellings at a cost that eliminated speculative profit. The state was to set the rules and standards and hold the power to condemn property that was ripe for redevelopment at a monthly apartment rent, in Manhattan, not to exceed $12.50 a room; the corporation (of three or more persons) was to provide one-third of its capital needs at a dividend return not exceeding 6 percent; private financial institutions were to lend the other two-thirds at an interest rate of not more than 5 percent, and the city was asked to exempt the new buildings from local taxation.

The legislation had been endorsed by the Advisory Housing Conference, an organization of more than fifty social welfare groups that was chaired by the equivocal Lawson Purdy but included Belle Moskowitz, a close associate and advisor of Governor Smith, and Bing, who headed the subcommittee on new housing for low-income groups. Mayor James Walker, however, had his own ideas. Making no effort to have the necessary supporting local tax exemption bill passed, he instead encouraged August Heckscher to go to Europe and report back on the housing programs there. A German immigrant and self-made millionaire, head of the zinc trust and social benefactor, Heckscher was seventy-eight years of age and a contemporary of Jacob Riis. His solution, announced publicly that fall, was to raise $500 million, half to be contributed by government, the other half to be obtained from 500 public-spirited citizens including himself donating $100,000 annually for five years. Two weeks later, with no support materializing, he modified his proposal to substitute mortgage loans for gifts. Countering a further suggestion that the city meet the entire cost, Walker asked Heckscher to set an example by redeveloping one block as a pilot project. At a dinner given on the Lower East Side, with Heckscher as the guest of honor, a group of its former inhabitants who now controlled more than a billion dollars worth of real estate heard with indifference Walker's plan for model housing. Disappointed in such "moral slackers"[6] but not dispirited, Heckscher organized the National Housing Committee for Congested Areas. Meanwhile, Walker, when accused of stalling a local tax exemption ordinance, expressed innocence and explained that it was still under consideration by his advisors. This housing subcommittee, part of a citizens' committee of 500 that had been asked to report on the future growth of the city, was headed by Veiller, who was currently attacking the proposal in his magazine *Housing Betterment*.

Applying pressure, Governor Smith invited a group of influential New Yorkers to dinner at the Biltmore Hotel, but he was equally unsuccessful in obtaining promises of money, only Alexander Bing offering $100,000; and when Heckscher (who was one of the guests) commented that capitalists were always "dilatory, timid and looking for an inordinate profit," his remarks were, according to the *New York Times* "received in silence."[7] One outcome, however, was a citizens' advisory committee that led to a conference of bankers who studied a proposal for redeveloping a typical Lower East Side area and gave suggestions for making limited-dividend investments more attractive. For, as Lawson Purdy observed, few wealthy people seemed "willing to hazard for so small and so uncertain a return the sums necessary for large-scale building operations."[8]

The failure of Heckscher's attempts to raise capital made the mayor more amenable to tax exemption, and after narrowing its term from the building's life (as proposed by the State Housing Board) to twenty years, he pushed the bill through in June 1927. Concurrently, Heckscher was developing another plan. Believing that the $12.50 rental of the State Housing Law was too high for ordinary wage earners, he sought a way to provide lower-priced dwellings at minimum expense to the city. The counsel to the Citizens' Union, Leonard Wallstein, provided the answer. A 1913 provision in the state constitution and city charter permitted the city to take over more land than was actually needed for its public works and then sell or lease abutting building sites. The opposition to such a radical solution was swamped by emotional support for it. All we want for the poor, wrote Attorney General Albert Ottinger, is "light, air, a patch of garden and a breathing spot."[9] Walker guided the bill through city hall from London, England, where he was vacationing, and that November the electorate, roused by the appeal, "Every child is entitled to a little sunshine. Vote for them and see that they get it,"[10] did so overwhelmingly.

The site selected for the experiment was the band of seven blocks between Chrystie and Forsyth streets, roughly parallel to, and one block east of, the Bowery. Chrystie Street would be doubled in width. The building sites alongside would be leased for 99 years at a rental based on 4 percent of the land cost which would cover the repayment of the money borrowed to purchase the property. A 10 percent return on a developer's investment would provide rooms at a rental of $8 monthly, or less than two-thirds of that required by the State Housing Law. A year passed while negotiations took place, until the mayor, having expressed to a city hall gathering of 100 Chrystie-Forsyth landowners his indignation at their cold reception of his philanthropic project, threatened revision of their property tax assessments—and then announced the project's cancellation because of their attempted profiteering. Hints of secret negotiations for land nearby concurrently caused a local speculative boom. Organizing themselves, the Chrystie-Forsyth property owners appealed to the mayor to reconsider his decision and promised to make their land available at the normal 25 percent above assessment valuation. With regained confidence, Walker expressed the hope that John D. Rockefeller would be the major lessee, and the city approved the purchase of the land (though the condemnation awards by the courts turned out to be another 25 percent higher than had been planned for, or around $16 a square foot). Three months later came the depression.

The era of the Coolidge administration had been one of unparalleled prosperity. From 1924 through 1931, Manhattan experienced a building boom that produced an average of nearly 10,000 apartments a year at a time when the borough's population was rapidly diminishing. That is (taking demolitions into account), during the 1920s extra accommodation was provided for over 150,000 persons, while there was a decrease of over 400,000. In this decade the Lower East Side's population dropped by 40 percent.[11] The Tenement House Department statistician explained: "The younger generation is greatly responsible for the exodus from the cheap tenements. They go to school and visit the homes of their classmates and see how much better they are living in the Bronx, Brooklyn or Queens, with all modern improvements at a little more rent. They prevail upon their parents to move and when the latter give in to the children it means a vacancy that is hard to fill. The standard of living has increased. People want electric light, bath rooms, heat, cold and hot water and clean

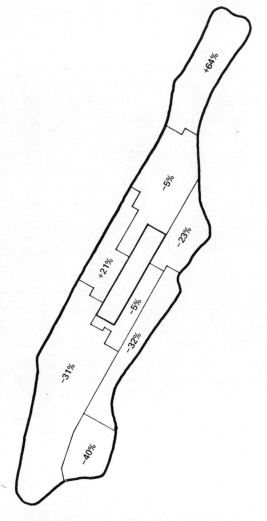

Population changes, 1920-1930, map

Source: New York Building Congress, Committee on Land Utilization, *Research Bulletin 1* (1933).

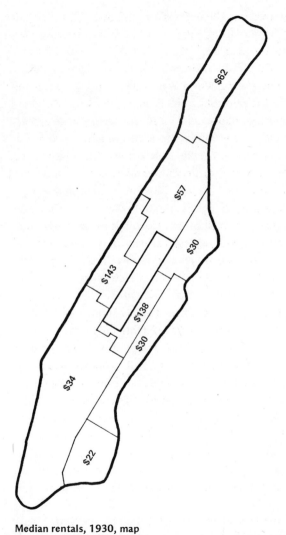

Median rentals, 1930, map

Source: New York Building Congress, Committee on Land Utilization, *Research Bulletin 1*, (1933).

rooms."[12] After a year of the depression the Lower East Side had a vacancy rate of one in four, and one out of every thirty residential buildings was boarded up.[13] Nevertheless, a quarter of a million people remained, almost entirely European immigrant families.

Unlike the period during World War I, there was no reopening of tenements and little doubling up. Then, spiraling uptown rents and a housing shortage had caused relatively secure wage earners to share substandard accommodation. Now home relief kept unemployed worker families together, while it was the unsupported white-collar class that overcrowded newer apartments in the outer boroughs. The Lower East Side was therefore an area that seemed ripe for redevelopment, being a ten-minute walk from City Hall and twenty minutes from Wall Street. Now that those who created the slums have left, argued a real estate operator, why not remodel the tenements as had been done successfully in Greenwich Village?[14] This is what the Regional Plan of New York and its Environs proposed: a white-collar district with pedestrian ways down to a waterfront park. "In a decade or two," commented the *New York Times*, "it may again become a residential district of distinction."[15] The idea of substituting rich for poor was supported by other specialists. The housing reformer Carol Aronovici wrote: "It would seem to me logical that we should quit trying to rehabilitate lower Manhattan for the poor and give it back to the well-to-do by building expensive, luxurious and well planned apartment houses in which the rich could live close to the financial district."[16] In the meantime, it was being used by bums covered with "Hoover blankets" or newspapers, with "cinders for a couch, a blue or gray sky for a canopy, and the rattle of the elevated in their ears."[17]

Frustrated by the lack of interest generated by the State Housing Law and the dearth of interested developers, Mayor Walker proposed a legislative amendment to the city charter permitting it

to mortgage the land it had acquired to provide the capital necessary to sponsor its own developments. Such a move would have
rendered the State Housing Board ineffective in the city by assuming its powers while discarding its controls. Supported by real
estate interests who thought it the lesser of two evils, the State
Housing Board persuaded Governor Roosevelt to veto the bill.
Undaunted, Walker disclosed that the new City Planning Department, with the help of Rockefeller's housing architect Andrew
Thomas, had prepared plans for the Chrystie-Forsyth area that
were "so attractive that if they were to be made public now I
should fear a general exodus from Park Avenue to the lower east
side."[18] His quip came with the announcement that he was rein-
troducing his housing bill under the city's home rule powers. Six
months later the bill was forgotten in committee, while the Sea-
bury investigations uncovered yet another episode of Tammany
corruption and Walker took off for Europe, having hastily resigned.

The affair of Chrystie-Forsyth, which had begun in 1927,
dragged on. Different proposals for the area included one for 24
nine-story buildings on columns with playgrounds below, by the
architects Howe & Lescaze, exhibited at the Museum of Modern
Art ("Battleship design,"[19] commented Veiller); another, for
Heckscher, had twelve- and nineteen-story buildings. All were opposed by city staff, and when finally Heckscher's proposal was
approved by the Board of Estimate, it was totally rejected by the
State Housing Board. At the beginning of 1934 the saga came
abruptly to an end when the new mayor Fiorello LaGuardia made
the area into a park.

During this period only one limited-dividend corporation had
been organized in Manhattan. Veiller had earlier pointed out that
the rent levels permitted by the State Housing Law would push out
local manual workers and replace them by white-collar workers,
that is, supplant those who paid $5 a room for substandard hous-

ing by those who could afford $12.50 for new apartment rooms. He foresaw that redevelopment would either cause the poor to invade surrounding neighborhoods or to be dispersed to outlying areas. And he was rightly skeptical about the demand for living on the Lower East Side. The proposals, he wrote, were formulated "without considering where the tenants are to come from that are to inhabit the new dwellings to be erected on the sites razed; without considering how it is going to be possible to induce people who are willing and able to pay a rent of $12.50 a month per room, or $50 to $75 for their housing accommodations, to move out of those portions of the city which they now inhabit and come down and live in the slums in the midst of slum dwellers, with people in the next block and all the blocks surrounding them living in what are called 'slums'; without school accommodations of the right kind, without neighbors of the right kind, without shops of the right kind, without social advantages, or recreation of the right kind. How they expect such a population to come and seek the new tenements is undisclosed."[20] Twelve years later a Federal Housing Administration study calculated that it would take all the Manhattan families with an income of over $2000 a year to fill the Lower East Side in new low-rise apartments. To achieve even a moderate 30-acre development would require an independent community with low-density luxury apartments and its own schools and shopping centers linked to other parts of town by a private bus line that would circumvent the remaining slums by taking its passengers along the East River Drive. And then, the report added: "After all these private and public expenditures have been made in rebuilding a small portion of the Lower East Side most of it will be left."[21]

It was clear that the Chrystie-Forsyth area was too much of a gamble for entrepreneurs to take. The rising middle class, whose whole ambition had been to get out of the slums, was making little effort to get back in. A survey by the State Housing Board found that with a land coverage of roughly 60 percent compared to the 85 percent or so of the old dumbbell pattern, there were 70 blocks below Fourteenth Street that were theoretically cheap enough to redevelop at the maximum rents allowed.[22] The first project to take advantage of the new law (though it had been initiated prior to it), took 400 families *out of* the Lower East Side to the Bronx, where they were able to pay less rent for better accommodation. The same sponsor, the Amalgamated Clothing Workers of America, also produced the first limited-dividend project in Manhattan. Encouraged by Governor Roosevelt, Lieutenant-Governor Herbert Lehman, and a member of the State Housing Board, Aaron Rabinowitz, purchased the site of the printing press factory of the Hoe family (which had been represented on the jury of the 1879 model tenement competition). This block on Grand Street on the Lower East Side was then redeveloped as 234 elevator apartments in six- and seven-story buildings and sold as cooperative units. Requiring an equity investment of $500 a room plus a monthly rental of $12.50, the accommodation was obviously too expensive for most wage earners, and Lehman and Rabinowitz offered personal ten-year loans to reduce down payments to $150 per room. As in 1930, when the Amalgamated Dwellings were completed, over half the tenant families of Manhattan paid less than $50 a month rent,[23] and few ordinary wage earners were capable of accumulating investment capital, it is evident that the success of the redevelopment was not in housing lower-income workers but in retaining those who had climbed the economic ladder out of the neighboring slums. Unfortunately, these pioneers found few followers. During the next couple of years as the depression worsened, only 181 other families were rehoused in three smaller limited-dividend projects (including 93 units that were demolished just over ten years later when the eighteen-block Stuyvesant Town was built above Fourteenth Street). Summarizing the situation at the beginning of 1933, the State Board of Housing scorned architects who could now "derive little comfort from the empty skyscrapers that they designed," instead of the housing projects that might have been. "For five years the Board has tried to interest private enterprise in the job of constructing houses for families of low income. The building industry was too busily engaged in other directions during the period of prosperity to explore a field which was distinguished for the absence of the glamour of speculative profits.[24]

Developers were hardly to be blamed for declining to be social benefactors. Even Smith, when he failed to win the presidency in 1928, took the state examination as a real estate broker and headed the company that built the Empire State Building. At the time it seemed that there were simply better investments to make. In Manhattan in 1929, $190 million went into residential buildings, $230 million into hotels.[25] The years before the depression did see a relatively large number of apartments built, but few of these were in lower Manhattan, and of four years' supply only 113 out of 30,000 rented for under $12.50 a room, while two-thirds rented at more than double that amount.[26] After seven years of trying to implement the new law, the State Board of Housing admitted defeat: "limited dividend corporations have been unable to assemble any large slum areas for reconstruction or to undertake a comprehensive plan for the reconstruction of any blighted area as a whole."[27] The partnership of government and entrepreneur had failed.

One of the major objections to the state's housing policy had been its insistence on city tax exemption. The proposition that landowners, builders, and landlords should not profit unduly from the supply of a basic necessity such as housing was easy to defend. The arguments for the local tax exemption were more tenuous. Different assessments of how much this would reduce rents varied from about $1.50 to $2.25 a room monthly.[28] Even the maximum deduction did little to bring rents within the range of the bottom third of Manhattan tenants. The $12.50 ceiling had been fixed pragmatically as the cheapest rent that would cover the expense of socially acceptable housing. If people wanted new housing, this is what they would have to pay. However, as many families could not easily afford this level of rent, any method of lowering it still further seemed to be desirable.

By doing so, the concept of a middle class was blurred. On the previous occasion that local tax exemption had been used in the early 1920s, the aim had been to encourage the construction of new middle-class dwellings at a rental competitive with those existing during a period of inflated costs. The law passed six years later provided for the tax exemption rebate to be passed directly on to the occupant. In other words, government this time was not stimulating the supply of housing but subsidizing those who could not afford the rents on the open market. The vacancy rate in 1921 had been 0.18 percent; in 1927 it was nearly 6 percent—that is, above the level accepted by the state as necessary for equitable landlord-tenant bargaining. The conclusion was that the middle class could no longer afford the standard of housing that was considered its due. When August Heckscher objected that garment workers did not need tax exemption because they earned more than $10 a day, he was ignored; but a later report showed that the average weekly income under full employment for occupants of the Amalgamated Housing Corporation's limited-dividend project in the Bronx (nearly a third of whom worked in the needle trades) was $52.88, and they were spending only 18.4 percent of this on their rent.[29] For the first time not only the poor were being protected but now middle class values were also being subsidized. Money not spent on rent purchased household appliances, better clothes and food, and automobiles began to appear on the Lower East Side.

At the same time housing standards continued to rise. In 1929, Veiller's "new" tenement law was superseded by the Multiple Dwelling Law (itself an upgrading of nomenclature), which, with the support of both professional housing experts and real estate interests, consolidated the middle-class demands of the time. That such housing was apparently beyond the means of most families was beside the point. This was their right; how they were to pay for it was another matter. The city, wrote Heckscher, "will have to house the poorer classes, will have to do so in adequate homes at a cost which they can afford and will have to raise through taxation the loss thus entailed."[30] Government was not quite ready to do that. What it did do was not to collect some of its taxes so that the lower middle class might enjoy better living conditions and still have money left over for those little luxuries that marked it off from the poor and gave it motivation to work in a free-enterprise economy.

While the euphoria from the boom years of the 1920s lasted, it was possible to believe that a rising standard of living would make poverty obsolete. As the depression spread and the bread-lines lengthened, the hope that the housing problem would simply evaporate disappeared. Not only the poor were feeling the strain. From a 1925 peak of nearly one million dwelling unit starts in the United States, housing production steadily fell, until eight years later the number was only 93,000. Concerned with this trend, President Hoover convened a President's Conference on Home Building and Home Ownership in the fall of 1931. At the end of that year 3700 delegates who had gathered in Washington heard him declare: "I am confident that the sentiment for home owner-ship is so embedded in the American heart that the millions of people who dwell in tenements, apartments, and rented rows of solid brick have the aspiration for wider opportunity in ownership of their own homes. To possess one's own home is the hope and ambition of almost every individual in our country.... Those immortal ballads, *Home Sweet Home, My Old Kentucky Home,* and the *Little Gray Home in the West,* were not written about tenements or apartments."[31]

III

The state must meet the difference between
what is economically possible and what is
socially necessary.

Carol Aronovici

Government Resolves

The principal outcome of the president's conference was the endorsement of the administration's proposal for a national home loan bank system supported by federal credit. However, as 97 percent of Manhattanites rented apartments, this initiation of a homeownership policy had little direct impact, although it subsequently encouraged the buildup of the suburbs, which hastened the exodus of middle-income families. Of greater immediate apparent use was another of Hoover's measures to stimulate the economy, the establishment of the Reconstruction Finance Corporation under the Emergency Relief and Construction Act of 1932. Authorized to make loans on self-liquidating projects including low-income family housing and the renewal of slum areas, the corporation required cooperation from other levels of government, and while several states thereupon passed enabling legislation, only New York had the necessary organization to regulate limited-dividend companies and reduce rents to an acceptable level through tax exemption. However, although numerous applications for loans were received, they were for projects that were considered either too small, too costly, too speculative, or in unsuitable areas, so that finally only one project was approved: Knickerbocker Village on the Lower East Side, housing 4000 persons on five acres in twelve-story blocks around inner courts. According to its developer, Fred French, it took over 50 trips to Washington to get his loan of $8 million for a housing development that had a density double that recommended by the government (but necessary, so French maintained, for a satisfactory investment).[1] By that time the housing activities of the Reconstruction Finance Corporation had been transferred to the Public Works Administration, and Franklin D. Roosevelt had been elected president.

Soon after the establishment of the Reconstruction Finance Corporation, a group of social workers and other concerned professionals had met at the Greenwich House settlement to organize a campaign for workers' housing. Presided over by its director, Mary Simkhovitch, the meeting was addressed by Edith Elmer Wood, Carol Aronovici, and Clarence Stein. Calling itself the Public Housing Conference, it recommended a state housing bank and a local housing authority to carry out slum clearance and low-rental housing. Its proposal that the city request a $25 million loan from the Reconstruction Finance Corporation was treated with skepticism by Mayor Walker, but with Simkhovitch's associate Helen Alfred as secretary (and Lillian Wald of the Henry Street settlement and the Socialist leader Norman Thomas on its committee), the Public Housing Conference pressed for action through the city council. During the last months of Walker's administration and then through the interregnum before the next municipal election, it continued its agitation, which included the submission of its own Chrystie-Forsyth proposal. Pressure was mounting for the initiation of projects that would help those who currently suffered from normal conditions of poverty, now aggravated by unemployment. Through 1931-1932, such bills that were introduced into the state legislature and Congress had been defeated, but the Democratic presidential victory, the breakdown of the banking system, and the peak of 12 million unemployed, brought about a merging of interests between those who sought a way out of the depression and those who wanted decent housing for the poor.

In the summer of 1933 when the Roosevelt administration was preparing its National Industrial Recovery Act, Mary Simkhovitch went to Washington to ask for housing to be included in its program of public works. Just over a decade earlier, the idea of government housing in peacetime had been politically indefensible. The editor of *American City,* Harold Buttenheim, had summed up the pre-depression attitude correctly in 1929 when he said in a paper presented at a national conference on housing: "We then come to the moot questions of tax exemption, state credit, and municipal ownership. . . . The question of where to draw the line is a difficult one. All—or almost all—of us would draw it this side of government housing."[2] The collapse of the world's most vital economy changed many people's minds. Even Simkhovitch herself wrote in her autobiography, *Here Is God's Plenty,* how while preparing a talk on housing she realized what little progress had been made and how the great mass of people still lived "in their old congested squalor," so that by 1931—that is, when she was sixty-three years old and after twenty-nine years as a settlement worker—"the cumulative impressions of the housing picture I had witnessed since childhood resulted in my conversion to the necessity of government housing for persons unable to pay commercial rents."[3] Backed by her considerable prestige and that of John O'Grady of the National Conference of Catholic Charities, the proposals that she brought from the Public Housing Conference were incorporated into the new legislation that permitted the construction, reconstruction, alteration, or repair under public regulation or control of low-rental housing and slum clearance projects.[4] A few weeks later a federal housing division was set up under the direction of Robert Kohn, who, since his employment with the Emergency Fleet Corporation, had been both continuing presi-

dent of the New York Society for Ethical Culture and, more recently, president of the American Institute of Architects. As part
of the Public Works Administration, headed by Secretary of the
Interior Harold Ickes, its impact was initially restricted by suspi-
cion and caution. Intended to make jobs rather than housing,
which was incidental to its main economic purpose, the public
works program authorized 30 percent capital grants and 70 percent low-interest loans to public bodies, and 85 percent low-interest loans to private corporations; but as at first there were no
municipalities with the necessary legal authority to take advantage
of its terms, only limited-dividend companies were eligible to
apply. Of 533 applications, only seven projects were authorized,
mostly because of the sponsor's lack of equity. Rejecting private
enterprise as a means of providing low-rental housing, Ickes announced the incorporation of a Public Works Emergency Housing
Corporation with the authority to clear slums and build low-
rental apartments nationally, and the power of eminent domain,
though this was subsequently denied by the courts. With $100
million allocated to it by executive order of President Roosevelt
(though intervention by the comptroller general forced its conversion back to a more legally constituted Housing Division), its staff
toured the country, encouraging local requests for housing. In
1935 the Emergency Relief Appropriation Act allotted a further
sum of $450 million for housing and extended the life of the Pub-
lic Works Administration until mid-1937.

The movement to formulate a local program for New York was
activated by the federal housing director, Kohn. At his suggestion
a citizens' committee was organized in October 1933 to promote
the creation of a municipal housing authority. Named the Slum
Clearance Committee of New York, its establishment coincided
with the election of Fiorello LaGuardia as mayor. For tenement
house commissioner he chose Langdon Post, a former state assem-

blyman who had previously supported a state housing bank and was a member of the Slum Clearance Committee. Within this group, three housing lawyers, Carl Stern, Ira Robbins, and Charles Abrams, wrote the necessary enabling legislation that was passed by the legislature with the support of Herbert Lehman, who had succeeded Roosevelt as governor. Faced with the closure of funds after the turn of the year, the Slum Clearance Committee had obtained a promise of federal support. Prior to the enactment of the Municipal Housing Authorities Law and three days after taking office, LaGuardia received a telegram from Ickes offering $25 million. Obtaining it, however, proved more difficult. Though the New York City Housing Authority came into existence in February 1934 with Post as chairman, Simkhovitch as vice-chairman, and Roberts Moore of the Catholic Charities of the Archdiocese of New York, Louis Pink, a lawyer who had earlier served as a settlement worker and was on the State Housing Board, and the veteran Socialist and general manager of the *Jewish Daily Forward*, Charney Vladeck, as commissioners, negotiations with the federal government proved unproductive. Ridiculing an anecdote by Robbins on the importance of a semicolon in the state housing bill, LaGuardia complained of the "semi-colon boys"[5] in the Public Works Administration. Post later criticized it for "indecision, red tape, semicolons and a general fear of doing something."[6] (Ickes was equally uncomplimentary, calling Post "a stuffed shirt without any stuffing.")[7]

In the meantime, the administration had passed its National Housing Act of 1934. During the previous decade, few professionals had concerned themselves with government housing policy. The years of idleness (there were over 2500 persons registered as unemployed with the Architects Emergency Committee in the New York region during the depression)[8] gave them the opportunity to become more involved. When Post organized a model housing competition in mid-1934, there were 1775 entries, but only 22 of these, according to jury member Frederick Ackerman, then Housing Authority technical director, had any "real knowledge" of housing.[9] Studies abounded. The Housing Study Guild, set up in the summer of 1933 by the Lewis Mumford, Clarence Stein, Henry Wright group, had the active assistance of 30 or more persons. A survey of surveys by the New York Building Congress (itself reactivated under the presidency of Robert Kohn), listed over 200 pieces of current research.[10] Surpassing them all in comprehensiveness was the two-volume, 1000-page *Slums and Housing* carried out under the auspices of the Phelps-Stokes Fund. Edited by James Ford, who had previously been associate director of President Hoover's Conference on Home Building and Home Ownership and editor of the twelve volumes of its proceedings, it included a 27-page bibliography of writings on a century of housing activity in New York. However, his viewpoint that the chief cause of slums was human selfishness and that their elimination involved a fundamental change in attitudes was no longer fashionable by the time his work was published in 1936. (Nor was his recommendation that those who were unable to earn the necessary $6 per room per month for housing should be placed under social and medical care in rural colonies where they might live at minimum public expense.) Government housing was no longer as Ford proclaimed "a last resort" but the basis of a new panacea.[11]

Roosevelt's National Housing Act was therefore disappointing to the advocates of the new policies. Continuing Hoover's philosophy of supporting homeownership at a time of spiraling foreclosures, it encouraged investment in single-family housing by guaranteeing mortgages and providing loans for repairs and modernization. The reformers' reactions to these policies were published in the catalog of an exhibition held at the Museum of Modern Art that was organized under the chairmanship of Carol Aronovici with the collaboration of the Columbia University Orientation Study, of which he was director, the Lavanburg Foundation, the Welfare Council, and the Housing Authority. Catherine Bauer considered the new act "an empty hoax"; Lewis Mumford called it "a fake program." "Sabotage on the part of property-owning and mortgage-holding interests has nearly wrecked the modest program for low-cost housing which the United States Government projected as a minor part of the national reconstruction program," wrote Aronovici.[12] Only Edith Elmer Wood propounded the philosophy of the moderates: the top third of the income range would be housed by private enterprise, the middle third by limited-dividend corporations and cooperatives, and the bottom third by government agencies.

With the continuing movement of commerce and industry uptown and into the outer boroughs, the character of Manhattan's population had changed. The opening up of the area between Pennsylvania and Grand Central stations, the retail establishment around Rockefeller Center, and the wholesale move toward Times Square had turned the Lower East Side into a backwater. In the early part of the century the garment industry had been largely below Fourteenth Street; by the mid 1930s its manufacture of women's wear had almost ceased, while that of men's wear had been cut in half. Since 1910 over four-fifths of the city had lived within half a mile of rapid-transit lines.[13] The extension of the subway system and the increase in automobiles (337,000 New York families owned one in 1934, including 40 percent of all those living in Queens),[14] plus the pre-depression general rise in living standards, helped build up the outer boroughs and adjacent counties as middle-class suburbs. Manhattan's annual loss of 40,000 during the 1920s had been countered by a peripheral growth of seven times that number.[15] Generally, Manhattan rents reflected this trend. Half of all American families who paid $200 a month or more for their apartments lived on Manhattan, while 45 percent of its tenants paid less than $30 a month.[16] In Queens and the Bronx, in contrast, over 80 percent were in the middle-rental range. Extrapolating from the number of children involved in the change, the New York Building Congress Land Utilization Committee concluded that the move to the outlying areas was mainly by middle-income families.[17]

The emptying of the slums on the Lower East Side focused attention on the plight of those who still lived in them. A few weeks after Post took office, seven children died in a tenement house fire. A thousand others marched on City Hall with placards reading "We Don't Want To Burn." Post later wrote of how this provoked him into action when his chief inspector asked what to do about another dilapidated building. " 'I suppose you could order the building vacated,' he said. 'Vacated? What do you mean by that?' 'Order the people out. You have the power to do that if the building is unsafe and unfit for human habitation.' 'I have that power? I thought that belonged to the Health Department.' 'No, the Tenement House Department has it also.' 'You mean to say,' I shouted at him, 'that I can order people out of these houses without having to go to the courts?' 'Oh, yes, the department has had that power ever since 1901,' was his calm answer. He started to go out. 'You get up that vacation order and bring it in right away,' I said."[18] Climbing onto the roof of 500 East Eighteenth Street and knocking a couple of bricks off its parapet with a crow-bar, Post (who had once heard Jacob Riis talk at his preparatory school) inaugurated a city program to raze its slums, and the Tenement House Department burst into the sort of activity that had not been seen since the beginning of the century when Veiller had first brought it into existence.

The peak of demolition had previously been reached in 1930 when 9462 Manhattan units were demolished. However, one-fifth of these were less than thirty years old. While only 20,000 units were demolished during Post's four years of office, 90 percent of them were in old-law tenements. The major difference was in the number of demolitions relative to new apartments built. During 1926-1929, the ratio was roughly 1:2; during 1934-1937 it was 5:2. That is, old-law tenements were now being torn down not to make way for new developments but because they were slums.[19]

Unfortunately, the slums were also spreading. In 1921 an observer had described Harlem as giving "an impression of spaciousness, of cleanliness, of prosperity, of success."[20] The depression put an end to that. By 1932 12 percent of its inhabitants were out of work, families were doubling up or moving into one room, and it had the highest rate of infant mortality, twice the normal venereal disease rate, and three times the tuberculosis death rate of the city.[21] A later state investigation declared that one block in Harlem had the highest density in the world, capturing the title from the Lower East Side. Harlem's problem was not that its buildings were physically obsolete (over four-fifths of them were reported to be in good condition) but that its tenants could not afford or make proper use of what they had. In a typical area the average monthly income was $76.80, the monthly rental $30.39.[22]

Two different situations therefore existed: an emptying slum on the Lower East Side that needed only partial renewal for lower-income families; and a burgeoning slum in Harlem of middle-class housing that had been taken over by people who were both economically and socially unable to utilize their accommodation properly. The result was a neighborhood that had all the characteristics of a slum except that instead of containing ramshackle tenements it had solid buildings of the wrong type. In the real estate inventory of the city carried out in 1934 by the Housing Authority with the support of the Works Progress Administration, a survey that occupied 6000 persons for eight months, no differentiation was made between the two types of slum. The inventory recorded 17 square miles of blight or slum in the city, of which 10 square miles were unfit for habitation and ripe for renewal. Of these, 4.4 square miles were in Manhattan.[23]

The first direct government attempt to rehouse slum dwellers was initiated by Langdon Post. Still without the promised federal funds in the fall of 1934, he later recalled how he was walking in Central Park, when he saw the zoo that Robert Moses as park commissioner was having built with money from the Federal Emergency Relief Administration. Flying to Washington, he convinced its director, Harry Hopkins, that housing human beings was as legitimate as housing monkeys. With the promise of relief support, Post accepted Vincent Astor's offer to take over a group of tenements on the Lower East Side in exchange for 3½ percent Housing Authority bonds. Unfortunately, the site was divided by two tenement houses under separate ownership, and, unable to agree on purchase terms, the Housing Authority was required to deposit $34,000 pending a court decision. The ruling in its favor in 1936 by the court of appeals in the judgment of *New York City Housing Authority v. Muller* became the legal precedent upholding the right of the state (rather than the federal government) to condemn slums and replace them with low-cost housing. However, lacking money of its own and with none forthcoming from the city, its efforts would have been stopped without the offer of a low-interest loan from financier Bernard Baruch. The following year the first municipal housing project in New York was completed by demolishing every third building in a tenement row on Avenue A between Second and Third streets (a method of opening up blocks previously suggested by the Congestion of Population Commission chairman 25 years earlier), completely renovating three of the remainder, and erecting five new buildings, all with men and money from federal and state relief. Symbolically named

First Houses, the project contained a playground, a health center, nine stores, a laundry, recreation and community rooms, and 122 apartments with central heating and hot water in four-and five-story walk-ups renting at an average of $6.05 a room—half the rent of those built under the limited-dividend corporations. Post was exultant: "They told us we could not issue bonds—we have issued bonds; they told us we could not condemn—we have condemned; they told us we could not build with relief labor—we have built with relief labor; they told us we could not operate even if we did build—we are operating; they told us we could not get tenants from the slums—all our tenants are from the slums."[24]

Others were less enthusiastic. The project had previously been criticized as being structurally, economically, and socially questionable. Walls had collapsed, windows had sagged, unions had picketed against the use of cheap labor. On completion of the project, the *Real Estate Record* charged that while its estimated cost had been $328,000, its real cost was $1.55 million, or $2389 a room, compared to $1500 in limited-dividend projects.[25] The *New York Times* noted that "with adequate resources and equipment anyone can turn coal into diamonds"[26] and quoted one critic's reaction: "Come, come now brother, surely you would not apply cost accounting to the Pearly Gates."[27] Even Post seems to have been more elated by the initiation of a municipal housing program than by the actual work done, for when he discussed housing problems in his book *The Challenge of Housing*, published in 1938, he rejected the rehabilitation of slums as "a nice theory for the opportunist or even the sentimentalist" but socially undesirable and economically unsound. The only insurance against obsolescence, he declared, "is to create a community large enough to protect itself and open enough to afford the inhabitants a full life within its own boundaries. Little islands of good housing in a sea of slum are not good investments either financially or socially."[28]

This approach had an architectural history dating back to the 1920s. In Europe, Le Corbusier had publicized his Ville Contemporaine with its potent image of skyscrapers set in a park. In the United States, when designing Sunnyside Gardens in Queens for Alexander Bing's City Housing Corporation, Clarence Stein and Henry Wright had ignored the internal lot divisions of a city block and placed apartment buildings around an inner park. Their next project in Radburn, New Jersey, introduced the "superblock" of 30 to 50 acres with through vehicular traffic kept to the perimeter. This large-scale approach to urban design made earlier housing layout reforms seem timid. As Veiller had condemned previous tenement laws for failing to cope with interior courts, so Post in turn accused Veiller of ignoring the space around buildings, so that "the net result of the Tenement House Law of 1901, as far as planning is concerned, has been to produce greater economic evils than formerly existed. Today rows of tenement houses on block after block, for miles and miles of the city, back up against other houses almost within jumping distance. . . . The reform of 1901 did not even take into consideration the fundamental problems of land usage."[29] A special city housing adviser, Nathan Straus, afterward United States Housing Authority administrator, also stressed the need for open space in neighborhoods and added his criticism of Veiller's "so-called 'new-law tenements,' which involve conditions of overcrowding, lack of light and air . . . forbidden by law in practically every civilized country."[30] Large-scale renewal also permitted new block layouts, bulk purchasing, and site mechanization, which made production cheaper and quicker. Moreover, it fitted into the current demand for an overall city plan administered by a permanent planning commission (established in 1938, after its short-lived forerunner had been abolished in an austerity cut five years earlier).

There seemed only two choices: either rehouse the poor in their neighborhoods or build new communities in outlying areas. Specialists such as Clarence Stein and Catherine Bauer argued that well-designed neighborhoods with lower densities could be built only on cheap peripheral land and that as the demolition of slums inevitably displaced their occupants, they might as well move away to better conditions.[31] Other specialists contended that central sites were already intensively developed with services, that these huge costs would have to be duplicated in new suburbs, and that rehoused families naturally wished to remain near their social and business connections. Post agreed: building on new land drained "the city at its very heart leaving blight and decay behind. . . . It is just exactly what private enterprise has been doing for the past 50 years."[32]

If government was to rehouse its low-income population, the need was for mass production. Since the advent of Henry Ford and the evident efficiency of his assembly line, architects had looked to industrialization as a solution to the housing problem. Although little had been achieved since Grosvenor Atterbury's pre-World War I precast concrete panel housing at Forest Hills Gardens, he was still optimistic when he reported on "The economic production of workingmen's homes" in the *Regional Plan of New York and Its Environs*, published in 1931.[33] During this period, a Boston industrialist, Albert Bemis, had developed the theory of a three-dimensional modular grid as a prerequisite to rationalized design but had failed to market any of 22 different housing systems. In Europe, however, the evolution of a modern architectural style had associated itself with technological progressiveness. From Le Corbusier's aphorism that "a house is a machine for living in" through the light steel frame and panel houses designed by Walter Gropius for the 1927 Weissenhof Exhibition in Germany, avant-garde architects equated advanced technology with advanced aesthetics, though in practice appearances usually overrode technical considerations. The peak of industrial enthusiasm in American architects was reached at the 1933 Century of Progress Exposition in Chicago, for which George Keck designed a circular metal and glass "House of Tomorrow" that included not only a garage but also a space for a small airplane. A couple of years later, a four-room air-conditioned "Motohome" that was unveiled in Wanamaker's store by President Roosevelt's mother on April Fool's Day in 1935 attracted considerable interest but had little commercial success. Apparently, American attitudes were unready to accept the social, economic, and political consequences of this sort of housing solution. If the building fabric was not subject to a significant reduction in cost through mass production, then the only remaining possible economy was in the price of land.

Unfortunately, a report by Carol Aronovici showed that while a land value of $2 a square foot or less was required for low-rental housing, nothing at this price was available in Manhattan, where most blocks averaged five times that amount.[34] In response, President Roosevelt charged that New York land values were often "fictitious" and threatened that the Public Works Administration housing program would not operate without the municipal supply of cheap land.[35] As a mayor's commission report on conditions in Harlem put it, "it is apparent that property owners have long whip-sawed the community by blowing hot and cold as to the lives of properties. For income tax purposes, property owners claim short lives so as to procure high depreciation rates and substantial income tax savings. When, however, the property is up for condemnation, the property owner claims as much as a hundred-year life so as to procure more funds from the city treasury."[37] (The city was also believed to favor unrealistically high assessments so that its budgetary requirements could be met within the constitutional tax limit.) Reporting to LaGuardia in 1935, Nathan Straus recommended that no new housing be built in slum areas until prices dropped, as otherwise it would only bolster already inflated values.

The basic problem was that the cost of land derived its assumed value from the overcrowding of previous years. While housing specialists might consider old-law tenements to be substandard, this attitude was so remote to those involved in real estate that depreciation was seldom charged as an operating expense and mortgages were renewed without any reduction in principal. Given their average rate of demolition during the 1930s, one might expect that it would take another 80 years for them to be replaced. But as vacancies increased and their incomes dropped, owners were faced with a novel situation where their paper assets were greater than their realizable value. Unable to benefit from redevelopment by business because of the geographic isolation of the Lower East Side bulge in the Manhattan grid layout and its poor subway service, owners who wanted to sell had only two grounds on which to base an inflated asking price: a potential increase either in the level of rents or in the number of families housed on the site. That is, to satisfy the land costs of residential redevelopment at the sort of prices demanded by current owners, either the existing low-income tenants would have to be supplanted by middle-income households, or the density of land use would have to be raised. (Speculators, of course, hoped to do both like Fred French at Knickerbocker Village.)

With the historically satisfactory record of real estate investment, few owners were willing to admit that their properties had decreased in value. All one had to do was to wait for better times.

(Similarly, the city was accused of keeping up a standard of living it could no longer afford and was advised to lower salaries, municipal services, and taxes.) If slums were required to be redeveloped at a land cost based on its high point of use (on the assumption that the value of land can rise but never fall), then at 400 persons on each of its 1000 acres, over one-fifth of Manhattan's population would have to be housed on the Lower East Side. The seemingly unthinkable alternative was to force the sale of land at a price that would permit lower densities or open space. A report by the Citizens' Housing Council advocated patience. Originating from the cooperation of concerned social agencies under the auspices of the Welfare Council, this organization, presided over by Harold Buttenheim, had become the coordinating center of city housing interests. "Present high prices," it wrote, "are generally a hangover from earlier periods of speculation and are due to present overcrowding and to the expectation of new use and a rising density of development which would justify a higher price, and have no connection with realities. When zoning takes account of probability—for example, probable stabilization of population—by providing for much lower densities over the entire city, land prices are bound to be readjusted."[37] The slums of the Lower East Side were, however, more durable than expected. Notwithstanding their cheap materials, shoddy construction, and decades of misuse, the old-law tenements survived.

Manhattan's major housing needs therefore appeared to be the demolition of substandard occupied housing that was beyond reclaim and the rehousing of its occupants, and because no one seriously questioned the prevailing overuse of land, the creation of middle-class neighborhoods on the cleared land that remained. (Receiving less consideration was the renovation of salvageable housing, though the Brooklyn Real Estate Board later induced

LaGuardia to set up a Mayor's Committee on Property Investment, which initiated legislation to encourage renovations by waiving increased taxation.)

The housing movement of the 1930s concentrated on the first of these objectives. The impact of the Public Housing Conference in 1932 made New York the center of influence to the extent that Ickes quoted President Roosevelt as saying that he would not like the country to think that New York was running his public housing program.[38] Its initial legislation was drafted by the New York State Board of Housing counsel Ira Robbins; its sponsor was Senator Wagner of New York; the first director of the Public Works Administration's housing division was the New York architect Robert Kohn; the first administrator of the United States Housing Authority was to be Nathan Straus of the New York merchant family. When the local pressure group moved to Washington and became the National Public Housing Conference, its president remained New York's Mary Simkhovitch, who was a friend of Wagner and Ickes, and also of Eleanor Roosevelt.

The next few years saw the struggle to implement a permanent federal public housing program. "It is obvious," wrote Langdon Post, "that the battle lines are drawn. All intelligent, socially-minded persons stand unreservedly in favor of government low-rental housing: social workers, liberal clergymen, progressives in politics, untrammelled newspaper editors and thousands of other creators of public opinion. Only the spokesmen for reaction oppose it."[39] Unfortunately, President Roosevelt was not too keen about public housing either. Although Post had asked for 30,000 apartments a year over a ten-year period, at a cost of $1.5 billion, and LaGuardia had promised "more steam shovels and fewer typewriters,"[40] relatively few public-aided housing units were built during Roosevelt's first administration. The Public Works Administration was responsible for about 21,000 units, that is, just over

2 percent of the national output between 1934-1937. Of these only 2196 were in New York City, mostly at Williamsburg in Brooklyn, with a smaller project in Manhattan along the Harlem River.

The introduction of a public housing bill in the 1935 session of the Congress was therefore only for edification. The following year Wagner seriously tried to have it passed. The difficulty was not in the opposition of real estate and loaning interests, which automatically protested such legislation, but from the internal dissension among the housing program sponsors themselves. The National Public Housing Conference, dominated by Mary Simkhovitch and Helen Alfred, favored control by the Secretary of the Interior. Catherine Bauer, who advised the American Federation of Labor, demanded an independent agency. There were many other differences of opinion which to both sides were matters of principle, while Ickes wanted his staff to write a housing program that would be a continuation of his Public Works Administration policies. Disgruntled by seemingly endless arguments, Wagner pushed his own bill through the Senate without presidential approval, only to have it stalled in the House of Representatives. The year 1937 seemed more propitious; the tone was set by Roosevelt in his second inaugural address: "I see one-third of a nation ill-housed, ill-clad, ill-nourished. It is not in despair that I paint you that picture. I paint it for you in hope, because the nation, seeing and understanding the injustice in it, proposes to paint it out."[41] The principle of government responsibility had been firmly established. The only question was what to enact. Once more the experts deliberated forcefully and at length, and again a bill was approved by the Senate on Wagner's own initiative, this time with a much larger majority. "Remember," the National Public Housing Conference publication exhorted: "The wheel that squeaks the loudest gets the grease."[42] All the lobbying that could be mobilized was required to get the bill past the House committee. Ruled by an anti-public housing congressman from Alabama, the committee awaited a presidential directive, which through the spring and early summer never materialized. Finally, as the pressure mounted, Roosevelt instructed the committee to move. On September 1, 1937, after further interhouse compromise, the United States Housing Act was signed into law.[43]

The act set up the United States Housing Authority, with a single administrator under the secretary of the interior. From the sale of guaranteed bonds it could make 90 percent building loans for periods not exceeding 60 years at a rate of interest of one-half percent more than the prevailing federal rate, which was then 2½ percent. In addition, annual contributions were to be made to service the debt and generally reduce rents to the level necessary to cover only actual operating costs. Eligible families were defined as those whose total income did not exceed five times the rental, or six times if they had three or more minor dependents. Each unit built had to be matched by the demolition of a slum in the same locality, though this could be deferred during a housing shortage. The cost of dwellings (excluding land and demolition) was limited to $1250 a room and $5000 a unit in cities of over half a million. Power of condemnation remained with the local authorities, which also were to take over completed projects. Beyond the actual housing of the poor, certain requirements for open space or playgrounds could be made mandatory if they were necessary for the safety or health of children. No state was to receive more than one-tenth of the authority's funding.

The differences between the Public Works Administration, supported by influential members of the National Public Housing Conference, and their opponents within the housing movement had centered largely on means. The ends were also open to question. Under an amendment to the original bill proposed by Senator David Walsh, who had in the earlier years chaired its commi-

tee hearings, the aim of public housing was restricted from generally providing low-rental housing to the rehousing of slum tenants. However, his attempt to have the income requirements of
recipient families lowered to meet the act's definition of belong-
ing to the "lowest" income group[44] failed in that the program
both eliminated from its benefits the very poor and favored the
established working class.

At the same time there was a renewed shortage of even slum accommodation. Defining low-rental units as those renting for $40
monthly or less (at a time when the city median weekly wage was
about $20 a week), a Manhattan survey counted 267,850 in this
price range, that is, roughly one-half of the borough's housing
stock. Of these it is likely that a further one-half made up most of
the 130,000 or so dwellings that the 1940 census found to be in
need of either major repairs or lacking adequate plumbing facilities. Nevertheless, from a high of 20 percent in old-law tenements
in 1933,[45] the vacancy rate in low-rental units had dropped to 3.1
percent by 1939. Of these it was found that one-third were located
on the top floors of walk-up tenements, and one-half were considered to be substandard.[46]

The new shortage had various explanations: the depression had
drastically reduced new construction; unemployment had forced
families down the housing scale instead of up; households were
undoubling; the postponement of marriages had been followed
by a boom; and there was a large influx of blacks from the South
and the West Indies, so that in Harlem the vacancy rate was 1.1
percent. The problem there, Charles Abrams reported, was not
structural deficiency but segregation, high rents, low incomes,
and overcrowding.[47] In other words, an increase of families of
a smaller size, the lack of relative purchasing capability, and
racial discrimination were refilling existing slums and adding
new ones.

In the city at large the estimated number of substandard dwellings was somewhere over half a million.[48] Included in the calculation of the overall housing need by the Citizens' Housing Council (the State Division of Housing later arrived at a similar figure) was the effect of the filtering process whereby as housing aged or was superseded and made obsolescent, its rental value dropped, and it thus became available to lower-income families. Believing that the prevailing system of fixed-interest repayments forced owners to cut back on maintenance just as their buildings deteriorated and so encouraged the formation of slums, it recommended the amortization of mortgages so that declining interest payments could be accompanied by the reduction of rents (though later practice showed that owners ignored such issues in determining their annual profits). Yet even with some filtering, which it considered more theoretical than actual, an annual program of 29,000 public housing units was still required over a period of twenty years. At $5000 a unit for building construction, the cost of the slum replacement program would be $2.9 billion. With its initial allocation of $500 million increased by a further appropriation of $300 million, the United States Housing Authority allocated $80 million to New York State, of which New York City received $53 million. It was obvious that with the act's proviso of a maximum one-tenth for each state, the city's housing need was too great to be significantly remedied. The "only feasible method of undertaking a long range housing program," reported a city council committee, "is to regard housing as a city function, subject to the same budgetary requirements as any other city departmental service."[49]

At the beginning of 1938, to supplement federal financing, Mayor LaGuardia proposed a scheme whereby the city could allocate $500,000 to pay interest on a $16 million issue of city Housing Authority bonds. Then as the program got under way, the interest fund would be increased to approximately 0.5 percent of the city budget. To raise the initial capital, LaGuardia asked for a new occupancy tax, which came into effect that summer with a charge of from one to six dollars annually on all rented business premises.

At the same time the legislature also passed a bill permitting state, city, and financial institutions to invest funds in local housing authorities, so enabling them to raise their 10 percent share of the cost of federal housing projects; and approved a consitutional amendment permitting state and city loans to pay for slum clearance and low-rent housing by public housing authorities and limited-dividend corporations which was ratified in the next election. The following year the State Housing Law was superseded by the Public Housing Law of 1939 which authorized the state to borrow money ($300 million by 1946), of which New York City could receive two-thirds, and to pay annual subsidies to be matched by municipalities, largely in the form of tax exemptions.[50] It also permitted municipalities to incur a special indebtedness of up to 2 percent of their assessment of taxable property (approximately $325 million) to meet their additional obligations. The legislation and financing to permit a broad public housing program was now in effect at all three levels of government.

By this time New York's group of housing specialists had fallen apart. The conflict had erupted over LaGuardia's ban on the city's Housing Authority personnel participating in "star gazing" conferences with the new United States Housing Authority administrator Straus.[51] Seemingly incensed by the appointment of Straus rather than a protégé of Ickes whom he supported, LaGuardia acted petulantly, calling Charles Abrams, the Housing Authority counsel who had resigned in protest, a "pettifogging lawyer."[52] Post quit a few days later. LaGuardia immediately swore in his own secretary as chairman of the Housing Authority. "You haven't the power to name the chairman, Mr. Mayor," he was reminded by journalists. "They'd better elect him or there will be a new board," he retorted.[53] A statement of support for LaGuardia ("the white hope of the American housing struggle")[54] from the National Public Housing Conference, written by Helen Alfred, was immediately disavowed by Mary Simkhovitch and followed by the resignation of two of its directors. So the era of Langdon Post came to an end with his subsequent departure to the West Coast office of the United States Housing Authority. The age of public housing had officially begun.

15

Promise and Reality

In the few years remaining before World War II, 2941 public housing units were built in Manhattan.[1] A combined development of 24 six-story buildings financed through the federal and city housing authorities formed Vladeck Houses on the Lower East Side, and a group of six-, ten-, and 11-story buildings made up the federal project of East River Houses in East Harlem. In Brooklyn a similar mix of low- and high-rise buildings at Fort Greene Houses inaugurated the state housing program. Housing reformers were exultant when results quickly conformed to middle-class expectations. Brochures showed happy children in playgrounds, healthy teenagers at sports, proud adults attending social functions, as well as aseptic clinics and bright clean apartments. "Managers reported—with amazement—that they could see the difference in the children after a few months of living in the homes," declared the veteran housing specialist Elizabeth Wood some years later. "School teachers reported it, police officers reported it. We gathered statistics to prove it—statistics which weren't very scientific, I'm afraid, but which recorded the things we saw with our own eyes and felt with assuredness."[2] In the words of the wife of a $20-a-week stevedore when asked what she thought of her new public housing unit by a *Fortune* correspondent in 1940, it was "Glory to God, and it's heaven."[3]

That year, claiming that public housing was no longer an issue for reformers but "a big business proposition,"[4] LaGuardia replaced Post's successor by Gerard Swope, who had just retired from the presidency of the General Electric Company. In the years preceding the American entry into World War II, when Swope was called to Washington, the Housing Authority completed twelve projects containing 13,000 families, of which 88 percent were white, including 38 percent immigrants, and 12 percent were black. Confirming the overall success of the program, only $238 from a revenue of $3 million was reported lost because of rent delinquencies.[5]

The remaining wartime years permitted two projects to be completed for military use and sites to be acquired and plans drawn for eight further city projects that committed all allocated federal, state, and city funds. Presaging the future, LaGuardia also invited a black to serve on the Housing Authority board, and the appointment of Frank Crosswaith, organizer for the International Ladies' Garment Workers Union, was publicly announced to tremendous applause at a mass civil rights meeting in Madison Square Garden.

During this period, while the public housing program was suspended, nearly one million special units were constructed under the Lanham Act and related legislation, but, influenced by the real estate lobby, amendments required these to be sold or demolished within two years of the end of the emergency. The Congress also reintroduced rent controls. Not considered a center of essential industry, New York was at first excluded from its provisions; the city's middle-income apartment vacancy rate was comparatively high, and its workers were being drawn to out-of-town wartime jobs. However, as the suspension of nonessential building began to take effect, the situation drastically changed. Government permission was required for all construction projects; the War Production Board issued permits in accordance with the program of the National Housing Agency, which consolidated the functions of sixteen federal agencies including the United States Housing Authority (now called the Federal Public Housing Authority and later the Public Housing Administration). New housing construction was restricted to areas lacking facilities for wartime needs. In Manhattan, it fell from approximately 5000 units in 1941 to 1000 in 1942 and to zero in 1943—where it stayed.[6] Though there was no evidence of rent profiteering, according to the federal Bureau of Labor Statistics, housing availability fell to an all-time low.[7] Political pressures proved irresistible. With the rents of old-law tenements stabilized by a 1938 state enactment, subsequently extended annually, that prohibited any increase unless the accommodation was upgraded to the standards required by the Multiple Dwelling Law, and with growing vacancies on the Lower East Side and in Harlem, the outcry came mainly from the middle-income group, which found itself threatened with new annual fall leases with rent increases of up to 20 percent.[8] On November 1, 1943, the Office of Price Controls froze rents at their springtime level. A generation later, rent control remained a major civic issue.

By the end of the war, in common with the rest of the country, the city had an acute housing shortage. There were numerous causes for this: building had come to a halt; high prices and labor difficulties made new building uneconomic; and there was a rise in population and marriages. The problem was national. In 1946 it was estimated that 1.2 million couples were doubled up, 1.6 million veterans were returning to reestablish their housholds, and a further 1.3 million marriages would take place by the end of the year.[9] The government response to this crisis, after an initial attempt to control production, was to assume that private enterprise would respond to its market opportunities. This it did with over a million dwelling starts annually from 1949 on; but as more than three-quarters of these were single-family dwellings, they gave little direct aid to the urban homeless and poor.

The housing shortage affected both low- and middle-income groups alike. In the New York press, stories abounded on the tribulations of returning veterans. "Sweetest girl ever will marry lucky Navy lieutenant commander next month if he can find a furnished place to start housekeeping. Can you help?" ran one typical ad.[10] Others were even harder pressed. After fifteen months of living in the overcrowded apartments of their parents, disabled veteran William Sosa and his wife set their belongings and their five-month-old son in his crib outside the Housing Authority Vacancy Listing Bureau and demanded help. "We are trying to help," commented an official, "but we have to give preference to . . . those who have no relatives whatsoever to go to."[11]

Even before taking over from LaGuardia, who resigned at the end of 1945 after twelve years in office, the new mayor, William O'Dwyer, had appointed an Emergency Committee on Housing under the chairmanship of Robert Moses. Then fifty-seven years old and city park commissioner since 1934 (when he had been defeated as Republican candidate for governor by Herbert Lehman), Moses was an outstanding administrator and a highly controversial personality. Son of a prosperous merchant and a graduate of Yale, Oxford, and Columbia universities, he was both widely admired for his achievements and disliked, especially later, for his autocratic ways. Probably his greatest victory over those who opposed him through his many decades of influence was when he withstood President Roosevelt's attempt to force LaGuardia to fire him by getting Ickes to withhold Public Works Administration funds from New York on the grounds that Moses could not be both a city official and and chairman of the Triborough Bridge Authority (a similar combination of appointments also held by Langdon Post, who had been both tenement house commissioner and chairman of the Housing Authority).

The Moses housing committee report recommended a two-part program for supplying 127,000 permanent dwellings over the following three years plus 43,300 emergency units. These were to include 5000 two-family Quonset huts, the conversion of one- and two-family houses, summer resort bungalows, and army camps, the rehabilitation of boarded-up tenements, and the use of demountable houses and trailers.[12] Under the state's Emergency Housing Act passed at the beginning of 1946, 3720 units were made available to the city, Of the 149 that were supplied in Manhattan, 113 were in two converted schools, and 36 in two renovated tenements.[13] Only 1000 apartments were obtained through conversion of family houses, as costs proved prohibitive. The idea of winterizing resort bungalows failed because owners could earn more during the summer months than under all-year-round rent control. The federal government supplied 8600 units through the Housing Authority, the first Quonset hut being delivered in the wintry dawn by a Normandy invasion veteran landing craft with its wartime skipper and erected on a windswept sandy beach near Canarsie Pier in Brooklyn.

The projected permanent program included 54,000 units through private enterprise, 16,000 in limited dividend projects, and 57,000 units of public housing. A previous estimate by the State Division of Housing had set the city's housing need at 682,000 (to provide a 5 percent vacancy rate and eliminate substandard buildings),[14] while according to the City Planning Commission there was an overall requirement for a million units by 1970, a figure denied by Moses, who added that anyway it was "beyond our means" and "far too large to serve as the basis for any realistic program"[15] (though 22 years later about 850,000 units had been completed, and the city still suffered from a housing shortage).[16] By the end of 1947, however, only a fraction of the projected target had been built, the vacancy rate was nil, and at least 150,000 families were split or doubled up.[17]

The city's housing program assumed the same division of responsibility that had evolved in the years between the wars. The rich would buy their housing on the open market; the middle class would have their full burden of mortgage interest, profit making, and property taxation reduced; and the poor would be provided with suitable accommodation at a rent they could afford. The desirability of building public housing for those unable to be served by private enterprise had been reaffirmed by the congressional inquiry into postwar economic programs initiated in 1943. The federal government, observed the Senate subcommittee on Housing and Urban Redevelopment under the chairmanship of Robert Taft, "has an interest in seeing that minimum standards of housing, food and health services are available for all members of the community."[18] Unfortunately, some of Taft's colleagues did not share his concern. The 1946 Wagner-Ellender-Taft bill, which sandwiched provision for half a million public housing units between programs desired by the housing industry, was defeated in the House committee and was not reintroduced the following year. In 1948, in an attempt to nullify Taft's influence, a new congressional committee was arranged under the chairmanship of Senator Joseph McCarthy, who, agreeing with the National Association of Real Estate Boards that public housing was "the spearhead of the Communist front,"[19] refused to sign the report that once again advocated it.

Harry Truman's unexpected victory at the polls and the return of a Democratic Congress made the passage of the Housing Act of 1949 inevitable. Everyone, the President declared, had the right to expect "a fair deal." In housing this was "a decent home and a suitable living environment for every American family."[20] The four years of feuding reached a climax on the House floor when eighty-three-year-old Adolph Sabath from Illinois traded punches with sixty-nine-year-old Eugene Cox from Georgia. Be a "Fanatic for Freedom," urged the real estate magazine *Headlines*.[21] The administration had asked for 1,050,000 public housing units over seven years. It got authorization for 810,000 over six years. The following summer the advent of the Korean War caused Truman to cut back on the program to conserve essential materials and curb inflationary tendencies; the Republican victory of President Dwight Eisenhower at the next election reduced it to 35,000 for 1954. Twenty years of agitation faltered to a halt as McCarthy's assault on civil liberties exhausted liberal energies. Further setbacks to the cause of public housing were the ill health and retirement of Senator Wagner and the loss of widespread support from a middle-class population that was being adequately catered to by a house-building boom. But a major factor in the lack of dedicated advocacy was the reformers' own loss of belief.

Up to the early years of the 1950s, public housing in New York had been considered a success. Crime within projects was virtually nonexistent, their racial mix provided an appropriate melting pot, and even a banking study thought their financial operation was sound. "What New York City would be today without this twenty-year program can hardly be imagined," editorialized the *New York Times* in 1955. "It has demonstrated what can be."[22] But both intrinsic and external pressures were already undermining its achievements.

Physically, public housing was basically similar in form and character to private developments. Admittedly, closet doors were omitted in the belief that this might encourage tidiness and vandal-resistant materials were used instead of doorkeepers, but these differences were more petty than consequential or derived from suppositions about different class behavior. Given their position on the rental scale, public housing projects were what one might expect compared to other, more expensive accommodation. When Lewis Mumford coined the term "prefabricated blight,"[23] he was not referring to public housing but to Metropolitan Life's Stuyvesant Town, which rented at twice the amount charged by the Housing Authority. Completed in 1947 along the East River above Fourteenth Street, the project housed 24,000 people at 393 per acre, a density that Robert Moses claimed was "less than that of the finest hotels and apartments on Park and Fifth Avenues"[22] and Mumford called "that of a slum."[25]

Federal government policy had been against high densities from the beginning, and Straus had gently chided LaGuardia during the ground-breaking ceremonies at East River Houses, which included buildings up to eleven stories tall and had an estimated density of 354 to the acre: "You must beware lest you overcrowd human beings in even such a wonderful project as this."[26] It was not that public housing was incontestably overdense but that its occupants were ill suited to cope with that way of life. Commenting on the problems of living in tall buildings after studying a number of projects including Jacob Riis Houses on the Lower East Side, an anthropologist reported in 1952 that "the elevator-apartment is a relatively ineffective instrument for achieving many of the aims of public housing, insofar as they are related to families with children."[27] Furthermore, while Mumford continued to argue that high densities would create the superslums of the future, Herbert Stichman, the state housing commissioner, condemned the policy of rebuilding the slums as economic ghettoes, such segregation being "at odds with American ideals of social progress, breeding, as it must, class division and frustration."[28] (However, Mumford approved of this scale of renewal, while Stichman claimed that Americans took to high-rise buildings like the Swiss did to mountaineering.)

So long as the poor had prized the work-and-make-good ethic of the promised land, public housing had been a staging post to a better existence. However, when prosperity returned with the war and its aftermath and the average low-income worker was elevated to the ranks of the middle class, public housing became the gathering place for the dropouts from the American way of life. The Housing Act of 1949 set the maximum rent in public housing to be at least 20 percent below its marketplace equivalent. When this higher-rental capacity was reached, public housing tenants were required to leave. Though immediately after the war the state had raised permissible income levels to accommodate homeless veterans, at the beginning of 1949 the Housing Authority began eviction proceedings against 600 families whose annual income was $5000 or more when the allowable maximum was $3600. Another 2000 families were listed as having incomes above this amount, which was double that permitted for applicants.[29] In determining the selection of their replacements, the Housing Act of 1949 gave preference to families displaced by slum clearance projects and prevented discrimination against those on welfare. By the end of 1952 the Housing Authority's unarmed watchman service was being supplemented by special police officers in areas subject to increasing crime and vandalism.

As the earlier poor had succumbed to bad light, air, and sanitation, which were to a lesser extent shared and yet overcome by the middle class, so disadvantaged project families did not have the capacity to surmount the problems of mass living. Children, not brought up with respect for manners and property, and out of sight of parental control, could wreak havoc on unattended spaces. Corridors, elevators, halls, gardens, playgrounds—the communal areas normally maintained by middle-class apartment dwellers who expected and respected well-kept surroundings—became a no-man's-land between the housing administration and those who did not share its values. Even the living unit itself, which differed little from a middle-class apartment, seemed to those without the means for a fuller life the constraining walls of a boxed-in existence. Becoming the repository of the chronic poor, successful large-scale redevelopment institutionalized poverty.

To its advocates, public housing had been the answer not only to the physical slum but also to what were seen as its social consequences. Earlier reformers had termed it the tenement-house rot. Although would-be scientific investigators like James Ford had cautioned that housing conditions were only one causative factor in the ill effects of slums, other professionals had brushed aside such moderation. "Do we desire to have less prisons; do we desire to have less hospitals; do we desire to have less crime?" asked Senator Wagner during a debate on his 1936 bill. "Should we not . . . go right to the root of the matter, where the crime and disease are bred, and remove the cause?"[30]

Others had subsequently perceived that the relationships between physical and social circumstances were far more tenuous than previously imagined. The belief, wrote John Dean in 1949, is "Remove the slums and you remove the social ills! But it would be just as illogical to say that the ills of slum areas are caused not by substandard housing conditions, but by the absence of telephone service, which also correlates with indexes of social disorder."[31] Simply "to tear down old houses and build new, safe and sanitary ones," observed Anthony Wallace three years later, will not automatically "reduce death rates, morbidity rates, unemployment, divorce, desertion, illiteracy, juvenile and female employment, sex offences, gambling, family size, poverty, illegitimacy, delinquency, crime, venereal diseases, alcoholism, prostitution, suicide, mental disease, and . . . increase marriage rates, birth rates, educational levels, telephone service, and so on ad infinitum."[32] *Fortune* magazine put it more graphically: " 'Once upon a time,' says a close student of New York's slums, 'we thought that if we could only get our problem families out of those dreadful slums, then papa would stop taking dope, mama would stop chasing around, and Junior would stop carrying a knife. Well, we've got them in nice new apartments with modern kitchens and a recreation center. And they're the same bunch of bastards they always were.' "[33]

Many of these tenants were nonwhite Americans. Catering to the aspirations of young parents looking for a suitable environment in which to bring up children within their income capabilities and encouraged by government policies, builders had begun to sprawl single-family houses around cities in what became the phenomenon of suburban growth. By the early 1950s the Long Island counties adjoining New York were adding to their population by roughly 100,000 a year. This siphoning off of middle-class families was a major factor in reducing Manhattan's white population by over 350,000 during the decade. In the same period about 100,000 Puerto Ricans crowded into the borough. Overpopulation and economic depression coupled with cheap airline access had caused a mass immigration from the island. Together with the continuing drift of blacks from the South, these swelled the numbers of poor families in need of a place in which to live. By the middle of the decade over one-third of the Housing Authority's tenants were black.

Studying those in St. Nicholas Houses in Harlem, Elizabeth Wood, who had been with the Chicago Housing Authority, found that one out of every fourteen families was, in social work parlance, "seriously damaged."[34] Sixty-one families had parent problems of child neglect, alcoholism, drugs and sexual promiscuity; 30 families had problem children. Of course, there were also over 1400 normal families, but the antisocial behavior of the few easily undermined the lives of the many.

The laudatory articles of earlier years gave way to disillusionment. Writing on "The new ghettoes," Harrison Salisbury described his visit to Fort Greene Houses (where one-third of the families were on relief) to typify the failure of public housing: "The same shoddy shiftlessness, the broken windows, the missing light bulbs, the plaster cracking from the walls, the pilfered hardware, the cold, drafty corridors, the doors on sagging hinges, the acid smell of sweat and cabbage, the ragged children, the plaintive women, the playgrounds that are seas of muddy clay, the bruised and battered trees, the ragged clumps of grass, the planned absence of art, beauty or taste, the gigantic masses of brick, of concrete, of asphalt, the inhuman genius with which our know-how has been perverted to create human cesspools."[35]

This bitterness reflected the prevailing disquiet over the slowness of achieving social equality in the years when President Eisenhower had to call out the military to protect the civil rights of black students in Little Rock schools. It also gave confirming evidence to both those who blamed the establishment and those who expected nothing better from minority groups. This conflict of judgment also existed in the black community, so that when a couple of years later author James Baldwin described Metropolitan Life's limited-dividend Riverton Houses in Harlem in much the same terms that Salisbury had used, there was a shocked denial from the ten-year resident chairman of its tenants' association who asserted that its occupants were normal people "cut from the same fabric of the American community as others."[36]

Earlier, reacting to this spate of adverse criticism, the city administrator in 1957 had been asked to report on the Housing Authority's organization and management.[37] First commending its achievement of providing decent shelter at low rents to needy families regardless of race or creed in a financially responsible manner, he then listed its shortcomings: its buildings were inadequately maintained and consequently deteriorating; tenant complaints were not being taken seriously; problem families were being allowed in and not given social care; and as the needs of public housing tenants changed (with the increase in large families and single elderly persons), its facilities were not being adjusted to accommodate them. The problems, the report declared, were due to a confused managerial bureaucracy and a lack of social purpose. The first step in their solution came in 1958 when the authority's unpaid part-time board members were replaced by two full-time officials under a chairman more amenable to the Wagner administration. Its other problems were more complex.

The major issues that Elizabeth Wood had underscored were the admission of problem families, the eviction of those who prospered, and the racial stratification that accompanied poverty. To counter these problems, the Housing Authority raised its maximum income limits and later set up its own department of social services rather than relying entirely on outside agencies. It furthermore tried to maintain racial balance by using a quota system in its selection of applicants, a policy that was quickly condemned as discriminatory.

But as long as society denied its unequivocal responsibility for ensuring shelter to all its members regardless of their way of life; or public housing remained a separate building program for those with low incomes, thus effectively categorizing them; or the standard of housing they were provided was below that made normal by the majority; or administrative policies, however enlightened, assumed that persons could forfeit their right to decent housing by behavior otherwise not punishable by law: that is, as long as public housing was viewed in any way as a withdrawable charity, the Housing Authority's efforts alleviated conditions rather than answered them.

Though public housing was evidently physically superior to private slums and the city returned to more enlightened social policies after the 1950s, adverse experiences across the nation continued to feed the widespread antipathy of the middle class. "Why isn't the program popular?" mused Catherine Bauer in 1957, twenty years after she had fought for its adoption. "Life in the usual public housing project just is not the way most American families want to live."[38] Nevertheless, by the end of the next decade in New York City $1.7 billion in federal and state funds had supplied more than 120,000 apartments for half a million persons while another half a million persons waited their turn to move in.[39]

The New Poor

For nineteenth-century reformers, the definition of poverty was comparatively simple; those of the twentieth century were less confident. The basic requirements of shelter, food, and clothing no longer seemed to fit a society that owned tens of millions of automobiles, telephones, and radios and went to the movies once a week. Another way of looking at the definition of need was that a family deserved a way of life that was commensurate with prevailing standards. Those who could not reach this general ideal through no fault of their own seemed to merit some form of communal aid. This attitude was reinforced by the effect of two world wars that produced housing shortages unrelated to the historical needs of the poor. Veteran families were generally not intrinsically poor, though, being young, they were often at the lower end of the middle-income group. For many of them a reluctance or even inability to pay the proportionally high cost of accommodation was tempered by the expectation of a higher standard of living to come.

Assuming a diminishing influx of poor immigrants, one therefore could argue that public housing was a temporary requirement that would largely disappear as the economy boomed. The need in that case was not for great numbers of dwellings of the lowest possible quality that would quickly become inadequate but for medium-quality housing that could absorb the upcoming expanding middle class. The social corollary was equally plausible. Unlike the old countries of Europe, the United States was an ostensibly classless society. Public housing isolated the poor; classless (middle-class) housing embraced them. Support the living standards of decent families, and you provided the bulwark of democracy.

Appointed construction coordinator at the beginning of 1946, Robert Moses pushed for the creation of the sort of socially homogeneous city that reflected the aspirations of many Americans. His authoritarian domination lasted through the 1950s, to be finally thwarted by those he ignored—the minority groups who crowded into the city and failed to be assimilated into the established way of life. In 1940 the city had contained just over 500,000 blacks and Puerto Ricans; by 1950 this number had nearly doubled; in 1960 it was over 1,500,000. One reaction to this population trend was to try to neutralize it by favoring the dominance of the majority class.

Nineteenth-century builders had erected dwellings for the poor by keeping their product at a price that was affordable and a cost that permitted a profit. When legislated standards made this impossible, the poor were excluded from the purchase of new housing. The subsequent rise in standards was not the result of government enactment but occurred through the marketing practices of free enterprise. Seeking custom, new amenities were offered which made otherwise sound buildings obsolete. At the same time the relative increase in land and building costs further limited the group that could afford what was being offered.

One of the proposals for a countersaving was to encourage the plentiful supply of low-interest mortgage money such as that which opened up the suburbs to middle-class families. Another was property tax exemption, which was first used to stimulate medium-rental apartment building and to encourage middle-class

cooperatives to replace slums. In *The New Day in Housing,* Louis
Pink had cited the financial resources of the five largest insurance
companies as $6.5 billion.[1] The earlier law that had permitted the
Metropolitan Life project in Long Island City had expired in the
1920s but in 1938, as state superintendent of insurance, a position
to which he was appointed after serving on the New York City
Housing Authority, Pink supported a new bill that allowed insurance companies to invest up to 10 percent of their assets in low-
or moderate-rental housing (although it failed to specify any
maximum rent levels). The outcome was another Metropolitan
Life development, Parkchester in the Bronx, with over 12,000
apartments on 129 acres of vacant land that, because they did not
conform to limited dividend requirements, did not qualify for tax
exemption and averaged $14 a room. When other projects failed to
materialize, a bill formulated by the Merchants' Association in
1941 gave urban redevelopment corporations the right of condemnation after acquiring 51 percent of the area and assessed
value of land assembled by private transaction. Further compro-
mises during the following year climaxed in the amended Redevelopment Companies Law passed in 1943, by which time the
original 10 year tax exemption and 5 percent return had been
modified to a 25-year tax exemption and a more liberally calculated 6 percent return (based on the total project cost rather than
on the equity investment). Negotiated by Moses, other concessions made the city responsible for condemning the land and
selling it at cost and dropped the requirement that the redevelopment agency find alternative accommodation for those displaced.
Urged on by LaGuardia and the promise of another large Metropolitan Life project, Governor Thomas Dewey signed the bill with some
misgivings, and fifteen days later in a radio broadcast the mayor
announced the impending construction of Stuyvesant Town.

"East Side 'Suburb in City' To House 30,000 After War," head-lined the *New York Times*.[2] The euphoria was short-lived. Coming out of a public hearing before the City Planning Commission, Metropolitan Life's chairman Frederick Ecker announced: "Negroes and whites don't mix.... If we brought them into this development ... it would depress all the surrounding property."[3] The city council reacted with an antidiscrimination law prohibiting tax exemption for restricted housing, though not being retroactive, it did not apply to Stuyvesant Town. "If you don't want this contract," Moses had threatened the Board of Estimate, "I can assure you that it will be the last opportunity we'll have to attract private capital. It will mark the death knell of slum clearance by private enterprise."[4] With his support, Metropolitan Life later announced another project in Harlem (Riverton Houses, invoking an equal but separate policy), but three black veterans sued the insurance company for violation of their consitutional rights. Though their suit was turned down by the lower courts and the court of appeals and turned back by the U. S. Supreme Court, the dispute lasted until the end of the decade and, together with Metropolitan Life's difficulty in obtaining rent increases, discouraged further private limited-dividend housing.

When the Housing Authority proposed to build its own housing for this income group, however, Moses opposed it on the grounds that private enterprise could fulfill this need. The plan for building so-called moderate-rental garden apartments on vacant peripheral land had been worked out by Charles Abrams, Maxwell Tretter, who was the executive director of the Housing Authority, and Nathan Straus, under whose chairmanship of a group of representatives from veteran, labor, and civic organizations it was announced in mid-1946.

With the return of the veterans after the war, the housing situation in New York was critical. The vacancy rate in private housing had dropped to less than 0.1 percent;[5] during 1946 there were more units demolished than built;[6] and the postwar federal housing bill was stalled in the Congress. In his report to the mayor-elect, Moses had proposed that the federal law then under review be extended to permit housing at $10 a room monthly for the upper section of the lowest-income group. The Housing Authority proposed that it build housing with rents similar to those in limited-dividend developments.

The proposal came at a time when Mayor William O'Dwyer was trying to oust the Housing Authority's unpaid wartime chairman, Edmond Butler, a public-spirited lawyer (and son of the tenement house commissioner of the first decade) and to replace him by his own appointee, ostensibly someone more capable of carrying out large-scale construction. In the meantime the plan for moderate-income housing went unheeded until in mid-1947, after state enabling legislation, Butler was replaced by Thomas Farrell, an ex-army general and an engineer of wide experience and responsibility from the New York State Department of Public Works.

Although Tretter was also forced to resign (in the reshuffle Mary Simkhovitch, then eighty years old, was subsequently dropped after serving fourteen years as vice-chairman), the plan was fostered by Abrams through the column he wrote for the *New York Post*. Continuing to assert that the housing shortage would soon be overcome by private enterprise, Moses gave way and proposed that a maximum of 4600 moderate-income units be built at a cost of $56 million, a sum that could be raised by one of the various taxes on entertainment, telephones, patent medicines, tobacco, or vending machines, permitted by the Public Housing Law. When the adequacy of this program was questioned, Moses attacked his critics in his usual style: "I have been asked to reply to Councilman Stanley Isaacs"—a respected reformer on the city council who some years earlier, when he was Manhattan borough president, had continued to employ a declared member of the Communist party as a matter of principle. "My advice to him is to give up Karl and study Harpo Marx. He will get more sound advice out of *Horsefeathers* than out of *Das Kapital*."[7]

However, at the beginning of 1948, a week after Straus had again pressed for moderate-income housing over the radio station he owned, O'Dwyer, at a dinner sponsored by city groups critical of his tardiness, unexpectedly announced that he would accept a Housing Authority recommendation to use almost all of the approximately $325 million credit permitted by the prewar constitutional amendment to provide "unsubsidized" housing. Later details set the program as 6000 units to rent at $12.50 a room monthly with their operating costs underwritten by the city; and 17,000 units renting at $15-$16 to be self-supporting except for tax exemption.[8]

The aim was to provide housing for veterans at a price they could afford, but as over 12 million men had served in the American armed forces, the issue was not housing veterans but which veterans were to be housed. The raising of the city's debt limit by 2 percent of its property assessment had been specifically approved for clearing the slums and providing low-rental housing. While agreeing that there were over half a million slums to be cleared, the Housing Authority argued that the severe housing shortage made demolition impractical and minimum subsidization would make the most of its limited resources. It furthermore cited a survey to show that a majority of veteran families could afford to pay rents higher than the $8.50 a room monthly that was to be charged in the 26,000 public housing units to be built using state and city subsidies.[9]

The outcome was for the city to subsidize incomes up to $4500 a year when $3450 was considered sufficient for a modest but adequate way of life.[10] The issue, publicized by a mass meeting of

1000 persons in Queens, was why some nonpoor should be afforded favored treatment. In response a judge declared that anyone earning less than $4500 was poor. Dismissing a taxpayer's suit against the mayor's program, the court upheld the definition in the Public Housing Act that "families of low income . . . are those who cannot afford to pay enough to cause private enterprise to build a sufficient supply of adequate dwellings."[11] In this interpretation a person was poor if he could not induce manufacturers to cater to his basic needs. Of course, cheaper housing existed, but it was already occupied; the newcomer was being offered luxury goods at a price that was more than he was prepared to pay. His income level was therefore low relative to what private enterprise was offering—not to the cost of basic construction or to that of other necessities such as standard clothing or food. By permitting moderate-income families to keep their general purchasing capability and relating their accustomed expenditures on housing directly to what was then being marketed, the city made its case for subsidy notwithstanding the ability of these families to pay the $20 or so saved monthly through tax exemption (the figure given by its critics)[12] by cutting down on their other purchases. The city might have established the principle that it was responsible for housing any of its citizens when private enterprise declined to do so. It obscured this concept by pretending that it was doing so because they were poor.

The no-cash subsidy program, as it became known, initially produced over 21,000 units (none of the cheaper units ever received city subsidies to underwrite their running costs) mainly on vacant land, thus maximizing the saving in tax exemption, which was based on the difference between pre-and postdevelopment assessments. Another nearly 5000 similar units built during the rest of the decade completed its use of $300 million of its housing credit. The severe housing shortage had ostensibly made it impracticable to house moderate-income families on cleared slum sites. Shortly afterward, however, another program dispossessed the poor to make way for the established middle class.

Beside its public housing provision, the Housing Act of 1949 allocated $1.5 billion over five years for a slum clearance and redevelopment program known as Title I. This section of the act permitted land assembled by a municipality to be sold at a loss to a private developer, the difference being shared two-thirds to one-third by federal and local governments. At the end of that year, Moses added yet another title to his activities, that of chairman of the Committee on Slum Clearance Plans. Many housing reformers assumed that slum clearance meant low-rental housing replacement and was an extension of the public housing program. Moses thought otherwise. Years later in his autobiography, entitled *Public Works: A Dangerous Trade*, he observed: "Title I was never designed to produce housing for people of low income. The cities failed to understand that Title I aimed solely at the elimination of the slums and substandard areas."[13] In the ten years of the 1950s, Moses authorized the demolition of roughly 26,000 dwellings renting at less than $10 a room monthly and the erection of 28,000 dwellings renting at $25 up. In other words, he evicted the poor and replaced them with middle-class families. He also initiated Lincoln Center, the Coliseum, a new campus for Pratt Institute, new facilities for Fordham, Long Island, and New York universities and Brooklyn Hospital, three schools, three playgrounds, parking garages, an office building, and nine commercial buildings.[14]

In Manhattan roughly 18,000 housing units were built displacing an equal number of original tenant families.[15] The Housing Authority also built a similar number of low-rental units during the same period; but while the public housing program was theoretically rehousing the poor that it displaced (though a study showed that only one-third moved into the new housing after it was built),[16] the urban renewal program was not. Instead, the poor were being evicted from their homes to add to the overcrowding of other low-income areas. "There is a limit to the amount of disrupting of city life which can be tolerated at one time," the mayor had earlier reported. Relocation was a "new and very difficult obstacle."[17] Moses treated it as a necessary evil for the greater good. It was just unfortunate that it was the underprivileged who had to suffer so that the living conditions of the city as a whole could be improved.

The effect of slum clearance on its inhabitants had been previously studied. When 386, mostly Italian, families had been forced to leave the old "Lung Block" immortalized by Veiller to make way for Knickerbocker Village, four-fifths of them moved into other nearby tenements.[18] At Stuyvesant Town a survey showed that roughly three-quarters of the 3000 displaced families would move into other slums.[19] "If, each time a slum is demolished, the vast majority of the dwellers there are driven into other substandard housing, either new slums are created or old ones made worse,"[20] commented the Community Service Society of New York. With a minimal vacancy rate the problem was critical. By the mid-1950s there were two state and three city agencies involved with tenant relocation, and 50,000 households had been dislocated in Manhattan, overwhelmingly by public programs.[21] Those most affected were the incoming nonwhite groups, who often settled directly in the path of demolition. The solution to their problem was not solved by the $100 maximum compensation provided for under the law by the Housing Authority or even by the up to $500 allowed by the Board of Estimate for Title I evictees, though these were more than that given by private enterprise. Pushed out of the existing slums, they formed new ones. Thus, notwithstanding the new housing built, as many substandard units existed at the end of the decade as there had been at the beginning.[22]

In mid-1957 when the federal Housing and Home Finance Agency administrator complained that "the agency has had more trouble with Mr. Robert Moses than with any other single individual in all the cities of the United States. ... [He] is inflexibly bent on following his own course, whatever may be the outcome,"[23] the *New York Times* repeated the stock assertion that "there has never been the equal of Bob Moses for getting things done."[24] Even the Capehart investigations of 1954 had left his reputation unmarred. Then, in a national housing scandal investigated by the U. S. Senate Committee on Banking and Currency (which was concerned mainly with the multiple-rental housing program of the previous administration that had provided builders with loans that had exceeded by nearly 15 percent their actual costs), it was revealed that large sums were also being made illegally through Title I projects. One of these was Manhattantown in New York.

While federal rules for Title I projects required the drafting of a development plan and its approval before a developer was found, Moses first selected a developer, collaborated with him in drawing up a plan, and then pushed it through city hall; for as he said, "when it comes to action, reaching even limited objectives in the rough and tumble of American politics calls for more fighting equipment, nerve, guts and endurance than the average bureaucrat ... can muster."[25] During the 1950s he was more than a match for the "smark aleck" "paper planners" he despised, with their "hokum," "bunk," "tripe," and "mumbo-jumbo."[26] In other cities the government relocated the residents, cleared the slums, and invited proposals. In New York the land was discounted to the developer, who assumed responsibility for relocation and demolition. Acquiring profitable slums at a fraction of their market value, the new owners were sometimes in no hurry to proceed.

In 1951 the city had bought six blocks off Central Park West known as Manhattantown for $16 million and sold them to a developer for $3 million. Under examination by the Capehart committee, various questionable procedures were uncovered, including the purchase of the area's appliances by the company secretary's son-in-law, who leased them back for one year at a charge of $115,226 and then sold them back at their original cost. When in 1957 the city was owed over $400,000 in taxes, no building had been done, the land was not yet cleared, and a judge had ruled that some of it could be used as a parking lot, the Committee on Slum Clearance Plans recommended foreclosure.

Manhattantown was bought out by other developers and became Park West Village, but by the end of the decade public approval had turned to animosity. Critical newspaper articles were climaxed by a special issue of the *Nation* entitled "The Shame of New York," which called urban renewal "a program administered from the top, arranged among private business interests, City Hall and Moses . . . in which the people involved have only a token voice."[27] The press attack centered on graft in the dealings of the Committee on Slum Clearance Plans, which was largely under the control of its vice-chairman, Thomas Shanahan, who was both the major fund raiser for the Democratic party and president of a bank that financed Title I developers. Other critics underscored the plight of the poor, who were often black or Puerto Rican. These were joined by professional planners (sometimes incensed by their own conflicts with city hall) who were disillusioned by the social effects of large-scale slum clearance and rebuilding.

As early as 1953 a report to the Eisenhower administration had pointed out the limitations of the Title I program and argued for its incorporation into a broader spectrum of housing policies. "A piecemeal attack on slums simply will not work," its authors wrote: "occasional thrusts at slum pockets in one section of a city will only push slums to other sections unless an effective program exists for attacking the entire problem of urban decay. Programs for slum prevention, for rehabilitation of existing houses and neighborhoods, and for demolition of wornout structures and areas must advance along a broad unified front to accomplish the renewal of our towns and cities."[28] Under the headings of conservation, rehabilitation, and redevelopment, the report stressed small-scale preventive actions to stop blight rather than large-scale bulldozer operations to remove it: the strict enforcement of neighborhood housing and occupancy standards, the lessening of congestion, the reorganization of street and traffic patterns, and the provision of parks and playgrounds. The consequent Republican Housing Act of 1954 permitted government-insured loans for housing in urban renewal areas, contributed to the expense of public works, such as schools, within them, and broadened earlier provisions to cover deteriorating areas as well as slums. It also extended the write-down formula to apply to the purchase and resale of buildings for rehabilitation.

Taking advantage of the offer of federal funds for surveys and preliminary planning, the New York City Housing Authority initiated a study of Manhattan's West Side. Ignored by Moses, who considered the rehabilitation of the area's brownstone housing uneconomic and was anyway against this type of approach, the City Planning Commission was asked to continue the study by Mayor Robert Wagner, the senator's son, who had been elected to the mayoralty in 1953, the year his father died. Limited to the twenty blocks between 87th and 97th streets and Central Park West and Amsterdam Avenue, the West Side Urban Renewal study was completed in 1958. The report, which stressed community participation, found a comprehensive approach both practicable and desirable because the "Promotion of economically and ethnically integrated neighborhoods is not only a proper objective of a publicly-assisted program, but the best means of assuring balanced, healthy and stable development."[29] As approved by the Board of Estimate in 1962, the $180 million project took over designated buildings in the area and used a mixture of federal, state, and city programs to achieve a socially mixed neighborhood in an area that had previously been degenerating into a slum. Notwithstanding later criticism of the lack of private investment and of the large subsidies required to attract middle-class residents, the attempt was unusually successful; and though without the overall visual impact of an architecturally integrated environment, the project illustrated a humane alternative to other extremes of redevelopment.

Responsibility for the implementation of the West Side Urban Renewal project had been given to an interdepartmental Urban Renewal Board under James Felt, the chairman of the City Planning Commission. A real estate broker who had been associated with the Metropolitan Life projects of Stuyvesant Town and Peter Cooper Village, he had more recently been on the New York City Housing Authority and stressed social goals and balanced neighborhoods. Felt was also responsible for the preparation of a master plan that Moses was accused by his critics of blocking because he wanted to retain maneuverability in his freewheeling deals.

In mid-1959, after Mayor Wagner had begun to countermand his orders and Moses in response had pronounced Title I a "dead duck,"[30] the mayor appointed Anthony Panuch, a lawyer and civic organizational authority, to report on the roles of government and private enterprise in the use of public funds. Panuch confronted the two opposing points of view. Moses insisted that it was a fact of life that redevelopment was initiated by private enterprise in the expectation of monetary gain and that the city's role was to encourage and cope with it. The planners argued that it should be through the initiative and under the control of the city administration and that it should fulfill community needs. The report praised both Moses and Felt, while proposing a central board to coordinate their programs, but just before it was released, Moses resigned his four city offices (though he kept three from the state) and accepted the presidency of the upcoming World's Fair.

The first phase of slum clearance had made way for low-rental housing. The second phase under Moses replaced slums with buildings for the established middle class. The need to entice the middle-income group back into the city was stressed in the Panuch report. Previously, Mayor Wagner had observed: "No less than one-fifth of the families in substandard dwellings have annual incomes of more than $5000. Unfortunately, while these families are not eligible for the benefits of low-cost housing, private builders have not produced anywhere near an adequate supply of dwelling units for their needs. This unhappy phenomenon has resulted in driving some of our most valuable citizens out into the suburbs."[31] His citizens' committee on housing duly found that a substantial volume of middle-class housing was essential "to preserve New York City's vitality."[32]

In 1955 another program was enacted to achieve this result. Known as the Mitchell-Lama act, the Limited-Profit Housing Companies Law was, according to its sponsor State Senator MacNeil Mitchell of Manhattan, mainly for "white collar workers in urban areas who do not wish to be public dependents, but who would welcome government aid which helps private enterprise supply their housing needs. These families are the backbone of economic, social and political stability in our nation, and their needs cannot be ignored any longer."[33] The act (while maintaining the pretense that it served those with low incomes) enabled the city to allocate part of its housing indebtedness to middle-income housing and also provided it with an allocation of $60.9 million in state funds over the next few years. Its long-term low-interest mortgages plus tax exemption produced a monthly rental of about $20 a room.[33]

There were now separate government support for low-, moderate-, lower-middle-, middle-, and upper-middle-income families, with subsidized rents ranging from about $10 a room monthly for public housing tenants up to the $55 paid by residents of the Title I Coliseum Park apartments.[35] If it is assumed that by 1960 these represented the purchasing capability of families earning up to $10,000 a year, then roughly 80 percent of those who lived in Manhattan were considered worthy of subsidy. That is, to those poor families who could not afford any decent sort of accommodation anywhere were added those who could not afford to live up to their expectations in the center of the city. To stop them from being driven out by the indifference of the free market, which concerned itself largely with the rich, federal, state, and city governments were prepared to offer financial inducements of write-downs, tax exemption, and larger and longer mortgages at lower interest rates. Being poor in New York City no longer only meant living in the ghettos of the Lower East Side or Harlem with insufficient money for proper housing, food, and care. Now the family who not only ate well but also in restaurants; who not only had a television set but also went to the theater; who not only had an automobile but also a cottage to drive to; and who not only had air conditioners but also vacationed in Europe: these families were allowed to pay less than the unhindered market rate for their apartments because to do otherwise would require a lowering of the standard of life that was considered their due as middle-class Americans.

17

Running Standstill

Anthony Panuch's report summed up the state of housing administration in New York as it existed at the beginning of 1960.[1] There were thirteen housing programs under the jurisdiction of ten city, two state, and three federal agencies: federal, state, and city public housing, limited-dividend housing, redevelopment company housing, state and city Mitchell-Lama, Title I, urban renewal, neighborhood conservation, tenement rehabilitation, code enforcement, and tax exemption (now known as tax abatement). The federal departments involved within the Housing and Home Finance Agency were the Public Housing Administration, the Federal Housing Administration, and the Urban Renewal Administration. The two state agencies were the Division of Housing and the Rent Commission.

In the city, the City Planning Commission theoretically provided the coordinating control over all housing, urban renewal, and open-land developments, subject only to being overruled by a three-fourths vote of the Board of Estimate (which was made up of the mayor, comptroller, council president, and the five borough presidents, the citywide representatives having four votes each, the others two). In practice, what little authority it had as a branch of government without any power base had been undercut by the influence of the construction coordinator. While its decisions were supposed to be based on a master plan, this up to then consisted of only a highway layout and a general indication of areas suitable for development and redevelopment. By the end of the decade, however, it was reasserting itself, and its chairman headed the interdepartmental Urban Renewal Board. The largest city agency was the Housing Authority, with a staff of nearly 8000. Neighborhood conservation was under the office of the deputy mayor. Middle-income housing programs, permitted under the 1926 State Housing Law, the 1942 Redevelopment Companies Law, and the 1955 Limited-Profit Housing Companies Law, were under the comptroller, though little advantage had been taken of them during the 1950s. Others involved in housing were the departments of buildings and health, the local courts, and the Tax Commission, these having responsibility for code enforcement and tax abatement.

The 1950 census, Panuch claimed, had shown the city to have a housing shortage of 430,000 units, which were needed to replace 280,000 slums, relieve 100,000 overcrowded households, and provide a 3 percent vacancy reserve. Nine years (and about 280,000 new units) later, a City Planning Commission report declared the housing shortage to be the same. "This is a matter of simple arithmetic which cannot be blinked away by closing one's eyes to distasteful facts," it contended; "a world in which residential construction is very largely in private hands, where builders increase their rate of activity only in response to market opportunities, and a world where government—City, State and Federal —is too burdened with fiscal problems to purchase a solution with the public purse."[2] That year, however, believing the housing shortage to have been virtually eliminated by the home-building industry, which was supplying about a million single-family homes annually, President Eisenhower vetoed the housing bill passed by Congress because he considered it extravagant and inflationary.

A subsequent analysis by the Housing and Redevelopment Board declared Panuch's report "overly pessimistic," though this disagreement between the planning and implementational branches of city housing policy often reflected a different attitude toward their aims and responsibilities. Estimating the 1950 shortage to have been 488,000 units, the board claimed that ten years of construction had reduced it to 356,000 units.[3] Nevertheless, in Manhattan, while the 1950 census had reported 110,979 dwellings, or 18.5 percent of the housing stock, either dilapidated or without a private bath, the 1960 census (which included more one-room units in its definition) counted 148,197 dwellings, or 20.4 percent, in similar condition and also noted that a further 110,881 dwellings, or 15.2 percent, that had all their plumbing facilities were in the process of deteriorating. The reasons for this were analyzed by the Panuch report. The enforcement of minimum standards was inadequate, and a very low vacancy rate (0.4 percent in Manhattan) made slums an attractive investment when legitimized by controlled rent levels, enriched by tax depreciation, and ensured a steady tenancy because of demolition, the influx of minority groups, public welfare (on which 33,000 city families were paid to live in substandard housing), and the overcrowding of rooming houses, which accelerated blight.

Panuch's administrative remedy was straightforward: the establishment of a central agency headed by a three-person board to coordinate urban renewal and middle-income housing programs previously divided among seven separate city agencies and departments. This was promptly set up as the Housing and Redevelopment Board (one of its members being Robert Weaver, who had started his career as adviser to Harold Ickes and was almost immediately appointed U.S. Housing and Home Finance Agency administrator by President John Kennedy).

His policy proposals were less decisive. Beyond declaring that the profit should be taken out of the ownership of slums by reassessment and taxation, he based his recommendations on his belief in the effectiveness of the filtering process whereby the provision of large quantities of higher-rental housing encouraged by the blanket tax concessions he advocated would not only draw middle-class families back into the city but would open up vacancies lower down the line. This echoed a report by the Citizens' Housing and Planning Council entitled "How tax exemption broke the housing deadlock in New York City . . . a study of the post World War I housing shortage and the various efforts to overcome it"[4]—though both failed to suggest how the filtering process might work under changed circumstances. Considering the differences between the mobility of the Jewish and Italian immigrants of the 1920s, who at that time were entering into the mainstream of American life, and the existing constraints on the Puerto Ricans and blacks, it was difficult to see how catering to the middle class could significantly open up sound housing stock to poor minorities. In 1950 the city ratio of nonwhite and Puerto Rican to white had been roughly 1:7; in 1960 it was 2:7. How building for the middle-class white population had helped, or was going to help, the burgeoning minority poor was left unexplained. For a decade they had been the butts of the Title I controversy that was in itself the reason for Panuch's inquiry. To continue this neglect was politically hazardous. At the same time, whereas it was generally agreed that the tax abatements of the 1920s were a handout to builders to make up their profits while keeping their prices competitive, the middle class of the 1960s expected rent (and profit) restrictions in return—a give-and-take that had proved unattractive to investors for the past 34 years. One practical suggestion in

Panuch's report was to locate new housing in deteriorating commercial areas, thus minimizing relocation. Another, more fanciful proposal was for Congress to finance a massive slum clerance program in Puerto Rico and thereby reduce its emigration.

The city responded by withdrawing its support from the type of luxury developments previously favored by Robert Moses and emphasizing housing in the medium-rental range of from $25 to $40 a room monthly. In the fall of 1960, the Housing and Redevelopment Board announced the expansion of the state and city Mitchell-Lama programs, which up till then had been virtually restricted to cooperatives, in order to encourage the erection of middle-income rental apartments at a combined rate of from 15,000 to 20,000 annually, though, in fact, an average of less than 8000 units a year were completed during the remaining five years of the Wagner administration. Supporting this action, the president of the City Club, I. D. Robbins, explained that without it 86.8 percent of the city's families (that is, those earning less than $10,000 a year) would be unable to afford new housing.[5] The electorate of New York State soon confirmed the political acumen of this approach. In 1962 it refused the use of subsidies to enable low-income families to live in state-mortgaged middle-income housing. In 1964 it turned down an additional bond authorization and thereby virtually brought the state's public housing building program to an end after a quarter of a century and an expenditure of close to three-quarters of a billion dollars.[6]

On the other hand, government was now expected to underwrite the costs of housing the middle class. When the Limited-Profit Housing Mortgage Corporation (which was set up by the state legislature in 1959 to encourage the supply of funds from insurance companies and banks) failed in its purpose, with less than one-third of the target amount being pledged, Governor Nelson Rockefeller called for a state housing finance agency with a bond allocation of half a billion dollars. The following year he put forward a $4.75 billion proposal to build medium-rental housing for a million persons in ten years, utilizing untaxed, publicly owned air rights over tunnel entrances, piers, highways, schools, and storage tracks. However, the actual number of publicly assisted middle-income housing units completed in the city during the first half of the decade was 35,417. For lower-income families 21,748 public housing units were built.[7]

In contrast, during the same period, without the benefit of subsidy, a major boom of luxury private construction resulted from a rush to get building approval before the enforcement of a new zoning ordinance, passed in 1960, which decreased the amount of land allocated for residential use to an estimated city population of 12 million, and at the same time lowered the permitted floor-space to lot-size ratio. By forcing owners to redevelop their land immediately or suffer a potential loss of revenue from the smaller number of units allowed on the site, the new law prefaced a delayed slump with a glut of high-rental apartments that provoked the offer of free trips to Europe for prospective tenants and such advertising copy as "The whole town's talking about the return to low rentals" (around $300 monthly for a two-bedroom apartment off lower Fifth Avenue).

Such investment in high-cost construction was especially evident in the erection of Manhattan office buildings. The tight money, anti-inflationary policy of the Eisenhower administration, which was used as an excuse to cut back on federal housing support, did nothing to inhibit the construction of office space, over 30 million square feet being built between the close of World War II and the end of the 1950s. An even greater boom climaxing in 1963 added an equivalent amount in only five years.[8]

This speculative pressure on materials and manpower, which was aggravated by the demands of the New York World's Fair, pushed construction costs even higher and in turn decreased the potential market for new apartments. Nevertheless, in the first five years of the decade, the response by developers to a threat- ened reduction of their profits resulted in the erection of 120,000 high-rental apartments of which one-third were on the high-cost land of Manhattan.[9]

The result, according to city housing economist Frank Kristof, was a substantial improvement in the housing conditions of black and Puerto Rican families.[10] Contending that new construction plus the annual loss of white families to the suburbs opened up vacancies for minority groups, he cited statistical evidence for 1960-1965 to support his claim: the number of single-room oc- cupancy units had decreased by 24 percent from 129,000 to 98,000; overcrowding (measured as more than one person per room) had decreased by 26 percent from 292,000 to 217,000 households; and while one-quarter of all Puerto Rican families still occupied substandard units, the number of substandard units rented by blacks had dropped from 24 percent to 17 percent. Seemingly everyone was benefiting from the mass of high-rental housing being built.

However, in Manhattan, the roughly 63,000 new apartments built during this period represented only one-tenth of its multiple housing stock. In 1965, 200,000 old-law tenements still remained from the nineteenth century. Another 200,000 new-law tenements were from about thirty to sixty years old.[11] Many of these build- ings when not fit for demolition required renovation. In 1962 the city combined the Rent and Rehabilitation Administration to bring together two programs to encourage landlords to modernize their properties. New York City had maintained rent controls since World War II. When a Republican Congress had threatened to block their extension by President Truman, the state had ap- proved a standby law, which went into effect in 1950. Twelve years later its administration was passed along to the city after it had become a major issue in the preceding mayoralty campaign. The new administrator was Hortense Gabel, a social advocate who had previously been appointed to the deputy mayor's office to develop a neighborhood conservation program for the city's transitional areas and then served as Mayor Wagner's assistant responsible for housing. The plan was to force the updating of the city's housing stock by tying rent increases to renovations. A revised Municipal Loan Program (first introduced under LaGuardia prior to World War II) granted low-interest mortgages plus tax abatement on properties that were to be rehabilitated with controlled rents for restricted-income tenants. As it turned out, difficulties with existing mortgages, the inability of tenants to pay higher rents, and the problem of relocation inhibited its use until the advent of the next administration (when $90 million and six years later the program bogged down with charges of corruption and ineptitude).

"At worst," a spokesman for Mayor Wagner had remarked, "the city will make some headway in upgrading its housing and at best the law will work a little revolution."[12] The miracle was not to be. At the end of 1965, offering a different interpretation to Kristof's analysis of events, a $3.25 million study entitled *New York City Renewal Strategy/1965* concluded that 1,250,000 persons still lived in slum areas, while a further 1,750,000 were in areas requiring government help to restore them to a decent environmental standard.[13] The causes, the report noted, were the aging of both buildings and the population living off fixed incomes, as well as the growing concentration of poor minorities with few job opportunities for bettering themselves. Opposing previous policies, it urged a shift back to low-income housing so that a new middle class might arise from the poor.

Five years earlier, Panuch had set the city housing need at 430,000 units. Now a detailed calculation correlating the overall income/family-size demand and the rental/number-of-rooms supply found a shortage of 514,900 units, including 413,700 of various sizes renting under $50 an apartment (roughly $8-$20 a room) and 101,200 at the level of $120 up ($20-$50 a room).[14] Those most affected by the lack of adequate housing were all families earning under $3000 a year and large families earning less than $6000, a major proportion of these being Puerto Rican and black.

It was apparent that the supply of upper-rental housing was not forcing the sort of vacancies to filter down that could satisfy the needs and demands of low-income families. Notwithstanding Kristof's limited research finding that for every family moving into new housing, another 1.4 families moved up into superior accommodation that was thereby vacated,[15] other evidence suggested that the building of luxury apartment houses would do virtually nothing for minorities in their ghettos. Theorists might conceptualize a vacuum system of empty apartments sucking families up the pipeline, but the necessary sequential precision of each economic group moving into its next position as it became vacated was being counteracted by other social patterns of human needs and responses. The unabated black migration from the southern rural areas and the continuing influx and growth of Puerto Rican families were creating a transformation in the city that was equivalent in intensity to that which had taken place before World War I. Consequently, it seemed unlikely that this situation could be handled by building new housing for the diminishing white majority and letting its castoffs be handed down to the increasing nonwhite minority, which neither wished nor was able to share its particular way of life. Furthermore, even when these minorities moved into relatively better accommodation, it was inevitably at the lowest end of the housing scale and acutely susceptible to additional wear and tear whether due to tenant abuse or landlord overuse. The outcome appeared to be the complete abandonment of those buildings that had been vacated and the crumbling into slums of newly occupied areas. Thus, whereas in Manhattan, for example, during the past twenty years the slums of the Lower East Side had been contained and to a limited extent reduced, those to the north had consolidated between 96th and 155th streets and were spreading into Washington Heights.[16] Unlike the Jewish ghetto, which had filled its tenements to capacity and then emptied as its inhabitants prospered, the black and Puerto Rican settlements were shifting and expanding while taking with them the destructive concomitants of poverty. The observable evidence beyond any housing statistics was that their homes were deteriorating at a faster pace than any proposed filtering process or rehabilitation could match.

One reaction to the report was an announcement by the outgoing mayor of a Preventive Renewal Operations Program costing $12 million, with two-thirds coming from the federal government under legislation that authorized low-interest loans and nonrepayable grants for rehabilitation, plus funds for neighborhood improvements. The *New York Times* was not impressed. "Mr. Lindsay," it editorialized, "takes over a city in which housing shortages for families at lower income levels are more acute than ever, urban renewal has failed to touch the hardcore slums, and planning remains a polite charade. More than one-third of the population of a metropolis frequently billed as the greatest in the world lives in an unsound environment."[17]

In the years of President Lyndon Johnson's "great society," however, everything was thought to be capable of solution—at a price—and nothing was considered impossible. A professionally detailed report by a Housing and Urban Renewal Task Force, appointed by mayor-elect John Lindsay and chaired by Charles Abrams, set out the range of possibilities. Brought up in the Williamsburg tenement district of Brooklyn across the river from

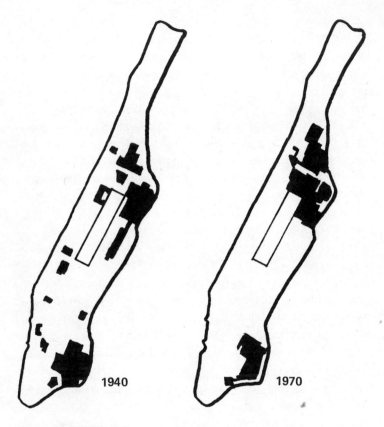

Slums, 1940-1970, map

Sources: New York City, City Planning Commission, *Master Plan, Sections Containing Areas for Clearance, Replanning and Low-Rent Housing* (1940); New York City Planning Commission, *Plan for New York City, A Proposal, 4: Manhattan*, Neighborhood Improvement Plan, Major Action Residential Areas (1969).

the Lower East Side, Abrams had made a fortune from real estate speculation in Greenwich Village after graduating from night school as a lawyer. At the same time his clerkship under Arthur Garfield Hays, who later became famous as defense attorney in the Scopes and Sacco-Vanzetti trials, encouraged a concern for civil liberties that culminated in his appointment during the latter half of the 1950s as chairman of the New York State Commission Against Discrimination. This combination of business acumen and liberal views had prompted his being invited to help draft the first public housing law and his subsequent appointment as counsel to the New York City Housing Authority. In his mid-sixties at the time of his report to Mayor Lindsay, he was renowned as an author and worldwide housing consultant for the United Nations and was chairman of the division of urban planning at Columbia University. His approach to the city's housing problems was therefore based on an intimate knowledge of government programs and their potential use in supplementing and influencing private enterprise—a comprehension that was increasingly rare as they proliferated during the 1960s.

As each recognized problem brought its own specific response, "omnibus" housing bills became ever more complex. In this decade public housing expanded to include rehabilitation, apartment leasing, and purchasing. The first rooming houses to be remodeled into public housing were brownstones in the West Side Urban Renewal area completed in 1962. In 1964, under state legislation, low-income families were permitted to be housed in privately owned nonprofit or limited-profit buildings with the difference between the actual rent and the comparable public housing rent being made up by state grants and additional tax abatement. A similar federal leasing program followed in 1965 under a new Section 23 that was added to the original housing act of 1937, though it was not funded until the following year after considerable Congressional opposition. This was also first used in the West Side Urban Renewal area as was another method of inserting low-income families by "skewing" the rents of a medium-rental building so that increased rents for four-fifths of the tenants compensated for the reduced rents of the other one-fifth. The Housing and Urban Development Act of 1965, in its encouragement of the greater use of existing housing, also permitted the Turnkey program, which allowed privately financed developers to sell new or rehabilitated buildings to local authorities at a fair profit, thus reportedly saving two to three years on the project development time and 10 to 15 percent on its cost (the first in New York being completed in 1969 in Brooklyn).

A low-to-moderate-rental program for those displaced by urban renewal or other government action was introduced in the Housing Act of 1961. Known as FHA 221(d)3 from its amendment of the Housing Act of 1954, it granted up to 100 percent mortgages at below market interest rates in return for income and rent ceilings and a restriction on the unit cost of the building (which limited its usefulness in high-cost areas like New York). The elderly (1959) and handicapped (1964) were correspondingly served. Another later moderate-income program, included in the Housing and Urban Development Act of 1968 and known as Section 236, provided subsidies to reduce mortgage interest rates to 1 percent.

With this mass of legislation, administrators juggled "piggybacking" federal, state, and city subsidies in their attempts to lower rents from an ever increasing open market rate that approached $100 a room monthly in 1968 to a figure that bore some practical relationship to the median annual incomes of $7000, $4900, and $4500 then received by white, nonwhite, and Puerto Rican families in New York City.[18]

Abrams was an expert at this type of permutational solution. In his report he insisted that there was "no single formula that will apply to all people at all times. Nor should there be one. For if one of our main objectives is to enlarge the choices available to the individual, there must also be a variety of housing formula— Authority-owned housing; rehabilitated, limited profit and non-profit housing; rent supplements; home ownership, rental and hire purchase housing; cooperatives and condominiums; planned neighborhoods and unplanned ones and above all a large supply of private housing with a multiplicity of landlords and a diversity of dwelling types."[19] However, no amount of ingenuity in the relatively small scale manipulation of personalized remedies could hide the fact that these were no match for the generic ills of the nation's major cities. For as a study group reported eight months later, "It is clear . . . that past and present programs of housing, city planning, and urban renewal have failed to defeat the problem or even significantly contain it."[20] The middle-class migration to the suburbs, the decay of city centers, riots in the ghettos; these seemed to be of a different order of events than how to package city, state, and federal subsidies.

The study report for the Institute of Public Administration was written by Edward Logue, who had been a member of Abram's committee. Prominent as Boston's redevelopment administrator, he was considered by Mayor Lindsay to be the ideal person to solve New York's housing problem. This problem, Logue declared, was not just physical but also social and economic. The city had overstressed housing supply and understressed such neighborhood facilities as parks, schools, cultural centers, and job opportunities. Regretting that the city still did not have a master plan, he topped Abrams's proposal for the greater concentration of housing responsibilities by recommending the coordination of planning, site selection, public and private housing, rehabilitation, relocation and rent control under a superagency which would be divided into ten area administrations. Logue calculated the city's housing need at 45,000 units a year—a figure that had been surpassed during 1962-1965. However, his demand for $1.5 billion in urban renewal funds over six years was five times the rate that the city was then receiving; and his public housing target of 15,000 units a year was double the existing quota.[21] Nevertheless, Logue had the reputation for being adept at securing federal funds and based his program on this. "If the defense effort, or the race to the moon, or the foreign aid program, do not permit a responsible level of Federal assistance to overcome the problems of New York's giant ghettoes," he exhorted, "then it is time to say so."[22]

That year a $1.2 billion Congressional authorization over three years permitted cities to receive supplementary grants of up to 80 percent of the nonfederal share of federally aided programs including those for new construction, rehabilitation, education, health, and economic opportunities. This was in line with the approach proposed by Logue, who recommended the designation of three city areas to qualify for funds under the Demonstration Cities and Metropolitan Development Act of 1966. These areas included Harlem-East Harlem, but, as a later report observed, the envisaged improvements were slow to take shape for the situation was "complex, delicate, and conflict riddled. . . . To build one vest pocket apartment in this part of Manhattan often requires the reconciliation of several ethnic, political and private community groups, as well as approval by one or more planning boards, the Harlem-East Harlem Model Cities Policy Committee and the City." Nonetheless, the report continued, what "separates the City's Model Cities program from other false starts is a recognition from the outset that the main job is not to superimpose another hierarchy of control, but to untangle the network of existing programs, organizations and interests so that real progress can be made."[23] (Seven years after its inauguration, the Model Cities program was included in President Nixon's freeze on government spending.)

As a natural choice to head the sort of housing, planning, and development agency he proposed (though the City Planning Commission and Housing Authority proved too independent to be merged), Logue was opposed by those who did not wish to revert to the autocratic ways of another Moses. In turn, the drastic reduction of President Johnson's majority in Congress and its likely impairment of federal funds, and yet another referendum defeat of an amendment that would have permitted cities to borrow money for housing on a larger property valuation influenced Logue in his decision not to accept the appointment. Circumstances anyway were against success.

Stressing support for the poor minorities, Mayor John Lindsay's electoral platform had pledged both to bring them into the decision-making process and specifically to increase their supply of new housing to a four-year output of 100,000 units (plus 60,000 more for middle-income families).[24] Unfortunately, this well-intentioned goal had no hope of realization under the prevailing conditions, which were largely beyond the mayor's control. Conversely, the move toward participatory democracy though commendable became a negative influence that helped reduce the city's housing output to its lowest level since the aftermath of World War II.

Part of the climate of the 1960s, citizen involvement encouraged immobilizing debates such as that which had ensued over the West Side Urban Renewal project where some black community spokesmen had argued that to rehouse all the existing low-income families in the area would perpetuate racial and social imbalances while Puerto Rican groups demanded more public housing and less middle-class intrusion. Such citizen involvement, with its precedents in antidiscrimination and antiwar demonstrations, could also explode into violence as in the riots at Columbia University, where one of the two basic issues was its expansion into adjacent Harlem. Though led by radical students, the protest was supported by the Congress of Racial Equality, the Harlem Committee for Self-Defense, and the Black United Front. Commenting on the central incident, the building of a university gymnasium in Morningside Park, the Cox Commission, which investigated the disturbance, remarked that it had come to "epitomize the conflict between the spirit of the civil rights movement and the attack on poverty, on the one hand, and on the other, the ways of an ancien régime."[25] Benevolent paternalism (for the intention was to have Harlem residents use part of the facilities) was undeniably effective for getting things done; it was simply unpalatable to a reawakened society.

"The need is for the surgeon followed by the bulldozer," reiterated Robert Moses, now in his eightieth year.[26] The prevailing philosophy was against it. Reacting against the massive projects of the previous two decades, the Housing Authority had in 1956 announced a new policy of inserting relatively small numbers of poor families into existing neighborhoods. This so-called (by New York standards) vest-pocket program was inaugurated in 1962 with the opening of a twenty-story block containing 168 apartments at 155th Street and Amsterdam Avenue. Such small-scale operations seemingly permitted racial and economic integration, utilized existing community facilities, and preserved neighborhood characteristics. They also permitted the employment of smaller contractors with consequent greater competition in bidding, but in fact a subsequent federal report calculated that a single apartment building in Manhattan cost the same per unit as multiple-building projects, while in the other boroughs it might be up to 10 percent more expensive.[27] Furthermore, larger developments were probably easier to plan, faster to build, and more administratively efficient (though a counterclaim criticized the Housing Authority's "numerous supervisory layers, dual channels of supervision, excessive central office hierarchy and failure to decentralize authority and responsibility to those closest to the project operations").[28] The social problem, however, was how to adequately integrate minority groups into the middle-class norm of city life by using small developments when the ratio of blacks and Puerto Ricans to whites in Manhattan, for example, was approaching 2:3. The overriding need seemed not just to produce housing but to use it to enforce balanced neighborhoods.

At the beginning of Lindsay's mayoralty the decision was made to build public housing in middle-class areas. The following year this scatter-site policy was endorsed by the U. S. Department of Housing and Urban Development, which ruled that projects for which it provided funds were to be located outside areas of existing minority concentration. Among the first group of localities selected for the erection of four fourteen-story buildings was the Corona section of Queens. When opposition was voiced, the project site was changed to one in Forest Hills. The first site was in an ethnically Italian community living in one- and two-family houses; the second, in a community of Jewish apartment dwellers who, with their inbred support of civil rights and their apartment building mode of life, seemed an ideal group to add to the token numbers of their nonwhite neighbors. The reality was otherwise, as city officials who had not even bothered to consult with local residents soon found out. The same process of forcibly taking over meetings ("Led by Mrs. Peggy Berry in a white pants suit, the women bounded upon the stage in the glare of the cameramen's lights and circled [City Planning Commissioner] Mr. Elliott and his companions in ring-around-the-rosy fashion chanting: 'Down with the project' "),[29] sit-ins, demonstrations, and the whole range of confrontation tactics that had become associated with minority activist groups were now taken over by the middle class, which added more sophisticated lines of action through the courts, the state legislature, and the federal cabinet. There were various expressions of shock that those inside the establishment should imitate others who, because they were outside it, had first by necessity but more recently through tacit encouragement made their views known in untraditional ways. Such appeals to fair play were lost in a battle of life-styles (equally vehement in the school system) that seemed to threaten the whole pursuit of middle-class values that had taken these families out of their own earlier ghettos. "They're scared to death," observed one Jewish official[30]— sufficiently so for them to resist until the protection of their way of life was ensured (a few years later the project was cut in half and turned into the country's first low-income cooperative).

If government could not impose integration, private enterprise would not. As one real estate spokesman put it, "Urban planners and elected officials may envision housing projects with a mix of low, middle and upper income housing. But the private investor will disagree as to its profitability, and when he does there is no wall around the city that will compel him to spend his money here."[31] There were other problems for developers who wanted to build housing. The eviction of long-term residents from their controlled low-rental dwellings at a time of minimal vacancies could be construed as an antisocial act. The increasing vilification of the developers' normal practices was aggravated by the time and money demanded from them by eviction proceedings and relocation. In response, a new wave of antitenant tactics led to a further increase in their unpopularity. The more orthodox approach of the real estate industry to free occupied buildings for redevelopment was to cut back on services until they became uninhabitable. A quicker method, where the tenants were used to victimization, was the hiring of a new specialty of hoodlum known as a building-breaker who employed such techniques as bringing in narcotic addicts, alcoholics, and prostitutes, vandalizing apartments, and arson and violence. The frustration of not being the master of one's own property, which was ripe for redevelopment at a windfall profit, was characterized by the landlord in Bernard Malamud's novel *The Tenants* who tells his last remaining novelist-tenant: "Rent control, if you aren't afraid to listen to the truth, is an immoral situation. The innocent landlord gets shafted. What it amounts to is you're taking my legal property away from me against the Constitution. . . . All I want is to be able to pull this sonofabitchy building down."[32] In fact, another writer, William Rueben, was paid $22,375 to leave his $72-a-month apartment on a site wanted for a Rockefeller Center addition. Reporting how the offer increased from an initial $250, he explained: "I had a deadline, and the Rockefeller agents kept harassing me with middle-of-the-night telegrams and phone calls. They couldn't seem to understand why anyone would 'hold up progress' just to write a book."[33] The conflict was between the profit-and-loss balance sheet of a major industry and the desire for places that people called home.

Because adding to or replacing low-rental housing was fraught with so many contradictory emotions, many people agreed with Governor Rockefeller's offhand comment at the height of the Forest Hills controversy that the city should concentrate on rehabilitating its existing housing stock.[34] To some, rehabilitation was a politic evasion. To others, it was a profession of faith in the texture of neighborhood life, with the added architectural merit of conserving a traditional urban scale. The idea of upgrading substandard buildings was not new. It had been debated since it was proposed by the New York State Reconstruction Commission after World War I, but it had fallen into disfavor during the intervening years. Even the West Side Urban Renewal study came to the conclusion that old-law tenements were too expensive to be saved (though it recommended the renovation of the brownstone housing in the area, which was later mainly sold off for upper-income occupancy).

However, in 1964 the city, with federal assistance, began an investigation into the problems involved in large-scale rehabilitation to determine what types of existing structures best lent themselves to upgrading by private sponsors using low-interest mortgage loans, how much relocation could be avoided, what social policies would be required to sustain physical improvements, and whether the rehabilitation of one area would trigger that of the surrounding neighborhood. That year, with federal and private foundation support, the first major rehabilitation project began with the gutting of 36 five-story tenement buildings on 114th Street between Seventh and Eighth avenues. At its inception, the chairman of the New York office of the Congress of Racial Equality had criticized the project's sponsors for "creating and maintaining a little oasis in the midst of one of the most dense ghettoes in the world." He asked: "why not use the $390,000 [from the Office of Economic Opportunity] for provision of housing in areas which are presently free of the social and environmental deficiencies which would still engulf 114th Street after rehabilitation?"[35] Hortense Gabel, who was reputed to have a close relationship with the black community, was more optimistic. Previous approaches to the problem of slums, she claimed, "were entirely architectural. They dreamed up things without concern for the families involved."[36] She employed a black sociologist and two community organizers. Six years after the first building had been completed, the New York Times reassessed the project: "Social and housing problems from the surrounding neighborhood have borne in on the rehabilitated buildings, the backers say, despite the effort of low income residents to maintain their apartments . . . vandalism is a frequent occurrence despite security measures . . . the primary lesson was that it is difficult to rehabilitate a blighted area in the 'inner core' of the city."[37] Rent delinquencies after a year of assertive management were at a level of about 17 percent (they had previously been as high as 38 percent). The executive director of the non-profit organization that administered the buildings observed: "a landlord needs to maintain an economic return. If we can maintain a zero gap [between income and expenses] we'll be happy."

The Citizens' Housing and Planning Council had already tried its own rehabilitation project for low-income tenants and failed. With a quarter of a million dollars donated by Laurence Rockefeller, two tenement buildings had been bought and renovated. The one on East Second Street in the East Village, which attracted students and artists, was a relative success. The other, a few blocks away on the Lower East Side, was occupied by people with "a completely different attitude." On an inspection of the building, a *New York Times* reporter was shown "broken windows, garbage a foot deep in the air shafts, defaced hallways and new mail boxes that already showed signs of being broken into, probably by narcotics addicts."[38] His guide, the council's executive director, Roger Starr, stated: "It soon became clear that you couldn't make anything at all. It simply costs more money to keep up your property than you collect from rents at this level of the economic system. Without subsidies rehabilitation is a snare and a delusion."

The head of the Housing and Development Administration disagreed. Rehabilitation, he thought, was feasible over large areas using sophisticated techniques. In 1967 the federal government contracted with the Institute of Public Administration to test the feasibility of the "instant rehabilitation" of tenements on East Fifth Street. Using a systems design approach with industrialized prefabricated components, the performance, which included the lowering of bath and kitchen units by crane through a hole in the roof by floodlight at night, was described in *Newsweek:* "At 10 o'clock one crisp morning last week, construction engineer Edward K. Rice blew a whistle outside a squalid tenement on New York's lower East Side and the first members of a 258-man renovation crew filed into the building. Their seemingly hopeless assignment: to transform the 72-year-old slum structure into a modern dwelling in just 48 hours. As an electronic clock ticked off the seconds in the project headquarters next door, demolition men started dumping debris into the street. Then, following a perfectly plotted schedule, relays of carpenters, plumbers, electricians, painters and laborers swarmed into the building to race the 48-hour deadline through the day and night. 'Hurry up, hurry up,' the workers called to each other. Finally, as the last touch was completed, Rice stopped the clock—at exactly 47 hours, 52 minutes, and 24 seconds."[39] The purpose of the experiment was to test its general feasibility. The results were inconclusive. In the words of the U. S. Department of Housing and Urban Development, the project could not "be considered a demonstration in the sense of the word that connotes a confident display of the merits of a developed product to potential buyers."[40] George Sternlieb generalized: "if new housing for the poor costs too much—and in new housing, remember, we have all the efficiencies attendant on mass production and standardization—then rehabilitation of existing structures, which means a much higher level of hand work and individualized expertise, is even more uneconomical."[41] "Thus far," Hortense Gabel wryly observed, "objective standards for evaluation of rehabilitation do not exist. Eighteen reports, statements, and evaluations, all prepared by highly respected scholars and practitioners, come to widely varying conclusions on costs to developer, government, and tenants and on acceptability and replicability."[42]

The general housing potentialities of industrialization were also being pressed by the federal government. In 1949 when Walter Reuther of the United Automobile Workers had proposed the use of idle aircraft plants for prefabricating housing on their assembly lines, his plan had been rejected by manufacturers who had investigated the possibility after World War II and found the costs prohibitive and restrictive codes and unions insurmountable. Twenty years later, ex-president of American Motors Corporation, George Romney, was appointed secretary of the U. S. Department of Housing and Urban Development in the first Nixon administration and inaugurated "Operation Breakthrough" to stimulate the development of industrialized building processes. Limited by the opposition of construction unions to use in experimental projects rather than utilized in housing to be built under existing federal programs, 22 building systems were chosen for the erection of 2800 units on nine sites, the closest to New York being in Jersey City. The hope was not only to increase the rate of supply to meet the requirement of the Housing and Urban Development Act of 1968 for 26 million units over the next decade but also to decrease its cost. In his annual report to the Congress in 1970, President Nixon observed that mobile homes were about all that many Americans could afford when the median price of conventionally built housing was $27,000, or 80 percent higher.[43] In Manhattan, a medium-rental apartment for three or four persons cost about the same amount.[44] As for a possible reduction in price, a detailed study of the "Cost and time associated with new multifamily housing construction in New York City" found that while building codes, labor practices, and administrative procedures did measurably increase costs, a saving of only 11.2 percent appeared feasible, half of this being achieved through three changes: by the shop fabrication of concrete steel reinforcement, the improved design of plumbing and hot water installations, and the substitution of a cheaper floor finish.[45]

The combination of forces affecting Lindsay's housing program had not been foreseen by his advisers. His campaign pledge had been simply unrealistic in the circumstances that prevailed. The result was a disillusioning failure not only to approximate election promises but even to come close to the output record of previous years. In the first four-year term of Lindsay's mayoralty, only 12,995 public housing units were completed, while middle-income programs added roughly 23,000 more.[46] Blame for this was reciprocally attributed to the lack of cooperation between city and federal housing officials, to the previous administration's lack of planning (though this did not prevent Lindsay from taking credit for completion of housing initiated by his predecessor), and to red tape, which included fragmented decision making and excessive checks and audits. A further setback resulted from the delays caused by the necessary reconsideration of overly expensive plans by well-known architects who were employed by the mayor to improve the standard of public-housing design. Further ill feeling between the two levels of government became evident in the wrangle over whether or not an unofficial cost ceiling of $20,000 a unit (that is four times the original limit) made the building of public housing in New York impossible.

Similarly, the high cost of capital and labor plus inflation also inhibited private investment. The federal government and state mortgage interest rates were allowed to climb above the historical limit of 6 percent in 1968; building construction costs rose from a decade average of 3.4 percent increase annually to 6.2 percent.[47] The result was that the average monthly rent of a new privately financed two-bedroom apartment that had been $200 in 1960 was $400 in 1970.[48] In 1967 private apartment completions plummeted from over 20,000 a year to a four-year average of less than 5000. Complicating the local situation were the new zoning law and rent controls. The former reduced the area of speculative potential. The latter, especially when extended to previously uncontrolled housing in mid-1969 during the mayoralty election campaign amid rumors of exorbitant rent increases, undermined confidence in investment by mortgage companies and developers.

If rent controls inhibited the construction of new high-rental housing, they could also be blamed for eroding the low-rental housing that remained. In 1968 the Housing and Development Administration had reported that about 4000 buildings had been certified as unsafe and ordered evacuated, and that another 2000-3500 were deteriorating.[49] Frank Kristof, then an assistant administrator, gave the actual count of boarded-up or abandoned buildings as 7100, containing approximately 57,000 units, and estimated the likely total at 100,000, so that during the period 1966-1969 the city's overall housing stock had decreased while the vacancy rate was 1.23 percent.[50]

The major causes of abandonment, Kristof believed, were "rent control, the attendant punitive and essentially political pressures upon landlords, and the intense landlord-tenant hostilities . . . exacerbated by racial issues."[51] His claim that rent-controlled housing was simply unprofitable was illustrated by an analysis of a typical building where he found a rent of $24 a room per month to be necessary to provide adequate maintenance, servicing, financing, and profit. As 570,000 city households were paying less than this, he concluded that these were being under-maintained and were therefore subject to deterioration and abandonment. In reaching his acceptable rental figure, however, Kristof included both items that were statements of their actual cost, such as heating, janitorial service, and maintenance, and those that were based on an assumption of value, such as financing, profit, real estate taxes and insurance. The first group came to $12.83; the second to $11.17.[52] As the building he postulated was fifty to sixty years old, the realistic assumption of a building (as opposed to land) value that was much lower than its assessment—or even zero— would have substantially reduced the resultant figure. His proof therefore seemed merely to show an inconsistency between assumed values and rents rather than any objective evaluation of an acceptable rental structure.

This concern for the effects of rent controls was the occasion for a splurge of city reports that peaked with a massive study by George Sternlieb entitled *The Urban Housing Dilemma: The Dynamics of New York City's Rent Controlled Housing.*[53] The size of the report, which cost the city a quarter of a million dollars, reflected the complexity of arriving at an understanding of the nature of real estate investment. The major concern of operators was the here and now—the so-called cash flow, which resulted from the rental income minus taxes, running expenses, and mortgage repayments. For the detached observer, however, there were more profound questions of the definitions of such concepts as *depreciation* when more than one-half of the apartments in Manhattan were over forty years old and more than one-quarter were over seventy years old, or of *profit* where the actual cash invested in a building might be nil, depending on its mortgaging or remortgaging in a period of general inflation, increasing replacement costs, and the possibility of speculative redevelopment. Sternlieb's major conclusions were that there was insufficient profit in rent-controlled housing to justify private investment, that there was not enough income to maintain properties, that financial institutions were withdrawing their funds, and that it was not the maligned real estate operator who was being made to suffer but the poor black or Puerto Rican landlord who owned and usually lived in nearly 40 percent of small old-law tenements and the smallest new-law tenements. The report suggested that these minority group members were being caused hardship by having their older properties reassessed disproportionately higher than better-quality structures (often owned by absentee landlords), and being prevented from charging higher rents; but the buildings they owned were probably slums, and it seemed that not only were they less efficient in the management of their properties but they were also less cautious in their investments, assuming excessive financial obligations that they hoped to pass on to their even poorer compatriots.

Sternlieb was from Rutgers University. Other concurrent reports to the city were by Robert McKay of New York University, Paul Niebanck of the University of Pennsylvania, and by the New York City Rand Institute. While they all agreed that rent controls should be at a level to permit adequate maintenance, Niebanck doubted that they had been a major cause of the housing shortage and listed the more important reasons as the high cost of land, construction, and money. Nor, conversely, did he consider the deterioration of the housing stock to be unique to the rent-controlled circumstances of New York. The same influences operated elsewhere: "structural obsolescence; unavailability of financing; general environmental decline; rapid tenant turnover; inadequate consumer protection; rising costs, and uncertain expectations."[54] It seemed that, rent control or not, the rents that poor people could afford were simply too low for adequate profit and maintenance. The New York City Rand Institute report summarized the situation: "Tenants are dissatisfied with low vacancy rates that limit residential choice and weaken their bargaining power, angry about recent large rent increases in the uncontrolled sector, and perpetually discontented with poor maintenance and limited building services in the controlled sector. Some view the landlord as a ruthless and greedy enemy against whom any tactics are justified. Landlords are dissatisfied with the yields of controlled housing, infuriated by destructive or irresponsible behavior of statutory tenants, resentful of the burdens and insensitivity of city regulations, troubled by the current illiquidity of rental housing investments, and discouraged by premonitions of capital loss in the future."[55] The Rand report proposed that middle-income families be made to pay an open-market rent and be forced to adjust their other living expenses. It also discounted the filtering theory that the supply of high-priced apartments would open up vacancies for lower-income groups, believing that this would require a rapid population growth and household formation (presumably of potential middle-class tenants) or a rapid increase of consumer incomes relative to building costs. Rather than employing a massive public subsidy to stimulate new building, it concluded that "the first priority of City housing policy should be to redress the existing imbalance between rental revenues and costs in a way that provides a long-run incentive for preventive maintenance,"[56] that is, give rent assistance to low-income families so that they could pay their landlords an equitable rent. The cost—$130 million a year. Opposing the whole idea of pumping ever more public money into private ownership, a critic responded: "The City has been using Urban Renewal, Model Cities, Mitchell-Lama and Public Housing with no success in stemming the tide of housing decay. The truth is that if the City were to continue to try to solve this problem by further subsidy of the real estate industry, the City (and the state and federal governments as well) would go bankrupt."[57] Nonetheless, by the end of the decade probably less new housing was being built in the city than was being lost through demolition and abandonment.

The response was even more agencies and programs. In 1968 an Urban Development Corporation was set up by New York State and headed by Edward Logue. Initially authorized to raise $1 billion in bonds, it was given very broad powers to condemn, demolish, and build urban structures and facilities, as well as to override the zoning laws and policies of local governments and communities in an attempt to circumvent the self-interest of limited groups. After preliminary skirmishing, the corporation was invited to operate in eight city renewal areas but only after the city had acquired and cleared the land and relocated its residents. A second state measure passed in 1971 was to shore up private confidence in housing investment by removing rent controls on vacated apartments.

That year the city also took two steps to increase its housing supply. It established a Housing Development Corporation with authorization to finance $200 million of slum rehabilitation and $500 million of limited-profit housing; and, reversing its earlier ideology, it supported private apartment construction through a tax abatement program that gave a sliding scale of tax abatement over ten years to builders who erected apartments on predominantly vacant or underutilized land at a rent that was 15 percent below the market rate (in exchange for an estimated reduction in operating expenses over the first two years of 20-25 percent).[58] The resultant monthly rents were about $120 a room in Manhattan and $85 elsewhere, but even these concessions did not fully satisfy developers (who continued to press for an increase in permitted densities), although they did result in a temporary spurt in private housing starts.

For those with lower incomes (though according to the city comptroller the Mitchell-Lama rental formula permitted tenants with incomes of up to $50,000 a year),[59] the federal government increased its level of subsidies, so that in 1971, when the national output first exceeded 2 million units, nearly one-third of these were erected with some form of government support.[60] At the same time the federal tax laws enhanced profits in housing investment through tax shelters with rapid depreciation write-offs and other financial inducements. For a person earning $50,000 a year, calculated an investment consultant who had formerly been a federal assistant housing commissioner (one of the many persons who over the years had turned a knowledge of government service to private use), Section 236 housing provided a 30 percent return on the first year of investment diminishing to 15 percent in the eighth.[61]

But while these fiscal policies certainly stimulated building, their social value was less spectacular. Even new housing in the older inner cities was highly susceptible to the vandalism and crime that prevailed where poverty remained. Conversely, building on open land on the urban fringe accelerated the decline of the inner city and undercut its reclamation. Federal housing programs, lamented the outgoing secretary of the U. S. Department of Housing and Urban Development, had led to poor site selection, bad construction, lax administration, and excessive profiteering by "fast-buck artists," "speculators," and "unscrupulous developers."[62] In response, at the beginning of 1973, all new commitments were halted on federal subsidies for housing and urban renewal. This "high-cost no-result boondoggling by the Federal Government must end," declared President Nixon.[63] The housing problem had passed from private enterprise through the various levels of government to seek a solution in the president's office. Unfortunately, others events were about to monopolize his attention.

Epilogue

The developer builds for that part of the population that can pay enough to make it profitable. In the nineteenth century this included a large proportion of lower-income families. Unfortunately, the standard of housing provided for them was so low as seemingly to cause danger, squalor, sickness, and immorality. The reaction of a concerned society was to impose minimum standards to prevent the worst of these abuses. The result was not only a rise in quality but also in price that took new housing out of the range of lower-income families. By this time, however, because of the previous rapid increase in urban population, there was a large stock of existing housing. This established the free enterprise housing supply pattern for the twentieth century. New housing was marketed for those who could afford it; those who could not lived in used housing.

To rationalize what had happened in the marketplace, a new theory of housing supply was evolved. Known as the filtering theory, it asserted that the construction of new housing in any price range would cause a reshuffling of the entire housing stock, so that everyone, including the poor, would benefit by either improved accommodation or lower cost. The reality has been otherwise except in limited special circumstances, and even then its wider effects have been injurious to the urban environment.

A basic assumption of the filtering theory is that there is some relationship between the number of units being supplied by private enterprise and the number of units required by society at large to keep pace with its needs. A community calculates its housing requirements by relating its households to its housing inventory, providing for replacements due to obsolescence and allowing a proportion of vacancies to permit adequate bargaining. The developer estimates his market by counting how many can pay for what he has to offer. He has no qualms about demolishing sound housing if it gets in the way of his developments. His vacancies occur only through miscalculation.

In the nineteenth century, when the purchasing pattern of society resembled a broad-based triangle with the poor at the base and the rich at the apex, developers built for almost the whole range of income groups. More recently, as the middle-income group grew and the low-income group decreased, the new housing market has continued to shrink because the increase in the cost of shelter relative to family income has caused the middle class to share the same fate as their poorer predecessors of being excluded from it. The result is that if the market were not underwritten with public funds, there would be fewer new dwellings built in the upper part of the price scale than are needed at the bottom, and the filtering process would end up with an overall housing shortage. This is just what developers prefer.

In the economist's seesaw of supply and demand, the consumer bargains by using or withholding his purchasing power and so forces the supplier to adjust to his demands. In housing, the customer has little choice unless the builder himself supplies it. When a shortage of a particular type of housing arises from such possible causes as an expanding population or the lack of building, it becomes an attractive investment. Developers increase their output. Their selection of location, size, standard, services, and price creates developments that more or less successfully fulfill the original housing need. The immediate evidence of oversupply, when the upward filtering of families stops, is in advertisements offering free rents and other enticements to fill newly completed units. In these uneasy circumstances, the average investor holds back until the market again swings in his favor. So while time lags, speculative errors of judgment, and external factors all combine to make the supply of housing more erratic than business acumen would like, developers instinctively try to maintain what the public regards as a housing shortage, and thereby they undermine the filtering process that they ostensibly support.

Society needs a stock of housing that will fit its population's needs. Private enterprise builds only for those who provide the most profit. The outcome is that the filtering of housing is inhibited by the unavailability of suitable housing types. Currently two major housing types are being marketed: multiple dwellings in urban areas and single-family houses in the suburbs.

Providing few bedrooms and a high standard of services, apartment building owners, by reducing the number of children allowed, hope to increase rents and to lower maintenance costs. While such buildings have their own filtering potential (from sharing young professionals to sharing students, for example), experience has shown that lower-income families cannot cope with apartment living. They are unable to contend with landlords or to utilize, when necessary, the power structure outside. Without the financial independence of the middle class, they cannot escape from the restrictiveness of their surroundings. Without the middle-class respect for property, they tend to be less careful with it.

The filtering potential of suburban housing is equally constrained. Vacancies are shielded from easy occupancy by nonconforming groups through limited access and restrictive practices, thus providing more of a refuge for the middle class itself than a prime source for subsequent use by lower-income families. Furthermore, the implied assumption that these families share the life-style aspirations of their economic betters is evidently untrue for some ethnic minority groups and may not be generally true for the ordinary working poor.

That this polarization of housing types exists is due to the exploitation of land as a profit-making commodity. The success of nineteenth-century urbanization raised the market price of inner-city areas so that they became potentially too valuable to maintain or to replace with single-family housing. Instead, developers moved to rural, and therefore cheaper, peripheral land and built up new areas of single-family housing that could agglomerate with the existing urban core and share in its value-increasing capability. In this commercial arena, each location is considered to have its own market use. High-rise and low-rise buildings are therefore placed, not where they are socially desirable, but where they fit into a land-cost-per-dwelling-unit formula. Though social policies of neighborhood preservation provide a rationale for their actions, even enlightened governments seldom attempt to reduce the overcrowding that usually exists in slum areas, and often take the densities that arose from entrepreneurial exploitation as the basis for their future redevelopments. Similarly, while the issue for government is clouded by functional and imagistic planning concepts supporting an urban form with a greater concentration of buildings and services at the center fading away to the surrounding countryside, in societies where land is treated as a market commodity, it too has tended to follow private enterprise and house high densities on high-cost land and low densities on low-cost land rather than combining them over areas of different market values.

What follows is the class division of our cities. In fact, the very essence of the filtering process is social segregation by economic groups. The wealthy move into superior housing as it is developed, leaving what then becomes less desirable housing to their financial inferiors. Currently, middle-income families occupy the suburbs, while inner cities are taken over by the young, the rich, the old, and the poor. The social ideal of mixed neighborhoods is undercut by the rule of the marketplace.

At the same time the filtering process also induces decay. Even when vacated housing drops in relative value, lower-income families can seldom afford to take over its use. The white-collar worker's excess of income over basic expenses tends to keep pace with the growth of his family; the manual worker's often declines. This gap becomes widest at the point where the maximum living space is required. The result is that lower-income families find it difficult to assume even reduced middle-class financial obligations. In practice, costs rarely fall significantly. Beyond the need for equity down payments and mortgage repayments, taxes are slow to respond to reduced values, heating and utilities must always be paid for, while maintenance costs actually increase as buildings age. Moreover, because seclusion is often one of the property's original qualities, transportation usually becomes a significant budgetary addition.

Faced with the prospect of reduced rents, landlords normally prefer to take in larger families or adult groups, which, though maintaining the immediate value of the property by retaining the level of its rental income, accelerate its decline. Similarly, inner-city houses usually will not fall in price but will increase their usage by accommodating lodgers or more than one family, or by conversion into rooming houses. The outcome in a free market is that as the older middle-class units are released by newer ones and become available for lower-income families, they tend to induce overcrowding, reduced maintenance, and consequently more rapid deterioration. Being in what was once a desirable area (reflected in the prices that previously could be obtained), they act as a neighborhood depressant. At first the values of properties may rise proportionately to the increased rents available, but as the original residents move away, the area deteriorates through the overuse and misuse of its facilities.

While the basic argument in favor of filtering is that new building causes prices to drop, the very opposite has been true for most of the twentieth century. When vacancies are low, the entrepreneur immediately charges what he thinks the market will bear. High vacancies, on the other hand, take an extended period of time before they bring about the lowering of rents. Landlords prefer to carry their losses or give concessions so that the paper value of their investment remains intact rather than make what might appear to be the first step toward bankruptcy. Since World War I the cost of replacing similar buildings has risen steadily, so that existing housing has actually increased in value rather than declined. In such an inflationary economy, the influence of vacancy rates on rent levels is overshadowed by that of building replacement value. The rising cost of mortgage money, land, and construction pushes up the costs and rents of new buildings. These create a new price level that in turn pulls up existing rents and prices, so that the market relationship between older and newer buildings is maintained. Where homeownership predominates, the result is merely inflationary. Landlords of existing dwellings, however, are able to raise their rents and pocket the difference. By the time the effect of what is usually a temporary glut is felt, any reductions are only the cutback of excess profits. Far from decreasing the value of existing buildings, the true effect of new housing can be seen in their increasing value when they are supposedly aging and depreciating.

Not only does the filtering process supply too few dwellings, of the wrong type, in the wrong place, at too high a cost; its very philosophy is equally antisocial. The essence of the filtering process is to cause obsolescence. The result at one end of the income scale is to raise housing standards unnecessarily; at the other end it leaves behind residual slums.

While the negative result of the filtering process has been the failure to maintain orderly renewal and growth and to satisfactorily house and socially integrate those with lower incomes, its major achievement has been the sprawl of middle-class suburbs. To those who believe that the deterioration of our urban environment is due to abstract socioeconomic forces beyond our control and not to the side effects of human actions and policies, suburbanization has wide appeal.

Consumers who are generally disinterested in the total life cost of their housing and really concerned only with their monthly carrying charges allow their suppliers ample latitude to include whatever profits they desire from the buying and selling of land, construction, and its overall financing. Although the public might focus on the sharp practices of local developers, this profit-making activity is underwritten by the national institutions of banks and insurance, trust, and loan companies, which wield enormous economic power. Furthermore, the house purchaser does not mind paying for what he gets when he knows that those who rent are even worse off than he is; for by increasing his equity over the years until he finally removes his debt and by holding for his own the capital gain that accrues through inflation or shortages, he has a relative bargain whatever his expense. At the same time he is supplied as if by right with the public services necessary to support his way of life even when, for example, the traffic he generates turns the existing urban core into a wasteland of pavement and parking lots. Facilities that are essential to the success of housing developments, such as access roadways, new schools, and transportation, are provided from public funds as if they were necessitated by natural causes rather than by specific acts of a certain group. Thus suburban housing is covertly subsidized by the community at large, which, conversely, has to foot the bill for the resultant obsolescence of inner-city facilities. The government's concern for its continuing count of housing starts is therefore matched by that of its influential middle-class constituency, which can withdraw to its own way of life and hope that those who do not yet share its values will somehow eventually benefit.

As a lasting solution, however, suburbanization is spurious: a shortsighted expedient that will bequeath to our grandchildren the same kind of problem that we inherited from our grandparents. Then, the response to the housing demand of an expanding industrial population was to provide whatever the workers could afford regardless of any long-term considerations. When it proved inadequate, this housing was not replaced, but developers moved on to the next circle of cheap land, leaving behind the slums of today.

The fact is that all buildings finally become obsolete or decay, even those in middle-class suburbs. If, when this occurs, the same private enterprise pattern of land value exploitation exists, the need will be to raise either their quality or their density to make them economic for rehabilitation or renewal, or to replace them by an expansion of commercial building space. These alternatives would necessitate a significant increase in either our population or our standard of living; otherwise, we would have overextended our area of urbanization. As yet no community has been able to match the extent of these growth demands of real estate developers. The assumption that urban growth must sometime come to an end was inherent in the approach of the turn-of-the-century theorist Ebenezer Howard, who by building peripheral new towns hoped to siphon off London's population and thus open up the city with parks. While this did not happen at that time, a similar movement did occur when the Lower East Side population emptied into the newly built-up boroughs of New York City. The lesson is that there is a limit to how much building stock society can sustain. Used to, first, the massive increase of population with industrialization and then its concentration into seemingly ever-growing conurbations, we easily assume that there will always be a market for more and denser buildings. But as the migration to the cities once depopulated the countryside, so the current migration to the suburbs is depopulating our cities. The further urbanization of rural areas will leave behind pockets of unneeded building space in the same way that the erection of high-rise buildings concentrates and absorbs the building requirements of low-rise neighborhoods and induces the decay of their existing facilities.

The familiarity of elevator buildings replacing the walk-ups of earlier days has rendered us insensible to the exponential growth required by private enterprise to obtain its traditional amount of profit from real estate development. Added to the expanding sprawl of housing encircling cities, the further exploitation of this mass of building stock by future generations will inevitably necessitate the intervention of government or result in an ever-increasing volume of unwanted disintegrating buildings. As it became imperative for the twentieth century to stop and then cope with the slum formation of nineteenth-century laissez-faire, so twenty-first-century legislation will have to put an end to unrestricted development and make good its excesses. For if improved transportation has made even more outlying areas accessible (leaving present suburban areas to stagnate), or if suburban deterioration makes urban rebuilding financially more attractive (inducing a return to the inner city), or if the suburban sprawl coheres into new urban centers (denuding the area in between), then our legacy to the future will be the same as we inherited from the past: a once plausible solution that can now be seen to have generated its own insoluble problems.

If the proliferation of suburbs has been the major accomplishment of private enterprise in the twentieth century, it has required the intervention of government to make it so. Theoretically, private enterprise reacts to public demand, but when consumers are left without a basic necessity such as shelter, then the consequent social and political disturbance provokes government action. In North America this has overwhelmingly been to support the price level set by private enterprise and so encourage its continuing supply. Two major approaches have been taken: giving entrepreneurs financial inducements to build; and increasing the size of their available market by either raising the purchasing capacity of its consumers or attempting to lower the price of the product.

The negative way for government to support private enterprise is not to restrict its activities. By permitting the intensity of building to be virtually set by developers, New York City, for example, allows overcrowding in a country of over 2 billion acres and the highest standard of living in the world.

Such blatant encouragement of profit-motivated practices has, however, been uncommon since the turn of the twentieth century when their effects were widely denounced. Instead, government has established minimum social standards and then used fiscal concessions to give the entrepreneur what he wants. In North America a major hidden subsidy has been the rapid-depreciation allowance, allowed as a deduction from the payment of income taxes, which is unrelated to a building's real aging process but is tied to the largely mortgage-financed cost of the property.

As an alternative stimulus to housing production, government has also provided monetary inducements to the house builder's customers, who are then assumed to be able to meet his price demands. Such concessions might also include fiscal arrangements such as the deduction from income taxation of mortgage interest payments or even direct grants of money; but typically they have taken the form of trying to reduce housing costs through one of its component charges of land, construction, financing, taxes, and profits.

This approach to the problem grew out of the belief that special circumstances, such as inflation or shortages, sometimes kept suitable housing just above the reach of otherwise self-sufficient families. Negative subsidies were therefore given to support this middle-class "poor": that is, the community did not collect their property taxes, did not charge them the market rate for mortgage loans, or did not receive from them the market value for the land it bought and sold for private development. At no time was it questioned that this middle-income group might be living above its means. On the contrary, as the cost of housing outran incomes, more income levels were subsidized to reach its open market price. Implicit in this attitude were two assumptions that seem to have become embedded in our way of life. One is that there is a relatively fixed percentage of income that can be applied to shelter; the other is that our prevailing standard of housing is essential to our well-being.

The historical rule of thumb was that a family should spend no more than a quarter of its income on housing. When the lower-income group spent more than this, health usually suffered from lack of food or clothing. Middle-income families have taken over the same formula but ignore the fact that whereas the remaining three-quarters of a small income buys only necessities, that remaining from a large income leaves a residue for luxuries. Conversely, the standard of accommodation that is now considered normal has largely evolved independently of other social goals. The result is that there are substantial qualitative differences between specific standards both within and among different societies: the conventional North American suburban house can be compared to a regulation Soviet apartment two-thirds of its area containing similar-sized families without any noticeable difference in comparative death rates, crime rates, educational standards, or even that old specter of overcrowding, immorality.

In a free enterprise system, where housing is another market commodity, an increase in what is regarded as the norm widens the gap between income groups and puts pressure on the rest of the community to conform. At the same time housing reformers find new criteria such as psychological and social needs, so that science combines with fashion to raise housing standards. In the process, housing that is built to last fifty years is rendered obsolete before the end of its life span. The solution requires a diminished growth rate of standards, which would follow from a lowering of public support for middle-class suburban developments.

The issue is one of social priorities. Our housing is probably too costly for our overall needs. The concept of a poor middle class is a contradiction in terms. The fact that custom-made clothing is nowadays too expensive for the middle-class clientele who used to enjoy it in the nineteenth century does not mean that it should now be subsidized to remain within their reach. The first phase of establishing housing standards put new housing out of the reach of the poor. Subsequently, higher standards have inadvertently taken new housing beyond the allocated means of the middle class. As yet it is unwilling to suffer the status consequences of reducing its other expenditures. In their search for what they consider better environmental forms, architects have used the goal of economy as the basis for their promotion of low-rise high-density housing. Developers for their part, in their attempt to serve the lower-income group, have pared down costs through poor location and cheap construction. While these means might seem undesirable, the controlled reduction of unnecessarily high standards for the middle-income group is obviously one way to lower the cost of its housing.

If the ordinary consumer is unwilling to lower his standard of living, developers are equally unwilling to lower their profits, of which a major source has been through the exploitation of land. Unlike the costs of an actual dwelling that can be seen to be based on materials and labor, the value of land is intangible and therefore conducive to hidden profiteering. The antisocial fringe of the real estate industry, like currency speculators, buys and sells land simply to make money. Others invest in land as if it were money in the bank, expecting it to compound annually. Generally, however, urbanization itself triggers a vicious circle of exploitation that is manipulated by developers and condoned by government, which benefits from it in increased property tax assessments. Demand for land causes its value to rise; higher values require higher revenues; higher revenues necessitate more expensive or intensive use. If the project is successful, its location becomes even more desirable; the land becomes even more valuable.

While more risk-taking developers might try for quick profits by building costly buildings on cheap peripheral or depressed inner-city land, most will accept the general rise of land values that comes with successful urbanization and will press for a change of use or higher density. It is simply unprofitable to replace worn-out buildings by their equivalents, as then no advantage is taken of this accrued value. The developer therefore prefers to replace farmland by family housing, family housing by apartments, apartments by offices, low-rise by high-rise buildings, and low rentals by high rentals. In so doing, a significant part of his profit derives from the increased value of the site due to its income-producing capacity.

In the past government has tried to lower the price of housing by paying off the excessive cost of urbanized land; more recently it has bought up farming land for future development. But where the subsequent erection of housing has been carried out by profit-motivated enterprise, the level of profit has been maintained regardless of the intervention of government; and if land is made unprofitable by limiting its charge or taxation, then either no housing will be built on it, or other devices such as leasing will return the profits in another form. It has long been recognized that the use of land as a market commodity is inimical to orderly urban redevelopment and growth. Until government is willing to exercise the powers that it holds to neutralize its exploitation, and if necessary to develop it itself, no amount of superficial tampering will alter the inexorable rise of its cost.

What constitutes a fair return on private investment in housing is a question of social judgment. It seems reasonable that its risks and annoyances should place it above gilt-edged securities, and yet it should not reach outright usury. The problem becomes complicated when one attempts to define what real estate profit is. When an owner has no actual money of his own invested in a building, then the profit should be only a management fee. Similarly, if a building is amortized over its acceptable life span and is periodically sold, its changing price should theoretically reflect its diminishing overall value. In practice, its current rental income potential is a more decisive determinant than any actual investment or original cost. Through shortage and inflation, the price of aging buildings has been as likely to rise as to fall. Much of a rental building's total life-span profits is hidden in these periodic gains. At the same time that part of the mortgage repayments which pays off the actual loan is recaptured by the vendor and treated as a bonus.

Whatever the complexities of profit definition, it is evident that a housing shortage encourages profiteering. Yet any move to curb this through rent controls diminishes the incentive for investors to build. The attempt by government to limit dividends in exchange for its fiscal support has had limited appeal except during economic recessions or when other additional concessions have made up the difference between the designated rate and the developer's expectations. Controlling the existing stock while permitting new housing to make a worthwhile profit favors middle-income families in their established households and discourages them from moving into new housing they could afford. On the other hand, it harms the poor by legitimizing the substandard housing in which they live. If government does not move in to satisfy its needs, the community is forced back into a free market to encourage production. Prices are allowed to rise. Another vicious circle is completed. It can be seen that only when government or other nonprofit suppliers are able to maintain a reasonable vacancy rate or housing surplus are customers in a bargaining position to induce competition and keep business profits at an equitable level.

Not only do the real estate industry and its customers keep prices high, but so does government through its control of the supply of money. Tied to national fiscal policies that are used primarily to manipulate the economy in the attempt to deal with such problems as unemployment and inflation, the mortgage loans on which housing depends are acutely sensitive to the fluctuations of interest rates. By tying the supply of housing to money, which is profit-making in itself, the government not only acts as a capitalist but often requires a rate of interest that once would have been considered usurious.

It is evident that the multibillion-dollar mortgage loan corporative system can be made more directly responsive to society's housing needs. Without further public control, however, the general lowering of mortgage interest rates may do more harm than good. Its immediate result is to raise the potential profit of existing buildings by lowering their mortgage repayments, thereby increasing their capital value. Typically operating as an incentive at a point of minimum vacancies, cheap money first encourages the selling and buying of rental properties before it works to stimulate the supply of new housing, thus consolidating existing rents at their highest level and encouraging inflated prices for new construction. Similarly, with single-family housing, the lowering of mortgage rates during a housing shortage pushes up prices to match the new bidding power of the consumer, whose borrowing capacity is a multiple of his level of monthly repayments, which can now buy more capital at the reduced rate of interest. Nevertheless, the role of government in supplying loans for housing seems to be shrouded in the mystique of tradition. When public funds are used for education, they are simply collected and spent. Few would expect its programs to rise and fall with the gross national product; no one has yet suggested that public education should be financially profitable. The right to a decent home, however, still appears to be a privilege that must be earned.

With the level of profits and standards as well as the price of land and money apparently almost irreducible within their socioeconomic context, the hope has prevailed since the beginning of the century that significant savings could be made by rationalizing housing construction, thus providing a technical solution to the problem of housing costs. Bemused by the phenomenal success of the automobile industry, professionals and government have challenged house builders to achieve the same results. Yet while the price of an automobile dropped sharply once the assembly lines went into production, it has since increased parallel with other commodities. A major cause is that whereas Henry Ford's initial achievement was to supply a new and expanding market with its basic automotive needs, he was superseded by those who realized that without a continual rise in salable performance standards, the market would contract. His competitors therefore introduced annual feature or style changes to induce obsolescence and thereby maintain the market demand for new cars. In this assault on consumer tastes, manufacturers were able to raise their output or their price to match the amount the public was willing to pay for its pleasures. In other words, private enterprise succeeds best when it can titillate the public fancy. Accomplishing remarkable feats of production, it has established social norms instead of fulfilling social goals. Accepting the most seductive offers made, we have endowed them with a symbolic mystique and absorbed them into our way of life while neglecting our basic needs.

However, even in those European countries where the demand for a continuing supply of standard housing is guaranteed by government, the benefit has been mostly in increased quantity rather than in the substantial reduction of traditional costs. In a less restricted economy the effect of a volatile market is worsened by the mobility of construction workers, who set the price of their labor by the overall demand of the industry and not by any one segment of it. Geared to the extravagances of prestige and high-income properties, wages soar with building booms and bear no relation to the price of would-be low-cost housing. On the other hand, even a significant reduction in construction costs will only marginally reduce monthly shelter payments if their other components of land cost, mortgage interest, property taxes, maintenance and operating expenses remain unchanged. At best, therefore, while any rationalization of housing production is desirable, a technical solution to the problem of housing supply in itself is only another illusion.

Throughout the twentieth century in North America, government has virtually limited itself to trying to maintain the flow of new housing in the mistaken belief that the natural forces of the marketplace would solve the complementary problems of aging, change, and growth. To achieve this, it has tinkered with the various components of housing costs and profits. As more and more fiscal support has benefited fewer and fewer people, and as the middle class has begun to share the traditional plight of its lower-income compatriots, there has been even more political pressure to further underwrite the housing industry. Yet if there are any doubts about the self-deceptions of suburbanization, there are none about the failure of private enterprise to protect our environment or cater to its poorer inhabitants.

Suburbanization makes its profit by supplying housing on rural land within connecting distance of existing urban services. It does not provide its own employment opportunities, utilities, or social facilities. Theoretically, government is therefore in a position to control it by providing or refusing such publicly paid for services as access routes or schools, but in practice where the sole housing supplier is private enterprise, government can only support its development proposals or take the risk of doing without. Faced with this dilemma, the majority of communities stumble along, pushed and pulled by speculative pressures, the turnover of professional planners being proportionate to the rejection of their advice. The result is that whereas other governments have evolved alternative urban growth patterns and constructed self-sufficient new towns, those in North America have been limited to trying to cope with the varied social consequences of haphazard urban sprawl.

While our cities resemble cancerous growths, their centers have been eaten away by decay. At the core of the problem is not just the need for provision of new housing but the conservation and replacement of existing residential areas. As government's role in the automobile industry has been to pick up abandoned automobiles off the streets after they have reached the bottom of the filtering process in the used-car trade, so its role in the housing filtering process has been to wait for neighborhoods to degenerate into slums before it buys them up to level them for redevelopment. Without the capacity to provide its own alternative accommodation, government has been unable to enforce minimum standards through the threat of compulsory vacation or demolition when there is either a general housing shortage or even one limited to low-priced dwellings. Additionally, it has preferred to accept the formation of slums rather than prevent them through the financial support of what it regards as a private capital asset (though it is not clear why this differs philosophically from new housing subsidy programs). Government has therefore been unwilling to insist on the maintenance of existing dwellings when this might require investment in their equity.

By not assuming responsibility for conservation, government has compounded the problem of replacement. Mass reconstruction should have been reduced by continuing physical restraints and supports. Instead the symbol of urban change has been the bulldozer. In the hands of developers it has scattered the poor; operated under the self-restraints of government, it has ghettoized them. Believing that some families would never be able to house themselves at a socially tolerable standard, nineteenth-century reformers sought the help of private philanthropists to build housing at a price the poor could afford by restricting the profit that was made on it. When these efforts proved insufficient, government was enlisted to provide the same sort of service. Along with the seemingly correlated need to clear the slums of the nineteenth century, so-called public housing carried over the irritations and stigma of charity into buildings specially erected for those ignored by private enterprise.

That government housing in North America has largely failed is not due to any inherent bureaucratic incapacity but is the inevitable consequence of its role as the residual supplier to those outside the regular system. Left with the castoffs of the marketplace, yet required to conform to its rules, government has been forced to produce unsuitable dwelling types in areas abandoned by private housing suppliers. While those early occupants, who were a small part of the mass of sufferers from the depression, welcomed their new housing as a benevolent social act, the subsequent re-widening of the gap between the middle- and low-income groups brought with it the sense of ostracism.

Belatedly recognizing that the physical division of economic groups, though intrinsic to the filtering process, was contrary to the ideals of a democratic society, government changed its policy to try to integrate the poor so that social unity might prevail. However, concurrently, a developing interest in sociology and the professionalization of social workers brought an awareness of community identity. In the supply of government housing these two points of view met head on and tended to produce paralysis. The particularizing of social needs helped bring about the rebuild-ing of slum areas into fixed lower-income enclaves, as occurred in the East End of London after World War II, and motivated the drive to rehabilitate existing low-income neighborhoods. The gen-eralizing of social needs showed itself in scatter-site or apartment-leasing programs that dispersed the poor among the rich in the hope that this would merge them into a classless society.

At the same time, forced into conforming to private enterprise patterns of land exploitation, government was maneuvered into providing multistory buildings unsuitable for low-income family living. While its professional advisers supported this approach for reasons of aesthetics, function, and cost, they failed to foretell the social reaction of their tenants, which passed from gratitude through resentment to hostility. Yet while government has been rightly criticized for its institutionalizing of low-income families, the supply of private enterprise housing for the middle class has been just as segregated in the suburbs or even more densely packed in cities. Furthermore, few would claim that government housing has been of a lower standard of design or construction. The major criticism is that it is unnecessarily slow and expensive, but it could be argued that an environmentally better product is worth waiting for and that often the savings of private enterprise are subsequently offset by excessive repairs and maintenance.

To escape such conscious planning and to allow families to make their own housing decisions, the current search for a solution has veered toward the direct subsidizing of people rather than property. Whereas prospective middle-income purchasers are primed largely for the open market by the negative process of reducing their required expenditures, low-income families would become prospective buyers with actual cash supplied by government. Limited in scope, this subsidy operates as a welfare rental supplement; extended, it would become a guaranteed annual income. From one point of view, such programs are simply humanitarian; from another, they are a public underwriting of rent levels established by the real estate industry, an interpretation borne out by private enterprise support for rental subsidy programs. Such a system assumes a responsible housing ownership that will set its rents according to value and not on what the traffic will bear—an idea completely foreign to entrepreneurial philosophy. The result would therefore inevitably be inflationary unless a suitable vacancy rate was maintained by the construction of nonprofit or limited-profit housing.

The housing industry trades on the knowledge that no Western country can politically afford to permit its citizens to sleep in the streets. Private enterprise is consequently able to force whatever concessions it insists upon from any community that does not have the capability to build for itself. In North America government has slowly attained the necessary expertise in face of tremendous opposition from the real estate lobby, but its role has been restricted to that of a charitable support.

Confronted by the self-interestedness of the housing industry and the paternalism of government, social reformers have turned to self-help groups as a way out of this dilemma. In turn, various low-income groups have been provoked into action by development plans that have ignored their human concerns. But the cooperative barnraising tradition seems out of place in an industrialized urban society. The question is whether it is possible that those without sufficient marketable skills to be part of the middle class have the ability to carry through projects of such complexity even when government and quasi-public organizations provide administrative and technical assistance.

More productive has been the provision of housing for cooperative purchase and management. While initially undertaken by social groups for the benefit of their members or constituencies, this method has lately been adopted by developers. It is plain, however, that government could equally provide such housing as a public service with a higher standard of design and construction and a lower appetite for profit.

Whether housing is provided by self-help groups, nonprofit sponsors, or government, the need is obviously for socially responsive organizations to guarantee the orderly supply of our housing needs, not by exhortation or fiscal manipulation, but by direct example, making the rules and setting the standards for entrepreneurs to follow. Although present-day Western economies bear little resemblance to nineteenth-century capitalism, in North America housing remains anomalous in the public-private balance of power. Few would insist that sewage disposal should be left to private enterprise rather than be part of a program of public works. Similarly, while our educational system includes the contribution of private schools, its standards are set and largely implemented through the public schools. With housing, as in education, the responsibility of government is to satisfy the essential requirements of its electorate.

That the housing situation in some places is not intolerable might suggest that under certain conditions the laissez-faire approach has worked. Generally, however, its results have ranged from muddling through to failure, especially in the provision of housing for the poor and in the quality of our overall environment. The belief has been that the process is fundamentally sound and only occasionally needs compensatory government intervention. Another reading of past events is that the process never worked, that it was socially unacceptable from almost the very beginning, and that is why government intervened in the first place; that there has always been a housing problem from the slum formation of the last century through the continuing exploitation of land and property leading to the inaccessible prices of today; and that even with massive government financial support, private enterprise with its single-minded profit motivation has been both unwilling and unable to cope. If the operations had been sufficiently profitable, private enterprise might have replaced slums, housed the poor, provided neighborhood choice, developed balanced communities, and created new towns; it did not. The result has been the North American failure of orderly urban growth and renewal.

In its turn, the halting efforts of government have been largely dissipated by lack of motivation. As each of its housing solutions has been undercut by the system within which it must operate, no effort has been made to make it effective, but another context-less panacea has been superimposed. Conservation, rehabilitation, urban renewal, low-rental housing, government mortgaging, mortgage interest subsidies, rent supplements—all would have succeeded if they could have been enforced by government control of housing supply, instead of being subsumed by the antisocial workings of private enterprise. For over a hundred years government has been trailing private enterprise, trying to plug its gaps and relieve its deficiencies. Yet the twentieth-century truth is obvious: private enterprise has no moral duty to provide us with adequate housing and a decent environment. If we want them, we must build them for ourselves.

References and Other Sources

Prologue

1. New York State, Select Committee Appointed to Examine into the Condition of Tenant Houses in New York and Brooklyn, *Report*, Assembly Document, Vol. 3, No. 205 (Albany, 1857), pp. 10-12.

1 The Problem Stated

1. New York City, City Inspector's Department, *Annual Report* (1834), p. 16.

2. John H. Griscom, *The Sanitary Condition of the Laboring Population of New York* (New York, 1845), p. 9.

3. Ibid., p. 23.

4. New York City, City Inspector's Department, *Annual Report* (1844), p. 680.

5. New York City, City Inspector's Department, *Annual Report* (1852), p. 289.

6. Jacob A. Riis, *How the Other Half Lives* (New York, 1890), pp. 35-38.

7. New York *Evening Post*, August 20, 1850, p. 2.

8. Charles Dickens, *American Notes* Vol. 1 (London, 1842), pp. 215-216.

9. New York Association for Improving the Condition of the Poor, *First Report of a Committee on the Sanitary Condition of the Laboring Classes in the City of New York, with Remedial Suggestions* (1853), p. 9.

10. New York State, Select Committee Appointed to Examine into the Condition of Tenant Houses in New-York and Brooklyn, *Report*, Assembly Document, Vol. 3, No. 205 (Albany, 1857), p. 25.

11. *New York Times*, July 21, 1871, p. 5.

12. Edward Crapsey, *The Nether Side of New York* (New York, 1872), p. 110.

13. *New York Times*, July 21, 1871, p. 5.

14. *Some Results of an Effort to Reform the Homes of the Laboring Classes in New York City* (1881), p. 14.

15. Charles F. Wingate, "The Moral Side of the Tenement-House Problem," *The Catholic World* 41 (1885):164.

16. New York Association for Improving the Condition of the Poor, *22nd Annual Report* (1865), p. 37.

17. New York Association for Improving the Condition of the Poor, *4th Annual Report* (1847), pp. 22-23.

18. *Morning Courier and New-York Inquirer*, January 30, 1847, quoted in James Ford, *Slums and Housing*, Vol. 1 (Cambridge, 1936), p. 113.

19. *First Report of a Committee on the Sanitary Condition of the Laboring Classes in the City of New York, with Remedial Suggestions*, p. 13.

20. Robert W. de Forest and Lawrence Veiller (eds.), *The Tenement House Problem*, Vol. 1 (New York, 1903), p. 87.

21. New York Association for Improving the Condition of the Poor, *13th Annual Report* (1856), pp. 45-46.

22. Alfred T. White, *Better Homes for Workingmen* (New York, 1885), p. 9.

23. Lucy M. Hall, "Tenement-Houses and Their Population," *Journal of Social Science*, No. 20 (Boston, 1885), p. 94.

24. Select Committee Appointed to Examine into the Condition of Tenant Houses in New-York and Brooklyn, *Report*, p. 27.

25. New York City, *Corporation Manual* (1866), p. 756.

26. Select Committee Appointed to Examine into the Condition of Tenant Houses in New-York and Brooklyn, *Report*, p. 23.

27. *New York Times,* April 7, 1856, p. 8.
28. Select Committee Appointed to Examine into the Condition of Tenant Houses in New-York and Brooklyn, *Report,* p. 40.
29. Ibid., p. 26.

Other Sources

"James Allaire," *Dictionary of American Biography* (New York. 1928).

Lillian W. Betts, *Leaven in a Great City* (New York, 1902).

Robert H. Bremner, "The Big Flat: History of a New York Tenement House," *American Historical Review* (October 1958).

Citizens' Association of New York, Council of Hygiene and Public Health, *Report upon the Sanitary Condition of the City* (1865).

Charles H. Haswell, *Reminiscences of an Octogenarian of the City of New York* (New York, 1896).

Roy Lubove, "The New York Association for Improving the Condition of the Poor: The Formative Years," *New-York Historical Society Quarterly* (July 1959).

James Mullin, *The Story of a Toiler's Life* (Dublin, 1921).

New York Association for Improving the Condition of the Poor, *18th Annual Report* (1861).

New York City, Building Department, *Report* (1871).

New York City, *Record of Assessments* (1851).

New York State, Tenement House Commission, *Report* (Albany, 1885).

Real Estate Record, February 16, 1895.

Jacob A. Riis, *The Making of an American* (New York, 1904).

William H. Tolman, "Half a Century of Improved Housing Effort by the New York Association for Improving the Condition of the Poor," *Yale Review* (November 1896, February 1897).

Thomas Willis, *Facts Connected with the Social and Sanitary Conditions of the Working Classes in the City of Dublin* (Dublin, 1845).

2   First Step

1. New York City, Building Department, *Report* (1862), p. 12.

2. New York State, Select Committee Appointed to Investigate the Health Department of the City of New York, *Report*, Senate Document, No. 49 (Albany, 1859), p. 205.

3. Ibid., p. 8.

4. New York *Daily Tribune*, April 15, 1861, p. 4.

5. New York City, City Inspector's Department, *Annual Report* (1863), p. 12.

6. Citizens' Association of New York, Council of Hygiene and Public Health, *Report upon the Sanitary Condition of the City* (1865), p. 101.

7. Ibid., pp. lxxii-lxxiv.

8. Quoted in Stephen Smith, *The City That Was* (New York, 1911), pp. 99-100.

9. New York State, Senate Select Committee Appointed to Investigate Various Departments of the Government of the City of New York, *Proceedings*, Senate Document, No. 38 (Albany, 1865), pp. 451-478; see also Andrew D. White, *Autobiography*, Vol. 1 (Albany, 1905), pp. 107-110.

10. New York State, Laws of 1866, Chapter 74.

11. *New York Times*, March 6, 1867, p. 4.

12. New York City, Building Department, *Report* (1863), p. 55.

13. New York City, Building Department, *Report* (1864), p. 107.

14. New York City, Building Department, *Report* (1865), p. 157.

Other Sources

Address of the Committee to Promote the Passage of a Metropolitan Health Bill (New York, 1865).

John P. Comer, *New York City Building Control, 1800-1941* (New York, 1942).

John H. Griscom, *Sanitary Legislation, Past and Future: The Value of Sanitary Reform and the True Principles for Its Attainment* (New York, 1861).

New York Sanitary Association, *Reports of the Sanitary Association of the City of New York in Relation to the Public Health* (1859).

New York State, Metropolitan Board of Health, *Report* (New York, 1867).

New York State, Tenement House Committee, *Report* (Albany, 1895).

New York Times, November 4, 1865.

George Rosen, *A History of Public Health* (New York, 1958).

Speech of Thomas N. Carr in Support of Charges Against Francis I. A. Boole, City Inspector Before His Excellency Horatio Seymour (June 3, 1864).

Homer A. Stubbins, *A Political History of the State of New York, 1865-1869* (New York, 1913).

3   False Start

1. For new tenement building statistics for Manhattan during 1863-1898, see New York City, Building Department, *Annual Reports* (1863-1872); *City Record*, Quarterly Building Reports (1873-1880); Fire Department, Annual Reports (1881-1892); *City Record*, Quarterly Building Reports (1893-1898).

2. New York State, Assembly Committee on Public Health, Medical Colleges and Societies, Relative to the Condition of Tenement Houses in the Cities of New York and Brooklyn, *Report*, Assembly Document, Vol. 7 No. 156 (Albany, 1867), p. 11.

3. Ibid., pp. 14-15.

4. Citizens' Association of New York, Council of Hygiene and Public Health, *Report upon the Sanitary Condition of the City* (1865), p. 122.

5. New York State, Laws of 1867, Chapter 908, section 17.

6. New York *Herald*, November 14, 1875, p. 5.

7. *New York Times*, December 29, 1869, p. 4.

8. New York State, Metropolitan Board of Health, *4th Report* (1869), p. 59.

9. New York City, Health Department, *3rd Report* (1872-1873), pp. 43-44.

10. New York State, Metropolitan Board of Health, *3rd Report* (1868), p. 124.

11. New York *Sun*, April 13, 1870, p. 2.

12. *Real Estate Record*, 7(January 14, 1871): 17-18.

13. *New York Times*, August 11, 1877, p. 2.

14. Alfred T. White, *Improved Dwellings for the Laboring Classes* (New York, 1879), p. 41.

15. New York Association for Improving the Condition of the Poor, *35th Annual Report* (1878), pp. 35-36.

16. *American Architect*, 4(November 30, 1878): 178.

17. New York Association for Improving the Condition of the Poor, *35th Annual Report* (1878), p. 37.

18. New York City, Health Department, *5th/6th Annual Report* (1874-1875), p. 7.

Other Sources

Citizens' Association of New York, *Address of the Citizens' Association of New-York to the Public* (1871).

New York State, Senate Committee to Investigate the Several Departments of the Government in the City and County of New York, *Report* (Albany, 1876).

Real Estate Record, December 4, 1875, November 17, 1877.

Stephen Smith, *Addresses in Recognition of His Public Services* (New York, 1911).

State Charities Aid Association, *Annual Reports* (1887-1880).

4   The Competition

1. *Plumber and Sanitary Engineer*, 2(December 1878): 1.
2. *Dictionary of American Biography*, 5 (New York, 1932): 573.
3. *Dictionary of American Biography*, 8(New York, 1932): 137-138.
4. *American Architect*, 5(February 22, 1879): 57.
5. *Plumber and Sanitary Engineer*, 2(January 1879): 34.
6. New York *Daily Tribune*, February 14, 1879, p. 5.
7. For press assessments of the competition entries, see *American Architect*, 5(February 22, 1879): 61-62, 69; *New York Times*, February 10, 1879, p. 8; New York *Tribune*, February 14, 1879, p. 5.
8. "Report of the Committee," *Plumber and Sanitary Engineer*, 2(March 1879): 90.
9. Ibid.
10. *The Sanitarian*, 7(May 1879): 226.
11. New York *Daily Graphic*, March 12, 1879, p. 80.
12. New York *Tribune*, March 17, 1879, p. 1.
13. A. J. Bloor, "Suggestions for a Better Method of Building Tenement-Houses in New York," *American Architect*, 9(February 12, 19, 1881): 75-76, 87-88.
14. "A Model Tenement House for New York," *Municipal Affairs*, 3(March 1899): 138-139; New York *Tribune*, February 24, 1895, p. 12.
15. *American Architect*, 5(March 15, 1879):81.
16. *New York Times*, March 16, 1879, p. 6.
17. *Plumber and Sanitary Engineer*, 1(April 1879): 121-122.
18. New York Association for Improving the Condition of the Poor, *36th Annual Report* (1879), p. 42.
19. James Gallatin, *Tenement-House Reform in the City of New York* (Boston, 1881), p. 4.

20. *Plumber and Sanitary Engineer,* 2(June 1, 1879): 177-178.

Other Sources

Henry C. Meyer, *The Story of the Sanitary Engineer, Later the Engineering Record, Supplementary to Civil War Experiences* (New York, 1928).

5 Chandler Moves

1. *New York Times,* March 12, 1879, p. 2.
2. James Gallatin, *Tenement-House Reform in the City of New York* (Boston, 1881), p. 6.
3. New York State, Laws of 1879, Chapter 504.
4. *New York Times,* May 25, 1879, p. 6.
5. Ten scrapbooks of tenement house plans prepared for Professor C. F. Chandler, filed with the New York City Health Department (1879-1883?), and currently held in the Avery Library, Columbia University. See no. 633 for plan by James E. Ware.
6. New York State, Laws of 1867, Chapter 908, section 15; New York State, Laws of 1879, Chapter 504, section 2; *Tenement-House Reform in the City of New York,* p. 5.
7. New York *Tribune,* May 20, 1883, p. 6.
8. *New York Times,* December 9, 1884, p. 4.
9. William L. Riordan, *Plunkitt of Tammany Hall* (New York, 1905), p. 10.
10. New York State, Special Senate Committee Investigation of the Departments of the City of New York, *Report* (Albany, 1885), p. 183.

Other Sources

Committee of Nine, Tenement House Reform, *Final Report* (New York, 1879).

Robert W. de Forest and Lawrence Veiller (eds.), *The Tenement House Problem* (New York, 1903).

Henry C. Meyer, *The Story of the Sanitary Engineer, Later the Engineering Record, Supplementary to Civil War Experiences* (New York, 1928).

New York Sanitary Reform Society, *Annual Reports* (1879-1884).

New York Times, May 17, 1883, January 1, 1884, May 3, 1885, March 15, 1887.

New York State, Tenement House Committee, *Report* (Albany, 1895).

Real Estate Record, November 5, 1881, April 3, 1886.

Marcus T. Reynolds, *Housing of the Poor in American Cities* (Baltimore, 1893).

Jacob A. Riis, *How the Other Half Lives* (New York, 1890).

6   The Problem Solved

1. New York *Tribune*, February 18, 1884, p. 3.

2. New York State, Tenement House Commission, *Report*, Senate Document, Vol. 5 No. 36 (Albany, 1885), p. 56.

3. New York *Tribune*, February 6, 1884, p. 4.

4. Gregory Weinstein, *The Ardent Eighties* (New York, 1928), pp. 124-126; *Real Estate Record*, 39(March 26, 1887): 398, *The Epoch*, 1(May 13, 1887): 323.

5. *Report of Mass Meeting of Workingmen at the Cooper Union, Monday, February 28th, 1887 to Sustain Tenement House Reform*, stenographic report.

6. New York State, Laws of 1887, Chapters 84 and 566.

7. New York City, Health Department, *The Tenement House Problem in New York* (1887), pp. 21, 27-28.

8. Dwight Porter, *Report Upon a Sanitary Inspection of Certain Tenement-House Districts of Boston* (Boston, 1889), p. 22.

9. *Building*, 11(December 21, 1889): 221.

10. *American Architect*, 45(September 1, 1894): 77.

11. New York City, Health Department, *Annual Report* (1890), p. 50.

12. E. R. L. Gould, *The Housing of the Working People*, Special Report No. 8, U. S. Labor Bureau (Washington, 1895), p. 128.

Other Sources

Fiftieth Anniversary of the Ethical Movement, 1876-1926 (New York, 1926).

New York State, Tenement House Committee, *Report* (Albany, 1895).

Real Estate Record, February 26, March 26, 1887.

Tenement House Building Company, *The Tenement Houses of New York City* (New York, 1891).

William H. Tolman and William I. Hull, *Handbook of Sociological Information* (New York, 1894).

7   Comparisons

1. *American Architect*, 19(March 13, 1886): 126.
2. W. B. Tuthill, *The City Residence: Its Design and Construction* (New York, 1890), p. 38.
3. Ten scrapbooks of tenement house plans (see reference 5 for Chapter 5), plan No. 1276.
4. *Builder and Wood-worker*, November 1881, plate No. 84.
5. Ten scrapbooks . . . plan No. 302.
6. Ten scrapbooks . . . plan No. 783.
7. New York *Tribune*, April 14, 1885, p. 1.
8. New York State, Tenement House Commission, *Report*, Senate Document, Vol. 5, No. 36(Albany, 1885), p. 89.
9. New York *Tribune*, December 28, 1884, p. 4.
10. Tenement House Building Company, *The Tenement Houses of New York City* (New York, 1891), p. 18.
11. *Real Estate Record*, 35(March 7, 1885): 234-235.
12. State Charities Aid Association, *6th Annual Report* (1878), p. 138.
13. Stephen Crane, *Maggie* (New York, 1896), Chapter 5.
14. Jacob A. Riis, *How the Other Half Lives* (New York, 1890), p. 235.
15. Ibid., p. 131.

16. Helen Campbell, *The Problems of the Poor* (New York, 1882), pp. 90-92.

17. Jacob A. Riis, *The Battle with the Slum* (New York, 1902), p. 100.

18. Ibid., pp. 96-97.

19. *New York Times*, March 7, 1879, p. 3.

20. Tenement House Commission, *Report* (1885), p. 49.

21. Emma Lazarus, "The New Colossus" (New York, 1883).

22. *Real Estate Record*, 51(June 10, 1893): 905.

23. Helen Campbell, *Darkness and Daylight: or Lights and Shadows of New York Life* (Hartford, 1891), p. 102.

24. U.S. House of Representatives, Committee on Manufacturers on the Sweating System, *Report,* 52nd Congress, 2nd Session, Report No. 2309 (Washington, 1893), p. 184.

25. New York State, Bureau of Statistics of Labor, *2nd Annual Report* (Albany, 1884), pp. 180-181.

26. Morris Rosenfeld, "The Pale Operator," *Songs from the Ghetto* (New York, 1900).

Other Sources

Commissioner and Mrs. Ballington Booth, *New York's Inferno Explored* (New York, 1891).

John I. Davenport, *Letter on the Subject of the Population of the City of New York* (1884).

New York State, Factory Investigating Commission, *2nd Report* (Albany, 1913).

Proceedings of Meetings of the Property Holders of the West Side District of New York (1878).

Real Estate Record, December 2, 1871, April 5, 1884, September 22, 1888.

Jacob A. Riis, *The Making of an American* (New York, 1904).

Some Results of an Effort to Reform the Homes of the Laboring Classes in New York City (1881).

James B. Walker, *Fifty Years of Rapid Transit, 1864-1917* (New York, 1918).

Howard B. Woolston, *Prostitution in the United States* (New York, 1921).

8   Interlude

1. Jacob A. Riis, *The Making of an American* (New York, 1904), p. 248.
2. Jacob A. Riis *How the Other Half Lives* (New York, 1890), pp. 135, 113, 235, 263.
3. Ibid., p. 284.
4. Ibid., pp. 295-296.
5. Louise Ware, *Jacob A. Riis* (New York, 1938), p. 76.
6. New York *Tribune*, January 4, 1885, p. 10.
7. *The Epoch*, 1(May 13, 1887): 323.
8. New York State, Tenement House Commission, *Report*, Senate Document, Vol. 5, No. 36 (Albany, 1885), pp. 3, 56.
9. New York Association for Improving the Condition of the Poor, *44th Annual Report* (1887), p. 12.
10. New York Sanitary Aid Society, *Annual Report* (1887), pp. 2-3.
11. New York *Press*, September 24, 1893, p. 9.
12. New York *Press*, October 1, 1893, pp. 15, 18.
13. New York *Press*, October 22, 1893, Section III, p. 2.
14. New York State, Tenement House Committee, *Report* (Albany, 1895), pp. 4-5.
15. New York State, Laws of 1895, Chapter 567, Section 13.
16. Tenement House Committee, *Report* (1895), p. 162.
17. *Real Estate Record*, 56(September 28, 1895): 395.
18. New York State, Special Senate Committee to Investigate the Police Department of the City of New York, *Report* (Albany, 1895), p. 2329.
19. *New York Times*, February 26, 1895, p. 9.
20. *American Architect*, 47(March 23, 1895): 117.

21. New York *Tribune*, July 20, 1895, p. 13.

22. Tenement House Committee, *Report* (1895), p. 30.

23. *American Architect*, 45(September 1, 1894): 77.

24. Riis, *The Making of an American*, p. 370.

25. *Real Estate Record*, 34(December 20, 1884): 1277.

26. Riis, *The Making of an American*, p. 264.

27. Ibid., pp. 347-349.

28. New York *Tribune*, March 4, 1896, p. 2.

29. Improved Housing Council, *Conditions of Competition for Plans of Model Apartment Houses* (1896).

30. *Real Estate Record*, 54(July 7, 1894): 2-3.

31. New York City, Tenement House Department, *1st Report* (1902-1903), p. 139.

32. Edward Marshall, "Stamping Out the London Slums," *The Century Magazine*, 51(March 1896): 706.

33. *Real Estate Record*, 57(March 14, 1896): 432.

Other Sources

Citizens' Association of New York, Council of Hygiene and Public Health, *Report upon the Sanitary Condition of the City* (1865).

City and Suburban Homes Company, *1st Annual Report* (New York, 1896/1897).

Robert W. de Forest and Lawrence Veiller (eds.) *The Tenement House Problem* (New York, 1903).

New York Times, March 15, 1887.

New York *Tribune*, March 30, 1899.

Charles C. Parkhurst, *Our Fight with Tammany* (New York, 1895).

Real Estate Record, April 27, 1895, May 30, 1896.

The Triumph of Reform (New York, 1895).

U.S. Federal Housing Administration, Division of Economics and Statistics, *Four Decades of Housing with a Limited Dividend Corporation* (Washington, 1939).

9 The Problem Restated

1. E. R. L. Gould, *The Housing of the Working People*, Special Report No. 8, U.S. Labor Bureau (Washington, 1895), p. 439.
2. *New York Times*, April 3, 1901, p. 8.
3. *New York Times*, June 29, 1899, p. 6.
4. *Real Estate Record*, 64(October 7, 1899): 500.
5. *Real Estate Record*, 64(September 9, 1899): 366.
6. *Real Estate Record*, 64(September 16, 1899): 398.
7. *Real Estate Record*, 65(May 26, 1900): 915.
8. Lawrence Veiller, *Reminiscenses* (New York, 1949), p. 20.
9. Robert W. de Forest and Lawrence Veiller (eds.), *The Tenement House Problem*, Vol. 2 (New York, 1903), p. 95.
10. Ibid., Vol. 1, p. 287.
11. Ibid., Vol. 1, p. 257.
12. Ibid., Vol. 2, p. 427.
13. Ibid., Vol. 1, pp. 401-402.
14. Ibid., Vol. 1, p. 377, quoting the *Commercial Advertiser*, March 3, 1900.
15. Ibid., Vol. 1, p. 366.
16. New York State, Laws of 1901, Chapter 334.
17. de Forest and Veiller, *The Tenement House Problem*, Vol. 1, p. 40.
18. *American Architect*, 71(March 9, 1901): 73.
19. *Real Estate Record*, 67(April 13, 1901): 641.
20. *Real Estate Record*, 68(July 27, 1901): 111.
21. New York State, Laws of 1901, Chapter 466.

Other Sources

Mary Antin, *The Promised Land* (Boston, 1912).

Charity Organization Society, *1st Annual Report* (1882), *17th Annual Report* (1898-1899), *18th Annual Report* (1899-1900).

Committee of Fifteen, *The Social Evil* (New York, 1902).

Alfred Hodder, *A Fight for the City* (New York, 1903).

Roy Lubove, *The Progressives and the Slums* (Pittsburgh, 1962).

New York Times, June 26, 29, 1899.

Real Estate Record, May 14, November 26, December 24, 1898.

Theodore Lothrop Stoddard, *Master of Manhattan* (New York, 1931).

Lawrence Veiller, "The Charity Organization Society's Tenement-House Competition," *American Architect* (March 10, 1900).

10 The Rule of Veiller

1. Robert W. de Forest and Lawrence Veiller (eds.), *The Tenement House Problem*, Vol. 1 (New York, 1903), p. xix.

2. *Real Estate Record*, 72(October 10, 1903): 621.

3. Lawrence Veiller, *Reminiscences* (New York, 1949), pp. 45-46.

4. Quoted in *Real Estate Record*, 71(February 21, 1903): 338.

5. *Real Estate Record*, 71(February 14, 1903): 290.

6. *Real Estate Record*, 71(March 7, 1903): 430-431.

7. Charity Organization Society, *33rd Annual Report* (1914-1915), p. 61.

8. Veiller, *Reminiscences*, p. 67.

9. Ibid., pp. 69-70.

10. *Real Estate Record*, 85(March 19, 1910): 608-611.

11. Charity Organization Society, Tenement House Committee, *For You* (1914).

12. *New York Times*, April 18, 1917, p. 8.

13. Veiller, *Reminiscences*, p. 39.

Other Sources

Charity Organization Society, 35th *Annual Report* (1916-1917).

Charity Organization Society, Tenement House Committee, *Report, 1911, 1912, 1913* (1914).

Housing Betterment, September 1912.

Roy Lubove, *The Progressives and the Slums* (Pittsburgh, 1962).

New York Times, March 27, November 4, 1903.

Real Estate Record, August 15, 29, October 28, 1914; March 20, 1915; April 4, 1925.

11 The Filter Clogs

1. New York City, Tenement House Department, *2nd Report* (1903-1905), p. 59.

2. Quoted in Roy Lubove, *The Progressives and the Slums* (Pittsburgh, 1962), p. 181.

3. For new apartment building statistics for Manhattan for 1902-1930, see New York City, Tenement House Department, *11th Report* (1930), Table XXXIIIa.

4. Walter Laidlow, *Population of the City of New York, 1890-1930* (New York, 1932), p. 249.

5. "Italy," *Encyclopedia Britannica*, 12(Chicago, 1963): 810; Nathan Glazer and Daniel Patrick Moynihan, *Beyond the Melting Pot* (Cambridge, 1963), p. 185.

6. Abraham Cahan, *Yekl: A Tale of the New York Ghetto* (New York, 1896), pp. 28-29.

7. Moses Rischin, *The Promised City* (New York, 1964), p. 94.

8. E. Idell Zeisloft, *The New Metropolis* (New York, 1899), pp. 272-273.

9. Charity Organization Society, Tenement House Committee, *Report* (1911, 1912, 1913), p. 9.

10. *Real Estate Record*, 98(July 1, 1916): 3-4; New York City, Tenement House Department, *8th Report* (1915-1916), p. 8.

11. Great Britain, Board of Trade, *Cost of Living in American Towns* (London, 1911), pp. 22, 25.

12. Caroline Goodyear, "A Study of the Minimum Practicable Cost of an Adequate Standard of Living in New York City," 7th New York State Conference of Charities and Correction, *Proceedings* (Albany, 1907), pp. 41-42, 51.

13. Robert C. Chapin, *The Standard of Living Among Workingmen's Families in New York City* (New York, 1909), pp. 273, 281.

14. Ibid., p. 79; Louise B. More, *Wage-earners' Budgets: A Study of Standards and Cost of Living in New York City* (New York, 1907), pp. 131-132; *Real Estate Record*, 112 (October 27, 1923): 519-520.

15. Abraham Cahan, *The Rise of David Levinsky* (New York, 1917).

16. S. Willis Rudy, *The College of the City of New York: A History 1847-1947* (New York, 1949), p. 293.

17. *Real Estate Record*, 86(December 24, 1910): 1081.

18. *Real Estate Record*, 86(August 27, 1910): 354.

19. Great Britain, Board of Trade, *Cost of Living in American Towns*, p. 29.

20. New York City, Tenement House Department, *13th Report* (1932-1934), p. 6.

21. Charity Organization Society, Committee on Housing, *Housing Administration in New York City* [1938?].

22. New York City, Tenement House Department, *3rd Report* (1906), p. 9.

23. New York *Evening Post*, January 6, 1906, Supplement p. 4.

24. Lillian W. Betts, "The Italian in New York," *University Settlement Studies Quarterly*,1(October 1905-January 1906): 90-105.

25. New York City, Commission on Congestion of Population, *Report* (1911), pp. 7, 84.

26. Ibid., p. 12.

27. Committee on Congestion of Population in New York, *The True Story of the Worst Congestion in Any Civilized City* [1910?], p. 3.

28. *Real Estate Record* 71(September 6, 1902): 321.

29. For vacancy rates for 1909 and 1916-1925, see New York City, Tenement House Department, *Report on Housing Conditions in New York City* (1925).

30. *Real Estate Record*, 79(January 26, 1907): 153.

31. *Real Estate Record*, 72(October 10, 1903): 624.

32. Robert M. Haig, *Some Probable Effects of the Exemption of Improvements from Taxation in the City of New York* (New York, 1915), p. 133.

33. New York *Tribune*, July 6, 1905, p. 4; July 7, 1905, p. 10; July 12, 1905, p. 10.

34. Emily Dinwiddie, "The Rent Strike in New York," *Charities and the Commons*,19(January 4, 1908): 1312; Charles Bernheimer, "High Rents on New York's East Side," *Charities and the Commons*, 19(January 18, 1908): 1403-1404.

35. Charity Organization Society, *24th Annual Report* (1905-1906), p. 11.

36. New York City, Tenement House Department, *4th Report* (1907-1908), pp. 268-269.

37. See Gilbert Osofsky, *Harlem: The Making of a Ghetto* (New York, 1966).

38. Rollin L. Hartt, "I'd Like to Show You Harlem!" *The Independent*, 105(April 2, 1921): 334-335, 357-358.

39. New York *Sun*, January 3, 1908, p. 1; New York *World*, January 3, 1908, p. 9; January 6, 1908, p. 5; January 8, 1908, p. 16.

40. Rischin, *The Promised City*, pp. 247-252.

41. *Real Estate Record*, 89(February 17, 1912): 317-318.

42. *Real Estate Record*, 87(February 11, 1911): 249.

43. New York City, Tenement House Department, *11th Report* (1930), Table XXXIIIa.

44. *Real Estate Record*, 120(July 9, 1927): 7-8.

45. *Real Estate Record,* 98(August 19, 1916): 252-254, 259; New York City Commission on Building Districts and Restrictions, *Final Report* (1916), p. 6.

46. *Real Estate Record,* 97(June 10, 1916): 864.

47. *Population of the City of New York, 1890-1930,* p. 238; *Real Estate Record,* 120(July 9, 1927): 7-8.

48. *Real Estate Record,* 100(July 28, 1917): 103.

49. *Real Estate Record,* 103(January 11, 1919): 38.

50. *Real Estate Record,* 102(July 6, 1918): 5-6.

51. For statistics on the demolition of old-law apartments for 1902-1952, see Real Estate Board of New York, *Apartment Building Construction, Manhattan, 1902-1953* (1953), pp. 18-19.

52. New York City, Mayor's Committee on Housing, *Report* (1924), p. 13.

Other Sources

Charles Bernheimer, "Rent Strikes and Crowded Neighborhoods," *Outlook,* 88(January 18, 1908).

Robert W. de Forest and Lawrence Veiller (eds.), *The Tenement House Problem* (New York, 1903).

Paul H. Douglas, *Real Wages in the United States 1890-1926* (Boston, 1930).

New York City, Tenement House Department, *8th Report* (1915-1916).

Real Estate Record, September 27, 1902; November 24, 1906; December 30, 1911; August 9, 1913; June 10, 1916; February 22, 1919.

James B. Walker, *Fifty Years of Rapid Transit 1864-1917* (New York, 1918).

12   Stick and Carrot

1. For vacancy rates for 1909, 1916-1928, 1931, and 1933, see New York State, State Board of Housing, *Report,* Legislative Document, No. 112 (Albany, 1933), p. 29.

2. *Real Estate Record,* 103(February 22, 1919): 235.

3. New York State, Legislature, *Brief in Support of the Right and Duty of the Legislature to Prevent the Charging of Unreasonable Rents by Landlords, Until the Deficiency of Buildings Caused by the Restriction of Building During the War Is Made Up*, [1920].

4. U.S. Bureau of the Census, *Historical Statistics of the United States, Colonial Times to 1957* (Washington, 1960), p. 393.

5. *Real Estate Record*, 108(July 23, 1921): 105-106.

6. For investment returns, see Merchants' Assn. of N. Y., Special Com. on Housing, *Report* (1919); N. Y. State, Joint Legislative Com. on Housing, *Report*, Legislative Document (Albany, Extraordinary Session, 1920) No.1; *Real Estate Record*, 105(March 20, 1920): 371-372.

7. For apartment building statistics for 1902-1930, see New York City, Tenement House Department, *11th Report* (1930), Table XXXIIIa.

8. Paul H. Douglas, *Real Wages in the United States 1890-1926* (Boston, 1930), pp. 60, 210.

9. For real estate taxes, see *Real Estate Record*, 105(March 13, 1920): 337; for rents, see *Real Estate Record*, 105 (March 6, 1920): 308; 107(April 30, 1921): 553.

10. *Real Estate Record*, 104(December 20, 1919): 625-626.

11. *National Municipal Review*, 8(September 1919): 461.

12. Samuel McCune Lindsay, *Economic Aspects of the So-Called Emergency Housing Legislation of 1920 in New York State and the Alleged Housing Shortage in New York City* [New York, 1921], pp. 84-87.

13. New York State, Reconstruction Commission, Housing Committee, *Housing Conditions, Report* (Albany, 1920), pp. 11, 31.

14. *Real Estate Record*, 105(March 6, 1920): 308.

15. *Real Estate Record*, 105(March 27, 1920): 407.

16. *Real Estate Record*, 108(September 3, 1921): 297. See also 108(September 10, 1921): 325; 109(February 25, 1922): 231; 115(May 2, 1925): 5; 118(August 28, 1926): 8.

17. *Real Estate Record*, 112(August 11, 1923): 166.

18. For rents see New York State, State Board of Housing, *Report*, Legislative Document, No. 85 (Albany, 1927), p. 48; New York State, Commission of Housing and Regional Planning, *Report*, Legislative Document, No. 91 (Albany, 1925), p. 19.

19. New York State, Commission of Housing and Regional Planning, *Present Status of the Housing Emergency, Report*, Legislative Document, No. 43 (Albany, 1924), p. 36; *Housing Conditions, Report* (Albany, 1920), p. 12.

20. Federated American Engineering Societies, Committee on Elimination of Waste in Industry, *Waste in Industry* (Washington, 1921), pp. 52-93.

21. New York State, Reconstruction Commission, *Housing Conditions, Report* (1920), p. 4.

22. *Real Estate Record*, 103(May 17, 1919): 653.

23. Roy Lubove, "Homes and 'A Few Well Placed Fruit Trees': An Object Lesson in Federal Housing," *Social Research*, 27(Winter 1960): 469-486.

24. Tenement House Department, *Report on Housing Conditions in New York City* (1925).

25. New York State, Commission of Housing and Regional Planning, *Tax Exemption of New Housing, Report*, Legislative Document, No. 78 (Albany, 1924), p. 11.

26. *Real Estate Record*, 110(August 19, 1922): 230.

27. *Real Estate Record*, 109(June 24, 1922): 773.

28. *Report*, Legislative Document, No. 43 (1924).

29. Charity Organization Society, *42nd Annual Report* (1923-1924), p. 25.

30. Douglas, *Real Wages in the United States 1890-1926*, pp. 106-107.

31. *Real Estate Record*, 116(November 21, 1925): 7.

32. New York City, Mayor's Committee on Housing, *Report* (1924), p. 13.

33. New York State, Commission of Housing and Regional

Planning, *Permanent Housing Relief, Report*, Legislative Document, No. 66 (Albany, 1926), p. 28.

34. National Industrial Conference Board, Inc., *The Cost of Living in New York City, 1926* (New York, 1926), p. 34.

35. Herbert S. Swan, *The Housing Market in New York City* (New York, 1944), p. 144.

36. New York State, Commission of Housing and Regional Planning, *Report*, Legislative Document, No. 91 (Albany, 1925), p. 44.

37. *New York Times*, August 24, 1920, p. 15.

38. Ibid.

39. For demolitions during 1902-1952, see Real Estate Board of New York, *Apartment Building Construction, Manhattan, 1902-1953* (1953), pp. 18-19.

40. *Report*, Legislative Document, No. 91 (1925), pp. 40-41.

41. Jacob A Riis, *How the Other Half Lives* (New York, 1890), pp. 4-5.

42. Commission of Housing and Regional Planning, *Permanent Housing Relief, Report*, p. 6.

Other Sources

Citizen's Housing and Planning Council of New York, Committee on Tax Policies, *How Tax Exemption Broke the Housing Deadlock in New York City: A Report of the Study of the Post World War I Housing Shortage and the Various Efforts to Overcome it* (1960).

Mary Conyngton, "Effect of the Tax-Exemption Ordinance in New York City on Housing," *Monthly Labor Review* (April 1922).

Robert W. de Forest and Lawrence Veiller (eds.), *The Tenement House Problem* (New York, 1903).

International Labour Office, *The Housing Situation in the United States* (Geneva, 1925).

New York City, Board of Alderman, *Proceedings* (March 16, 1920).

New York State, Joint Legislative Committee on Housing

and the New York State Reconstruction Commission, *Program of Architectural Competition for the Remodeling of a New York City Tenement Block* (Albany, 1920).

New York State, Joint Legislative Committee on Housing, *Preliminary Report* (Albany, 1920).

New York State, Joint Legislative Committee on Housing, *Report* (Albany, 1921).

New York State, Laws of 1920, Chapters 130-139, 949; Laws of 1922, Chapter 658.

New York Times, April 9, June 14, July 12, 29, August 5, September 3, 20, 1920.

Louis H. Pink, *The New Day in Housing* (New York, 1928).

Real Estate Record, June 24, 1916; April 19, May 3, 24, 1919; July 5, 1924.

Jacob A. Riis, *The Battle with the Slum* (New York, 1902).

Alfred E. Smith, *Up to Now* (New York, 1929).

Nelson S. Spencer, "New York City's Civil Service," *National Municipal Review* (January 1916).

Clarence S. Stein, *Toward New Towns for America* (Liverpool, 1951).

Charles H. Whitaker, *The Housing Problem in War and in Peace* (Washington, 1918).

Edith Elmer Wood, *The Housing of the Unskilled Wage Earner* (New York, 1919).

Edith Elmer Wood, *Recent Trends in American Housing* (New York, 1931).

13   Reluctant Partners

1. *Housing Betterment*, 15(June, 1926): 88.

2. *Housing Betterment*, 16(May, 1927): 28-29.

3. Clarence S. Stein, *Toward New Towns for America* (Liverpool, 1951), pp. 23, 33; New York State, State Board of Housing, *Report*, Legislative Document, No. 76 (Albany, 1928), p. 8.

4. New York State, Laws of 1926, Chapter 823; *Housing Betterment*, 16(May, 1927): 25; *Real Estate Record* 117 (May 8, 1926): 8.

5. U.S. Federal Housing Administration, Division of Economics and Statistics, *Four Decades of Housing with a Limited Dividend Company* (Washington, 1939), p. 22.

6. Louis H. Pink, *The New Day in Housing* (New York, 1928), p. 117.

7. *New York Times*, December 16, 1926, p. 1.

8. *Housing Betterment*, 16(May 1927): 9.

9. National Housing Committee for Congested Areas, *A Review of the Housing Situation* (Washington, 1927), p. 25.

10. *Housing Betterment*, 16(December, 1927): 268.

11. Herbert S. Swan, *The Housing Market in New York City* (New York, 1944), Table XI; U.S. Federal Housing Administration, *The Housing Demand of Workers in Manhattan* (Washington, 1939), p. 20.

12. *Real Estate Record*, 119(February 26, 1927): 7.

13. East Side Chamber of Commerce, Inc., *Research Studies of Community Problems*, No. 12 (1931); New York State, State Board of Housing, *Report*, Legislative Document, No. 84 (Albany, 1932), p. 41.

14. *Real Estate Record*, 122(July 7, 1928): 6.

15. *New York Times*, April 20, 1931, p. 18.

16. *Real Estate Record*, 129(March 26, 1932): 5.

17. *New York Times*, September 12, 1931, p. 19.

18. *New York Times*, April 2, 1932, p. 19.

19. *Housing*, 21(March, 1932): 13.

20. *Housing Betterment*, 16(May 1927): 27.

21. U.S. Federal Housing Administration, *The Housing Demand of Workers in Manhattan*, p. 63.

22. State Board of Housing, *Report* (1928), Tables 1 and 4.

23. *Real Estate Record*, 131(January 28, 1933): 8.

24. New York State, State Board of Housing, *Report*, Legislative Document, No. 112 (Albany, 1933), p. 11.

25. Swan, *The Housing Market in New York City*, Table XXXIII.

26. State Board of Housing, *Report* (1932), p. 21.

27. New York State, State Board of Housing, *Report*, Legislative Document, No. 41 (Albany, 1934), p. 11.

28. *Housing Betterment*, 16(May, 1927): 27; State Board of Housing, *Report* (1932), p. 34.

29. New York State, State Board of Housing, *Report on the Standard of Living of 400 Families in a Model Housing Project: The Amalgamated Housing Corporation* (Albany, 1931).

30. National Housing Committee for Congested Areas, *A Review of the Housing Situation*, p. 48.

31. President's Conference on Home Building and Home Ownership, *Publications*, Vol. 2 (Washington, 1932), pp. 1-2.

Other Sources

Housing Study Guild, Housing Surveys Committee, *Report* (New York, 1934).

New York State, Laws of 1926, Chapter 823; Laws of 1929, Chapter 713.

New York State, Commission of Housing and Regional Planning, *Report* (Albany, 1926).

New York State, Commission of Housing and Regional Planning, *Permanent Housing Relief, Report* (Albany, 1926).

New York State, State Board of Housing, *Report* (Albany, 1930).

New York Times, January 29, February 26, October 14, December 1, 3, 1926; June 14, July 8, 1927; September 27, 1928; September 24, 27, October 26, 1932; July 3, October 27, 1933.

Real Estate Record, December 26, 1925; January 9, March 27, June 19, 1926; February 23, 1929; March 22, July 5, 1930.

Alfred E. Smith, *Up to Now* (New York, 1929).

Lawrence Veiller, *Reminiscences* (New York, 1949).

14 Government Resolves

1. Fred F. French, *Housing in Lower Manhattan* (New York, 1934), p. 6.

2. Harold S. Buttenheim, "Must We Have Slums Forever?" *The Survey*, 62(April 15, 1929): 134-135.

3. Mary K. Simkhovitch, *Here Is God's Plenty* (New York, 1949), pp. 39-40.

4. Timothy L. McDonnell, *The Wagner Housing Act* (Chicago, 1957), pp. 29-30.

5. Michael W. Straus and Talbot Wegg, *Housing Comes of Age* (New York, 1938), p. 115.

6. Langdon W. Post, *The Challenge of Housing* (New York, 1938), p. 180.

7. Harold L. Ickes, *The Secret Diary of Harold L. Ickes*, Vol. II: *The Inside Struggle 1936-1939* (New York, 1954), p. 215.

8. "Unemployment Relief Measures," *Architectural Record*, 72(December, 1932): 354.

9. *New York Times*, July 25, 1934, p. 19.

10. New York Building Congress, Committee on Land Utilization, *Research Bulletin 4* (December 1933), pp. 2-4.

11. James Ford, *Slums and Housing* (Cambridge, 1936), pp. 858, 849-850, 855.

12. Carol Aronovici (ed.), *America Can't Have Housing* (New York, 1934), pp. 23, 18, 69.

13. Consolidated Edison Co. of New York, Inc., Industrial and Economic Development Dept., *Population Growth of New York City by Districts 1910-1948* (1948), p. 2.

14. New York City Housing Authority, *Real Property Inventory, City of New York* (1934), Summary of Five Boroughs, p. B.

15. New York Building Congress, Committee on Land Utilization, *Research Bulletin 1: Manhattan and the Decentralization Trend* (June 1933), p. 2.

16. Robert H. Armstrong and Homer Hoyt, *Decentralization in New York City* (Chicago, 1941), p. 19; *Real Property*

Inventory, City of New York, Summary of Five Boroughs, p. A.

17. *Manhattan and the Decentralization Trend,* p. 2.

18. Post, *The Challenge of Housing,* p. 31.

19. Herbert S. Swan, *The Housing Market in New York City* (New York, 1944), Table XI; Real Estate Board of New York, *Apartment Building Construction, Manhattan, 1902-1953* (1953), pp. 18-19.

20. Rollin L. Hartt, "I'd Like to Show You Harlem!" *The Independent,* 105(April 2, 1921): 334.

21. The Children's Aid Society, *The Negro Children of New York* (1932), pp. 18-21.

22. New York Building Congress, Committee on Land Utilization, *Harlem Family Income Survey* (1935), Table 4A.

23. New York City Housing Authority, *Toward the End to Be Achieved* (1937), p. 7.

24. New York City Housing Authority, *First Houses* (1935), p. 5.

25. *New York Times,* September 25, 1936, p. 25; September 27, 1936, section II, p. 3.

26. *New York Times,* December 4, 1935, p. 22.

27. *New York Times,* September 26, 1936, p. 14.

28. Post, *The Challenge of Housing,* pp. 230, 234.

29. Ibid., p. 89.

30. New York City, Special Housing Commissioner, *Low-Cost Housing Here and Abroad, Report* (1935), p. 30.

31. *New York Times,* January 25, 1925, sec. X, p. 1; Catherine Bauer, *Modern Housing* (Boston, 1934), p. 245; Charles Abrams, "Slum Clearance or Vacant Land Development?" *Shelter,* 2(February 1939): 23-24.

32. Post, *The Challenge of Housing,* pp. 222-224.

33. Regional Plan of New York and Its Environs, *Regional Survey,* Vol. VI (1931), pp. 336-347.

34. *New York Times,* March 22, 1934, p. 18.

35. *New York Times,* March 24, 1934, p. 17.

36. New York City, Mayor's Commission on Conditions in Harlem, *Preliminary Report on the Subject of Housing* [1935], p. 4.

37. Citizens' Housing Council of New York, Committee on New Housing, *Report and Recommendations* (1938), p. 17.

38. Ickes, *The Secret Diary of Harold L. Ickes*, Vol. II, p. 231.

39. New York City Housing Authority, *Wages, Slums and Housing* (1936), p. 4.

40. *New York Times*, May 2, 1935, p. 7.

41. *New York Times*, January 21, 1937, p. 14.

42. Quoted in McDonnell, *The Wagner Housing Act*, p. 307.

43. U.S. Public Law 412, 75th Congress 1st Session (1937).

44. Ibid., section 2 (2).

45. New York State, State Board of Housing, *Report*, Legislative Document, No. 112 (Albany, 1933), p. 29.

46. New York City Housing Authority, Vacancy and Rehousing Bureau, *Housing in New York City: A Study of Low Rental Vacant Dwelling Units in the Borough of Manhattan* (1939), p. 6.

47. Edith Berger Drellich and Andrée Emery, *Rent Control in War and Peace* (1939), pp. 88-89; City-wide Citizens' Committee on Harlem, Subcommittee on Housing, *Report* [1942].

48. Citizens' Housing Council of New York, Committee on New Housing, *Report and Recommendations*; New York State, Division of Housing, *Report*, Legislative Document, No. 70 (Albany, 1940), p. 30.

49. New York City, Council, *Proceedings*, Vol. 1 (1938), p. 1175.

50. New York State, Laws of 1939, Chapter 808.

51. *New York Times*, November 23, 1937, p. 11.

52. *New York Times*, November 24, 1937, p. 5.

53. *New York Times*, December 3, 1937, p. 1.

54. *New York Times*, December 22, 1937, p. 5.

Other Sources

Albert F. Bemis and John Burchard, *The Evolving House* (Cambridge, 1936).

Alfred Bruce and Harold Sandbank, *A History of Prefabrication* (New York, 1943).

George F. Keck, *House of Tomorrow* (Chicago, 1933).

New York City, Commission on Congestion of Population, *Report* (1911).

New York City, Local Law No. 18 (1938).

New York City Housing Authority, *Report to the Mayor on Its Investigations and Public Hearings on Living and Housing Conditions in the City of New York* (1937).

New York City Housing Authority, *Twenty Five Years of Public Housing 1935-1960* (1960).

New York City Housing Authority v. Muller (1936).

New York State, Laws of 1934, Chapter 4; Laws of 1938, Chapter 444, 461.

New York State, Temporary Commission on the Condition of the Urban Colored Population, *Report* (Albany, 1938).

New York Times, March 23, July 8, October 30, 1932; October 17, 1933; April 27, July 11, 1934; April 2, September 14, 1935; January 28, April 4, July 10, 1938.

Slum Clearance Committee of New York, *Maps and Charts, 1933-34* (1934).

U.S. Bureau of the Census, *Historical Statistics of the United States, Colonial Times to 1957* (Washington, 1960).

U.S. Bureau of the Census, Housing Census, 1940.

U.S. Bureau of the Census, Population Census, 1940.

U.S. Federal Housing Administration, *The Housing Demand of Workers in Manhattan* (Washington, 1939).

U.S. Public Law 520 (1932).

15 Promise and Reality

1. New York City Housing Authority, *10th Annual Report* (1944).

2. Elizabeth Wood, *Public Housing and Mrs. McGee* (New York, 1956), p. 3.

3. "It's Heaven, It's Paradise," *Fortune* 21 (April 1940): 116.

4. *New York Times*, December 12, 1939, p. 1.

5. New York City Housing Authority, *8th Annual Report* (1941).

6. Real Estate Board of New York, *Apartment Building Construction, Manhattan 1902-1953* (1953), p. 8.

7. Ibid., p. 11; U.S. Department of Labor, Bureau of Labor Statistics, *Post-World War II Price Trends in Rent and Housing in the New York Metropolitan Area* (Washington, 1967).

8. *New York Times*, July 19, 1943, p. 18.

9. Cited in Paul F. Wendt, *Housing Policy—The Search for Solutions* (Berkeley, 1963), p. 163.

10. *New York Times*, February 24, 1946, section IV, p. 44.

11. *New York Times*, June 23, 1948, p. 19.

12. New York City, Mayor's Emergency Committee on Housing, *Report to Mayor-Elect William O'Dwyer* (1945).

13. New York State, Executive Department, Housing Division, *The Emergency Housing Program of the State of New York* (Albany, 1955), p. 33.

14. New York State, Executive Department, Housing Division, *Report*, Legislative Document, No. 70 (Albany, 1940), p. 30.

15. New York City, City Planning Commission, *Housing Conditions in New York City, Report* (1948).

16. For housing completions and demolitions for 1941-1974, see New York City, City Planning Department, *Annual Net Change of Dwelling Units* (1975).

17. New York City, Mayor's Office, *Statement to the Joint Committee on Housing, Congress of the United States by Mayor William O'Dwyer* (1947).

18. Quoted in Richard O. Davies, *Housing Reform During the Truman Administration* (Columbia, Mo., 1966), p. 27.

19. *New York Times,* March 28, 1947, p. 16.

20. U.S. Public Law 171, 81st Congress 1st Session (1949), Section 2.

21. Quoted in Davies, *Housing Reform During the Truman Administration,* p. 109.

22. *New York Times,* June 3, 1955, p. 22.

23. Lewis Mumford, "Prefabricated Blight," *The New Yorker,* 24(October 30, 1948): 49.

24. *The New Yorker,* 24(November 27, 1948): 65.

25. Lewis Mumford, *The City in History* (New York, 1961), graphic section III: 46.

26. *New York Times,* March 3, 1940, p. 14.

27. Anthony F. C. Wallace, *Housing and Social Structure* (Philadelphia, 1952), p. 100.

28. New York State, Division of Housing, *Annual Report,* Legislative Document, No. 14 (Albany, 1952), p. 7.

29. *New York Times,* March 1, 1949, p. 28; March 2, 1949, p. 3.

30. *Congressional Record,* June 15, 1936, pp. 9345-9346.

31. John P. Dean, "The Myths of Housing Reform," *American Sociological Review,* 14(April 1949): 283.

32. Wallace, *Housing and Social Structure,* p. 31.

33. Daniel Seligman, "The Enduring Slums," *Fortune,* 56 (December 1957): 221.

34. Elizabeth Wood, *The Small Hard Core* (New York, 1957).

35. Harrison E. Salisbury, *The Shook-up Generation* (New York, 1958), p. 75.

36. *Esquire,* 54(September 1960): 16.

37. New York City, Office of the Mayor, Division of Administration, *Organization and Management of the New York City Housing Authority* (1957).

38. Catherine Bauer, "The Dreary Deadlock of Public Housing," *Architectural Forum,* 106(May 1957): 141.

39. New York City Housing Authority, *Project Data* (1974); *New York Times,* January 19, 1973, p. 1.

Other Sources:

Robert A. Caro, *The Power Broker* (New York, 1974).

Nathan Glazer and Daniel Patrick Moynihan, *Beyond the Melting Pot* (Cambridge, 1963).

Lewis Mumford, "Bigger Slums or Better City?" *The New Yorker* (June 24, 1950).

Lewis Mumford, "The Gentle Art of Overcrowding," *The New Yorker* (May 20, 1950).

New York City, Housing and Development Administration, Department of Rent and Housing Maintenance, *Rent Control and the Rental Housing Market in New York City 1968* (1970).

New York City Housing Authority, *22nd Annual Report* (1955).

New York State, Laws of 1938, Chapter 675.

New York Times, April 9, June 17, 1942; June 23, December 11, 1949; March 29, 1950; February 20, November 14, 1952; February 14, 1957; October 19, 1958.

Stanley Rowland, "Flight to Suburbia," *The Nation* (January 12, 1957).

U.S. Bureau of the Census, *Historical Statistics of the United States, Colonial Times to 1957* (Washington, 1960).

U.S. Bureau of the Census, Population Census, 1950, 1960.

U.S. Federal Public Housing Authority, *Public Housing Design* (Washington, 1946).

16 The New Poor

1. Louis H. Pink, *The New Day in Housing* (New York, 1928), p. 143.

2. *New York Times,* April 19, 1943, p. 1.

3. Quoted in Arthur Simon, *Stuyvesant Town, U.S.A.* (New York, 1970), p. 32.

4. *New York Times,* June 4, 1943, p. 23.

5. Real Estate Board of New York, *Apartment Building Construction, Manhattan 1902-1953* (1953), p. 11.

6. New York City, City Planning Department, *Annual Net Change of Dwelling Units* (1975), p. 1.

7. Robert Moses, *Public Works: A Dangerous Trade* (1970), p. 438.

8. *New York Times,* March 13, 1948, p. 1.

9. New York City Housing Authority, *13th Annual Report* (1947).

10. "Family Budget of City Worker, October 1950," *Monthly Labor Review,* 72(February 1951): 152-155.

11. New York State, Laws of 1939, Chapter 808, definition 18 section 2; *New York Times,* April 13, 1948, p. 22.

12. *New York Times,* April 22, 1948, p. 2.

13. Moses, *Public Works: A Dangerous Trade,* p. 454.

14. New York City, Special Adviser on Housing and Urban Renewal, *Final Report* (1960); *New York Times,* June 29, 1959, p. 1.

15. New York City, Committee on Slum Clearance Plans, *Title I Slum Clearance Progress* (1958).

16. New York City, City Planning Commission, *Tenant Relocation Report* (1954), pp. 48-49.

17. New York City, Mayor's Office, *Statement to the Joint Committee on Housing, Congress of the United States* (1947), p. 4.

18. Fred L. Lavanburg Foundation and Hamilton House, *What Happened to 386 Families Who Were Compelled to Vacate Their Slum Dwellings to Make Way for a Large Housing Project* (New York, 1933).

19. Simon, *Stuyvesant Town, U.S.A.,* p. 49.

20. Community Service Society of New York, Committee on Housing, *Housing Information* (January 1945), p. 8.

21. New York City, City Administrator, *Tenant Relocation and the Housing Problem* (1954); New York State, Temporary State Housing Rent Commission, *New Insights into the Housing Situation in Manhattan* (Albany, 1955).

22. Special Adviser on Housing and Urban Renewal, *Final Report*, p. 35.

23. *New York Times*, July 26, 1957, p. 21.

24. *New York Times*, July 29, 1957, p. 18.

25. *New York Times*, January 18, 1959, section VI, p. 71.

26. See *The New Yorker*, 24(November 27, 1948): 65-68, as an example of Moses's invective.

27. Fred J. Cook and Gene Gleason, "The Shame of New York," *The Nation*, 189(October 31, 1959): 263.

28. U.S. President's Advisory Committee on Government Housing Policies and Programs, *Recommendations on Government Housing Policies and Programs* (Washington, 1953), p. 1.

29. New York City, City Planning Commission, *Urban Renewal* [1958], p. 4.

30. *New York Times*, July 4, 1959, p. 1.

31. New York City, Mayor's Committee for Better Housing, Subcommittee on Middle Income Housing with Proper Use of Tax Concessions and State or City Credit, *Report* (1955), p. 1.

32. New York City, Mayor's Committee for Better Housing, *63 Steps Toward Better Housing for All New Yorkers* (1955), step 21.

33. *New York Times*, August 4, 1955, p. 16.

34. New York State, Laws of 1955, Chapter 407, Section 302; *New York Times*, April 19, 1955, p. 20.

35. *New York Times*, January 6, 1957, section VIII, p. 3.

Other Sources

Marquis James, *The Metropolitan Life* (New York, 1947).

New York City, Mayor's Emergency Committee on Housing, *Report to Mayor-Elect William O'Dwyer* (1945).

New York City Housing Authority, *13th Annual Report* (1947).

New York City Housing Authority, *Legislative and Fiscal Background* (1974).

New York City Housing Authority, *Project Data* (1974).

New York State, Laws of 1938, Chapter 25; Laws of 1941, Chapter 892; Laws of 1942, Chapter 845; Laws of 1943, Chapter 234; Laws of 1947, Chapter 579.

New York Times, February 26, June 25, August 12, 27, 1947; January 11, 14, February 20, 22, May 29, 1948; October 2, December 20, 1954; June 27, 1962.

Cleveland Rodgers, *Robert Moses: Builder for Democracy* (New York, 1952).

Nathan Straus, *Two-Thirds of a Nation* (New York, (1952).

U.S. Bureau of the Census, Population Census, 1940, 1950, 1960.

U.S. Public Law 560 (1954).

"World War II," *Encyclopedia Britannica* (Chicago, 1963).

17   Running Standstill

1. New York City, Special Adviser on Housing and Urban Renewal, *Final Report* (1960).

2. New York City, City Planning Department, *A Program for Housing and Urban Renewal* (1959), p. 1.

3. *New York Times*, May 11, 1962, p. 33.

4. Citizens' Housing and Planning Council of New York, Committee on Tax Policies, *How Tax Exemption Broke the Housing Deadlock in New York City: A Report of the Study of the Post World War I Housing Shortage and the Various Efforts to Overcome It* (1960).

5. *New York Times*, February 12, 1961, section VIII, p. 1.

6. For public housing statistics, see New York City Housing Authority, *Project Data* (1974).

7. New York City, City Planning Department, *Public and Publicly Aided Housing 1927-1973* (1974), pp. 10-11.

8. Real Estate Board of New York, *Office Building Construction, Manhattan, 1901-1953, Supplement Number Six 1947-1961* [1961]; for subsequent figures, see New York

City, City Planning Department, *Newsletter* issues.

9. New York City, City Planning Department, *New Dwelling Units Completed 1921-1972 in New York City* (1972), pp. 6-7, 15-16.

10. Frank S. Kristof, "Housing: The Economic Facets of New York City's Problems," a chapter from Lyle Fitch and Annmarie Walsh (eds.), *Agenda for a City: Issues Confronting New York* (Beverly Hills, Calif., 1970), pp. 3-7.

11. For apartment unit statistics for Manhattan for 1960-1965, see New York City, Department of Buildings, *Reports* (1960-1965); New York City, City Planning Department, *Newsletter* (May 1961-February/March 1965).

12. *New York Times*, March 19, 1962, p. 31.

13. New York City, City Planning Department, Community Renewal Program, *New York City's Renewal Strategy/ 1965* (1965).

.14. New York City, City Planning Department, Community Renewal Program, *An Analysis of Current City-Wide Housing Need* (1965), pp. 72, 33.

15. New York City, Housing and Redevelopment Board, *Report No. 12, The Pursuit of Housing Policy Goals in New York City* (1965), pp. 23-35.

16. Compare New York City, City Planning Commission, *Master Plan, Sections Containing Areas for Clearance, Replanning and Low-Rent Housing* (1940), p. 9, with New York City Planning Commission, *Plan for New York City, A Proposal, 4: Manhattan* (Cambridge, 1969), p. 12.

17. *New York Times*, December 28, 1965, p. 26.

18. New York City, Housing and Development Administration, Department of Rent and Housing Maintenance, *Rent Control and the Rental Housing Market in New York City 1968* (1970), p. 87.

19. New York City, Housing and Urban Renewal Task Force, *Report* (1966), p. 26.

20. Institute of Public Administration, Study Group, *Report: "Let There Be Commitment"* (New York, 1966), p. 1.

21. *New York Times*, October 2, 1966, p. 1.

22. Institute of Public Administration, *"Let There Be Commitment,"* p. 35.

23. Planning Commission, *Plan for New York City*, p. 122.

24. *New York Times*, October 15, 1965, p. 30.

25. *New York Times*, October 6, 1968, p. 83.

26. Robert Moses, *Public Works: A Dangerous Trade* (New York, 1970), p. 470.

27. U.S. Department of Housing and Urban Development, Office of Urban Technology and Research, *Cost and Time Associated with New Multifamily Housing Construction in New York City* (Washington, 1969).

28. Metropolitan Council on Housing, *A Citizens' Survey of Available Land* (1964), p. 9.

29. *New York Times*, May 21, 1971, p. 43.

30. W. Goodman, "Battle of Forest Hills, Who's Ahead?" *New York Times*, February 20, 1972, section VI, p. 63.

31. *New York Times*, February 8, 1970, section VIII, p. 6.

32. Bernard Malamud, *The Tenants* (New York, 1971), pp. 19, 21.

33. *New York Times*, August 20, 1968, p. 30.

34. *New York Times*, March 22, 1972, p. 28.

35. *New York Times*, February 13, 1965, p. 20.

36. *New York Times*, April 11, 1965, section VIII, p. 12.

37. Alan S. Oser, "Six Years Later: A Harlem Project Reassessed," *New York Times*, September 19, 1971, section VIII, pp. 1, 6.

38. *New York Times*, March 9, 1967, pp. 1, 34.

39. *Newsweek*, 69(April 24, 1967): 84-86.

40. Quoted in New York City, Housing and Development Administration, *The New York City Rehabilitation Experiments* (1970), p. 162.

41. George Sternlieb, "New York's Housing: A Study in *Immobilisme,*" *The Public Interest*, No. 16, Summer 1969, p. 135.

42. Housing and Development Administration, *The New York City Rehabilitation Experiments*, p. 8.

43. *New York Times*, April 2, 1970, p. 33.

44. *Cost and Time Associated with New Multifamily Housing Construction in New York City*, average of total development costs of five Mitchell-Lama high-rise projects.

45. Ibid., pp. 51, 55-59.

46. City Planning Department, *Public and Publicly-Aided Housing 1927-1973*, pp. 10-11.

47. Kristof, "Housing: The Economic Facets of New York City's Problems," p. 40.

48. First National City Bank, *Housing in New York City* (New York, 1970).

49. *New York Times*, November 13, 1968, p. 74.

50. Kristof, "Housing: The Economic Facets of New York City's Problems," pp. 12-13.

51. Ibid., p. 32.

52. Ibid., p. 19.

53. New York City, Housing and Development Administration, Department of Rent and Housing Maintenance, *The Urban Housing Dilemma, The Dynamics of New York City's Rent Controlled Housing* (1970, preliminary draft).

54. *New York Times*, February 27, 1970, p. 59.

55. The New York City Rand Institute, *Rental Housing in New York City*, Vol. 1: *Confronting the Crisis* (New York, 1970), p. 25.

56. Ibid., p. 29.

57. Metropolitan Council Community Improvement Fund, *Decent Housing for New York's People* (1970), p. 23.

58. *New York Times*, January 21, 1973, section VIII, p. 1.

59. *New York Times*, December 9, 1971, p. 32.

60. U.S. Department of Commerce, *Statistical Abstract of the United States* (Washington, 1973), p. 683.

61. *New York Times*, January 24, 1972, p. 1.

62. *New York Times*, February 1, 1972, p. 27.

63. U.S. General Service Administration, *Weekly Compilation of Presidential Documents*, Vol. 9, No. 10 (Washington, March 12, 1973), p. 226.

Other Sources

Mary Conyngton, "Effect of the Tax-Exemption Ordinance in New York City on Housing," *Monthly Labor Review* (April 1922).

Richard O. Davies, *Housing Reform During the Truman Administration* (Columbia, Mo., 1966).

Mayor's Rent Control Committee, *Report: Rent Control and Its Impact on Housing in New York City* (1969).

New York City, City Planning Commission, *Urban Renewal* [1958].

New York City, City Planning Department, *Newsletter* (September 1967).

New York City, Local Law No. 4 (1961).

New York City, *City Record*, July 9, 1960, November 4, 1971.

New York City, Committee on Housing Statistics, *Housing Statistics Handbook* (1966).

New York City, Department of Buildings, *Report* (1966).

New York City Housing Authority, *Annual Report: A Clearer Focus* (1962).

New York City, Housing and Development Administration, *Annual Report* (1968).

New York City, Housing and Redevelopment Board, *Annual Report* (1961).

New York State, Laws of 1959, Chapter 675; Laws of 1964, Chapter 272; Laws of 1968, Chapter 173, 349; Laws of 1971, Chapter 371, 551.

New York Times, February 13, 15, 1949; July 8, 1959; February 23, December 16, 1960; October 19, 1961; February 27, April 3, May 18, August 12, November 4, 1962; April 14, July 9, November 5, 1964; December 24, 1965; May 11, November 16, December 26, 1966; June 22, 1967; May 27, 1968; December 10, 1969; February 13, November 8, 1970; March 21, 1971; November 20, 1974.

The New Yorker, January 9, 1971.

U.S. Bureau of the Census, *Historical Statistics of the United States, Colonial Times to 1957* (Washington, 1960).

U.S. Bureau of the Census, Housing Census, 1950, 1960.

U.S. Bureau of the Census, Population Census, 1950, 1960.

U.S. Public Law, 372 (1959), 70 (1961), 560 (1964), 117 (1965), 754 (1966), 301 (1968), 448 (1968).

Index